Don't Let Them See You Cry

by: Milton G Stephens

Don't Let Them See You Cry

Author: Milton G Stephens

Copyright © Milton G Stephens (2023)

The right of Milton G Stephens to be identified as author of this work has been asserted by the author in accordance with section 77 and 78 of the Copyright, Designs and Patents Act 1988.

First Published in 2023

ISBN 978-1-915796-76-9 (Paperback)
      978-1-915796-77-6 (eBook)

Book cover design and Book layout by:
    White Magic Studios
    www.whitemagicstudios.co.uk

Published by:
    Maple Publishers
    Fairbourne Drive,
    Atterbury,
    Milton Keynes,
    MK10 9RG,
    UK www.maplepublishers.com

A CIP catalogue record for this title is available from the British Library.

All rights reserved. No part of this book may be reproduced or translated by any form or by any means, electronic or mechanical, including photocopying, recording or by any information storage and retrieval system without written permission from the author.

Unless otherwise indicated, all the names, characters, places and incidents are either the product of the author's imagination or used in a fictitious manner. Any resemblance to actual people living or dead, events or locales is entirely coincidental, and the Publisher hereby disclaims any responsibility for them.

Contents

Prologue: It's a girl! 5
Chapter 1: Something To Prove 7
Chapter 2: Nightmares 18
Chapter 4: Fiona Stanley 29
Chapter 5: Stell Aged 5 ¾ 40
Chapter 6: Mrs T 46
Chapter 7: Roger Theakston 48
Chapter 8: Fi's Dad 56
Chapter 9: Milesborough Old Boys Minis Under 9s 61
Chapter 10: A not so fond farewell 71
Chapter 11: Roger Theakston: Dirty Bastard 75
Chapter 12: Dinner Dance 83
Chapter 13: Carlton Edwards 92
Chapter 14: The Troubadours Experience 97
Chapter 15: Summer Training 104
Chapter 16: Post Training 109
Chapter 17: Crash Baggies 112
Chapter 18: Siobhan Owen 121
Chapter 19: Larry Mitchelle 128
Chapter 20: Summer Training 2 133
Chapter 20: The Northerton Vipers 139
Chapter 21: Reflections 146
Chapter 22: Warfare 151
Chapter 23: Aftermath: Rivenstoke Bears 20, Hammersmith and Fulham Ladies 5 161
Chapter 24: Defence Against the Dark Arts 168
Chapter 25: Masingford Away 177

- Chapter 26: He's Our Coach, Hands Off! 190
- Chapter 27: Roger Theakston Post Divorce 201
- Chapter 28: Court Martial 207
- Chapter 29: B.A.G.S. 218
- Chapter 30: The Dilemma of the Well-Meaning Precedent 233
- Chapter 31: Cowboys and Indians 243
- Chapter 32: An Inconvenient Truth 254
- Chapter 33: The Morning After the Night Before 262
- Chapter 34: Lunar Reflections 266
- Chapter 35: Something to Prove Too 272
- Chapter 36: Armistice 285
- Chapter 36: Armistice 2 289
- Chapter 37: Vengeance of a Gym Queen 300
- Chapter 38: Rochester Elms Away 308
- Chapter 39: Cake!!! 322
- Chapter 40: Fi's Meeting 328
- Chapter 41: Christmas Cheer 335
- Chapter 42: The Curious Case of Megan Mendez 342
- Chapter 43: Gwen's ILY Part 1 348
- Chapter 44: Gwen's ILY part 2 359
- Chapter 45: Would you allow your daughter to play rugby? 369
- Chapter 46: Stell's Party 379
- Chapter 47: Hammersmith and Fulham Combined 1st and 2nd team (Men's) vs New Quay Ironsides: Friendly 387
- Chapter 48: Indiscretions 392
- Chapter 49: Final Game of the Season: Kingston Away 402
- Epilogue 434
- (Endnotes) 438

Prologue: It's a girl!

They dress her in pink and give her mostly dolls to play with. They tell her how pretty she is and, all around her, she sees how pretty women are treated, respected, revered. They tell her to get an education so as to not waste the opportunity to be independent that possibly her mother (or maybe her grandmother) never had. After years of studying and getting the best grades she can, they tell her to get a job and a career.

In these brief, post-university years of independence (just before the compulsory "settling down with a nice, sensible man" phase that they will suggest, initially with vague hints, but with ever increasing conviction as the years progress), although perhaps struggling to get her foot on the career ladder and be taken seriously in her chosen profession, she will be in the prime of her life: young, attractive and free to do whatever she likes (and with whomever she likes!)

This freedom phase is strictly for a limited period only though as, if she is not picked before the sell-buy-date on "pretty" expires, a life on the shelf beckons. All the rose-hued dreams of playing with her own human dolls will be for other, prettier, more successful women. So then follows: marriage, mortgage, a nice house that she will fill with nice things, a decent car and nice holidays. Her career - for which she worked so bloody *hard* – will be put on hold and she will have her very own pooing, peeing, screaming dolls whom she will, if possible, send to a good school and raise as best she can and spend every F#&KING waking moment with until, when they are old enough, they will eventually leave home. She will be left with the house full of "nice things" and the sensible man whom she has hardly seen for the last 18 years. She may resume whatever is salvageable of her career and, eventually, her sensible man will die first[1]; she will join him sooner or later. This will be her life...

"Bollocks to that!" thought Stell and chucked the magazine in the bin.

Chapter 1: Something To Prove

"I had a professor once who liked to tell his students that there were only ten different plots in all fiction. Well I'm here to tell you he was wrong; there is only one: 'Who am I?'"

The Amazing Spiderman (2012)

Stell walked home from the pub.

Well, "walked" would be putting far too optimistic a spin on her general demeanour of "swaying from side to side with head pounding while all that beer[2] - gurgling away somewhere between her stomach and throat - struggled to not make another appearance". If it weren't for the fact that her legs were so used to the well-worn 10-minute journey between the Wheatsheaf and the "Theakston Mansion[3]", she probably would have ended up somewhere in Wandsworth ("South of the river, Aaarrrgghhh!")

Her heavy kit bag was doing its best to put as much pressure on her bruised shoulder as it could, the finger broken two seasons before but still not properly healed was throbbing with a life of its own now that the strapping had been removed and her knees just simply *ached*.

"So, this was: *The prime of my life*?" the captain mused, self-pity and sarcasm agreeing a temporary truce so they could both torment her soul in equal measure. "Owwwwww....."

One of the joys of living "back at home", where she had now retreated so she could save for a deposit for a flat, that she'd never be able to afford without a hefty contribution from Mum ("And maybe Dad. The bastard...," she thought), was that there would always be clean clothes, a permanently stocked fridge and some unconditional, even though completely uncomprehending, sympathy for whatever hardships the outside world had that day decided to heap upon her.

Stell's Mum, (Mrs T to all, even Stell), had bought The Mansion, a rather large, sprawling terraced house in the heart of Fulham, with the proceeds from the divorce, at a time when the only thing associated with Fulham was the rather unkind Trivial Pursuit question of: "Which rubbish football team did George Best play for after he left Manchester United?"[4]

Since the gentrification of the area, many of the older Fulham families who had bought houses after the war for the first few notes of a song (as opposed to the whole manuscript complete with chorus), now found they were asset millionaires and decided to go while the going was good, selling up and moving out of London to the leafier suburbs. Those who didn't own their own homes mostly stayed, feeling increasingly marginalised and squeezed in between the newly arrived, "Bank of Mum and Dad"-financed "Mobile Single Young Professionals" and the "Arrived-All-of-Five-Minutes-Ago Prosperous, Power Couple Young Professionals".

"...And the Too-Poor-to-Live-Anywhere-than-at-Their-Mum's *Very* Single Young Professionals," Stell bemoaned.

As she trudged past row upon row of the latest outlets of the huge coffee franchises along the Fulham Road, Stell couldn't help thinking that the normal buzz in the air on the Fulham streets had less to do with a younger, more affluent type of person moving in, and more to do with the amount of coffee everyone was drinking.[5]

Between work, where her boss Trish no longer even bothered to pretend to not hate her and the organising of the Ladies' Rugby Club, she just didn't have time to look for a boyfriend. Besides, the last forays into the dating field were particularly disastrous, with her preference for the "Intellectual Type" resulting in being introduced by well-intentioned friends to weedy, arrogant, self-obsessed bookworms needing more a mother figure capable of delivering a counselling session on the traumas probably suffered from being picked last for sports at school than a girlfriend ("Or more probably what they needed was a slap around the chops and being ordered to just grow a pair!" she thought). She'd been equally as unsympathetic to the last one of these prospective suitors and the relationship with the well-meaning introducer friends had been decidedly cooler since *that* incident.

She'd even considered internet dating and had come to within a click of signing her self-esteem away on a free trial period for "Perfect Mates.com: marriage guaranteed!"

"Nah, too sad," was the conclusion. She'd heard about the fat or withered, middle-aged men who were at least 30 years older than their profile pictures, or the "Desperate for a Shag" married men who'd built up whole alternate lives in order to convince their latest Cybervictim that they were indeed, single, or rich or both. "Besides, it's always possible to find someone to marry, the trick is in finding someone to marry that you'd *want* to be married to."

Then there was always the rugby-playing alternative that, despite her better judgement, she knew she still had a thing for...

"Absolutely NO WAY!" she protested aloud, remembering her father and the almost carbon-copy rugger buggers she knew. She looked around nervously to see if anyone had noticed her public outburst in the darkening evening, illuminated by the fluorescent light of the plethora of Estate Agents' windows. A respectable-looking middle-aged woman out walking her dog on the opposite side of the road pretended not to look in her direction (standard London procedure when encountering a "Nutter"[6]) but quickened her pace anyway in order to put good distance between herself, Fido and "big, Crazy Young Lady carrying unfeasibly large and ominous bag."

Her cheeks reddening at the tacit accusation of madness, Stell remembered her past experiences with rugby boys. To say they were only after one thing wasn't quite true. "That's the problem, they're after *everything*," she recalled. "Expecting one of them to be faithful is like expecting Fiona Stanley[7] to pass..."

One of her former Coaches, an ex-rugger bugger himself, had put it simply enough, during a post-match drinking session:

"Faithfulness is a short term condition brought on by the absence of opportunity."

"Thanks for that, Coach," she now thought dryly.

"And, can you imagine what would happen if you ever married one, had kids with him, and were completely dependent 'cos you couldn't work 'cos you're looking after the little monsters and he comes home late reeking of perfume with lipstick on his collar, inexplicable receipts for presents you'd never received, in his pockets, dodgy lingerie (in a much smaller size than I wear!) mixed up in his rugby kit and even dodgier text messages and emails on his phone and laptop?"

"Not that I'd ever check my partner's mobile and laptop," she quickly corrected herself. "Again..."

The very fact that most rugby boys, probably through the sport, were given so much confidence, were taught that "A penalty is only a penalty if the ref gives it" (translation: "Naughty is only naughty if you get caught") and were physically bigger and stronger Alpha-type males, meant that they were always on the hunt for new "totty", which often would give up without much of a struggle. It left you, as the girlfriend, constantly living in fear of the next "indiscretion" and permanently suspicious, leading to possessive and then, frankly, leading to a bit bonkers."

"Yes, there were definitely benefits to being single and living at home," she concluded, "for now at least."

She was comforted by the thought that Mrs T would probably have cooked when she returned home after the rugby earlier, so possibly there would be some of the Sunday roast hanging about. The idea of warm food to soak up all that beer brought back the afternoon's preceedings and the strange mood she had felt, just before her losing Captain's post-match speech.

"Losing to St Pete's wasn't that bad," she pondered, putting on a brave face through the dissipating alcoholic fog. "After all, it wasn't as if it were for the first time..."

However, over the last half-season, her reactions to the losses were no longer the habitual indifference. She felt something in her was definitely changing, possibly as a result of her body telling her that her rugby-playing years would soon be coming to an end.

She was almost constantly injured now, Stell reflected. Her right shoulder throbbed from the tackling, her broken finger from the other season hadn't ever really healed properly and the ubiquitous aches and sprains didn't fade away until the off-season, when she'd stop all physical activity completely in order to just recuperate. Then, within weeks, just when she was feeling almost 100%, even though the summer clothes were starting to get just that little bit tighter round the waist and bum ("And breasts!" she thought, brightening a bit. On reflection though, this wasn't necessarily a good thing as to most men, her face then became invisible, which was really annoying) the Club Fitness Coach, Ian the Sadist, would commence the gruelling and dreaded Summer Training.

How or why, for so many years of her life now, she willingly acceded to put her body through sheer running hell from end of June until the end of August, was something she'd never fully understand. The players would work physically so much harder during these long, long weeks than they *ever* would need for the rest of the season and it was enormously rare for them to even *see* a rugby ball for the first month of Summer Training, just grass, grass, sick and more grass.

Stell would try to delay her first attendance at Summer Training for as long as possible, with either holidays or recuperation from injuries or friends' weddings or, if no other excuse were available, by simply not answering the phone or responding to emails.

Problem with that though was that the longer you delayed starting, the harder it was and the more behind the others you were when you eventually began. Long ago, she'd worked out that the best way to avoid the complete shock to the body of going from doing absolutely nothing for two months from the end of the season to being fully fit and raring to go at the start of Summer Training was to *stay* fit for the whole summer!

"Nah," she'd concluded after many, many milliseconds of deliberation.

Kicking and screaming, she would be forced to "get fit" again, whatever that meant, as the tightening of abdominals, the expanding of lungs, the lowering of heart rate and hardening of thighs and calves, had absolutely the opposite effect on her ankles, hips and knees which, like the well-known breakfast cereal, snapped, crackled and popped when she extended her legs the morning after. "And fizzed as well," she thought, even though not strictly part of the breakfast cereal's repertoire.

"Scar tissue breaking free from fraying cartilage, probably," she added. "Too many more years playing on these and I'll be reaching for the Zimmer frame before Mum!" she consoled herself with the black humour. Being black humour, it wasn't very funny. Her mood darkened further.

But WHY was she doing it all? She didn't enjoy the losing, she liked the drinking (huge smiles!) but didn't like the feeling sick part which inevitably followed. She **LOVED** the end of August visual change in her body after those two months of pre-season training, where "a bit flabby" would transform into "lean, taut, rippling with glistening muscle", just like the "after" picture on the front of one of those "Who Do You

Do (magazine of the stars!) minor celebrity loses weight and looks fab again" stories.

Those two weeks, just before the aches and pains of the rugby re-started in September and by chance co-inciding with holidays, was the *best* time of the year ("Even though, most expensive," she thought. "Maybe holiday companies are all secret rugby trainers?"): she knew she'd look fabulous and she'd be able to take her pick of all the holiday hunks in Ibitha or Ayia Napa or Majorca, lining up to wine her, dine her and, knowing them, probably 68^8 her. Thoughts of the usually disappointing, drunken and sun-burned sex bit of the initially "oh so promising" holiday romances seeped into her memory, causing the dark mood to creep back. Her mind drifted back to the rugby.

"All that training, all that physical and mental commitment, all that organisation of games and medical supplies and kit and dragging people along to watch (largely unsuccessfully so far), it had to mean more than just an excuse to get drunk on a Sunday night. Musn't it?"

Determined to answer her own question before the usual cross-examination by Mrs T commenced,[9] Stell made an attempt to review the afternoon's preceedings.

"True: everyone had given 100%, smashing into the opposition for their lives' worth, running as much as any of them had for centuries. Well," she smiled, "as much of 100% as we had left after the night out with the men's team." She couldn't believe Gwen had turned up for the game that afternoon with last night's conquest's shirt on and kit, obviously not having had time to go home to find her own. "Classic!!"

Her smiling continued: "True: St Pete's thrashed us the previous time, so we're getting better!"

Stell's mood brightened even more; this brain-storming session was getting good!

"We would have won too if it weren't for Fi!" she repeated to no-one in particular.

Consoled now and having arrived at the Mansion, Stell searched in her bag for her keys. Somewhere under the damp, heavy kit, she was sure they were lurking, probably having wilfully buried themselves in the middle of her manky, muddied towel, deliberately delaying her entry into the warmth of the family home and with it, the disappearance of the disappointing memories of the afternoon.

However, those extra seconds fumbling around on the doorstep brought with them the realisation that the previous moments' reflections were no more than clutching at straws: rationalising defeat and ignoring the ache in her heart.

"Also true:" she heard herself thinking ("No, no, stop!!!"), "no-one from the men's team watching even offered any commiserations. Not a single: "Unlucky, well-played's. Nothing, nada. Zip."

"Also, also true," she continued, "Fi was more concerned about winning Man of the Match for the opposition than with the fact we lost. She was actually *smiling*, when we all know that, if we lose the next two games, we *will* be relegated!"

The straws snapped and so did her momentary good mood. Adrift now in her despair, her fingers discovered the keys' hiding place and while she fished to retrieve them, it suddenly hit her:

"Everyone *expects* us to lose!

"That's why the boys don't care, that's why our best player," she hated to admit it, but it was plain for everyone to see, "really isn't bothered how the team performs, because she, and everyone else, thinks we're *shit*!"

Mrs T had sensed someone at the front door and pulled the net curtain of the bay window back slightly to get a good look. Her only daughter, keys in hand, was deliberating on the front step, disturbed expression on her face.

"Probably boyfriend trouble," Mrs T concluded, and let the net curtains fall back into place.

Stell thought back to the reasons why she had started playing rugby at Uni in the first place: she and her teammates **knew** they were regarded as being strange, scary, *different* to the other girls. They had been called all sorts of names, ranging from butch lesbians to drunken sluts and virtually everything in between, by male and female alike (but normally behind their backs), but they **liked** the fact that they were regarded as different, as being apart from all the other girls who only did what was *expected* of them and "would end up miserable, sad, lonely and *unfulfilled*." Now though, girls playing rugby was more or less acceptable, but not taking it seriously, playing it badly and losing all the time was *expected*.

"Aaaaaarrrggghhhh!, I've become the monster I've been fighting against!" she wailed internally, remembering her Nietzsche from Uni. She peered into the corner glass of the bay window to detect any signs of monster in her reflection; Mrs T took a step back to avoid detection.

Then there was the question of Fi. What do you do with someone too good to leave out, but definitely a massive disruption on the pitch? If Stell looked like an "after" photo for two weeks a year, Fi managed to do so for a whole 52!

"Probably 53..." she thought. Fi quite clearly believed she was a superior being to the rest of the team and somehow, non-verbally, always managed to let the other players know it. The worst thing though was that all the other players did know it, Stell included...

"That's enough boyfriend squabbles, she needs to get ready for work tomorrow," Mrs T decided and rapped on the window to let her daughter know she was being watched.

Instantly snapped back to the present, Stell inserted her key into lock.

"True: we would have won it at the end if Fi weren't such a big-headed egomaniac who should maybe pass once in a while," she repeated to herself.

Straws thoroughly re-grasped, she hauled herself ashore and into the family home.

Chapter 2: Nightmares

Stell's body was asleep, but her brain had other ideas.

The game earlier on that day had somehow managed to find the "record" button in the Captain's mind and was not going to switch itself off until it had played through the whole match, with any especially embarrassing bits displayed in super-slow motion for "added cringe" effect.

It had been a filthy afternoon. One of those afternoons in winter when the freezing wind finds a way through any number of layers of clothing you may have on, instantly numbing the fingers of anyone silly enough not to be wearing the thickest gloves, thrust as far down into the deepest pockets, you could possibly imagine. In fact, being at home with the central heating on full, watching a good movie with a nice glass of something hot, or better, alcoholic, after your hunk of a partner has made a delicious Sunday lunch would definitely be the preferred option of any sane young lady.

But no.

The freezing rain had torn across the open, muddy field, whipping almost indiscernible pellets of ice into you, leaving almost imperceptible but nevertheless stinging marks on cheeks and bare thighs. Sounds of thunder could be heard not too far off and the tiny number of drenched figures on the sidelines huddling together for mutual comfort - including Mrs T and Fred (Stell smiled in her sleep at the thought of her small mongrel)- ankle deep in mud and peering out from their waxed hoods, knew that the lightning and the next torrent of rain wouldn't be too far away either. The sky was black.

"Forget her, she'll be fine," Stell had shouted (blonde-brown hair tied in a bun struggling to keep on top of her head against the weight of the accumulated mud).

She "wasn't being callous, just practical", Stell tried to convince herself, (although cringing in her sleep).

She hadn't even looked in Siobhan's direction (Welsh, cool, composed, well-known borderline psychopath) as her teammate had lain in the mud, a sticky, steadily expanding patch of dark blood oozing through her raven black hair. The sneaky penalty she'd won for the Hammers, at the expense of her own physical well-being, would do no harm to her reputation. A St John's Ambulance person had knelt at her side, doing the best he could to apply a bandage with numbing fingers, but clearly wishing it had been somebody else's shift that day.

Stell heard her voice boom, "We need to focus on the next 10 minutes. St Pete's whipped our arses last time and we now have the opportunity to turn this round. Ladies, I fucking guarantee that the beer will taste sweeter tonight if we have a "W" on the leader board." She had no idea why she'd sworn (to sound harder, maybe?) but her face grimaced at the memory. Stell rolled over in bed and tried to bury her head in the pillow, seeking the sanctuary of fluffiness.

The thirteen other mud-caked, sweating, exhausted young women huddled closer in a tight circle, linking arms around the shoulders as Zoe, fresh from the sidelines in clean kit, wriggled between their bodies to join them.

Stell's voice screamed: "We're going for the scrum which we will win. We'll do a blind-side move off 8 with Fi heading straight for their Winger, back row in support. Right, everyone on three: one, two three..."

All joined in together, "A-roo, a-roo, a-roo, HAMMERS HAMMERS HAMMERS!"

"Scrum down red ball!" called the ref.

The eight largest girls on each side had formed themselves into well-drilled phalanxes. Canadian Mel, by far the shortest of the forwards, raised her arms above her head like a phoenix about to rise, hands bent slightly outwards. Mads (Madeleine, a tall, very often inappropriately blunt Australian Systems Analyst, normally rake-thin at home, but since arriving in London on an ancestry visa, significantly chubbier[10]) and Gwen (also Welsh, rugby in the blood, incredibly pretty, with a reputation for being over-friendly with any reasonably fit members of the men's teams) joined her on either side and wrapped their left and right arms respectively around her, slightly tugging her to their side in turn, as if about to spin her like a top. Mel dropped her "phoenix arms" over their shoulders, slightly askew as Mads was a lot taller, and grabbed their shirts tightly to form a closely bound trio.

"Get lower!" she hissed to Mads through her mouthguard. They crouched down preparing for "the hit".

Hannah (a trainee solicitor, working all the hours God sends and very engaged to the love of her life) and Stell linked arms and got on one knee each behind their front row, threading their free arms up between the legs of Mads and Gwen to grip their shirts just below their slightly rounded bellies. They nestled their heads between the pairs of knee joints on either side of Mel and slid themselves directly upwards, so that their heads fitted snugly between the hips of the girls in front.

"Thank God for scrum caps," Stell thought (though obviously, she'd never say that to anyone), throwing her pillow to the floor to free her hair from the remembered heat of the scrum.

Hannah's ears had been raw, but with all that wild red hair, no scrum cap would ever have stayed in place without frying her head. She preferred to tape her ears down to avoid them being rubbed off altogether.

Mrs T, as usual, had been trying to control the mounting panic in her heart. She had experienced this moment many times with her daughter in the past, being the Hammers' no.1 (and often only) supporter, but no matter how many times she saw Stell in the middle of "that scrum thing", she couldn't help worrying about the effect a particularly hard blow to any of the soft bits to Stell's body could do. She remembered the strange mixture of feelings that had coursed through her body when her ex-husband Roger, a former player himself, had been lying in that hospital bed injured, broken. The annoyance at his basically self-inflicted wound (sprained vertebrae in the back) vied with a feeling of helplessness as there was simply nothing she could do to ease the obvious pain of her bruised warrior. "But it was different for girls..."

Mrs T had said nothing though and instead, bit her lip in anguish, as she had gotten used to over the years.

Zoe (a Surveyor from "Opp North", working in London after Uni) and Mands (Amanda, a no-nonsense, hard-as-nails Samoan) had loosely bound on the sides of Stell and Hannah and Fi (Fiona Stanley, the Golden Girl) normally a no. 7 but playing at 8 due to Sib's injury, gripped firmly on to the back of Stell and Hannah's shorts with her arms outstretched as if she were about to chariot race.

At the thought of Fi, the duvet began to press Stell into the bed, trapping her, paralysing her. She kicked out to let a current of fresh air slip under the covering and temporarily allay the momentary panic she'd felt.

Stell's thoughts now settled on Fi ("Oh no, please Gods of Rugby, let me think of "Newsnight", "UK Talent Is Here!", "Celebrity Pancake Master Cook", anything but HER!"). The Gods of Rugby were strangely silent.

So, what about Fi? Short-bobbed blonde hair, beautiful, the sort of body that you only get given if God is your, well, Godfather and your Dad owns a gym: in Fi's case, a chain of gyms in the States. Fiona's father, a former Zimbabwe rugby international[11] had the huge slice of luck (or, depending on to whom Jimmy Stanley was telling the story, the great prescience of mind) to, when Fi was only 6, sell the family farm outside of Kariba and move to California, buying up huge tracts of rundown warehouses and converting them to gyms.

Fi's preferred position was no.7, or Openside Flanker [12].

Fi had only been playing for a couple of years and, quite annoyingly for some, had the potential, as well as the correct psychometric profile, to be very, very good: and knew it.

"Oh, it must be in the blood," was her usual response when she won another Man of the Match award, with her "butter wouldn't melt in the mouth" West Coast accent (including a slight touch of Zimbabwean, when stressed). Everyone of course knew this was nonsense as she was *definitely* a secret trainer and, with the vague promise by her love-struck Coach back at College to potentially try out for the USA Women's Eagles national team upon her return, saw "The Mighty Hammers" as a stepping stone to bigger and greater things. Be it rugby, hopscotch or life in general, Fi had to constantly prove to everyone, or maybe just to herself, that she was "the best".

Involuntarily and while Fi was still on her mind, Stell gave the duvet a couple more meaningful kicks. Feeling partially avenged, she smiled subconsciously as the dream continued.

"Crouch," called the referee and the two packs of forwards had collectively bent down low, while keeping their heads up facing forward. Mel, Mads and Gwen, one metre away from the opposing front row - muddied monsters staring right into them – had stared straight back, deep into their eyes, searching for any possible sign of weakness or doubt just before "the hit".

"Touch."

Mads and Gwen had extended their free arms to lightly touch the shoulder of the girls in front of them. "I'm gonna fuck you up, you cow," the St Pete's no. 2 seemed to mouth. Mel's shoulder was starting to hurt; Mads was still too high and she just couldn't get the binding right. The thought "I really don't want to dislocate my shoulder again," was starting to grow at the back of her mind...

"Pause......"

The tension grew in Stell's stomach as she lay in bed, even though the physical clash had happened several hours before.

"This is it, this is it...."

"ENGAGE!"

The thud and groan of 16 bodies crashing together for "the hit" was heard from the touchline 15 metres away. The front rows' heads had joined and were immediately locked together, as both sets of forwards threw their combined weight into this panting, heaving mass of flesh, mud, sinew and strain. Katy had rolled the ball in between the two teams and Mel, suspended in the air between her props, had swung her right boot to divert the ball's path in between Mads' legs. The Hammers front row had buckled and the opposition drive was on. Feet slipped and slid in the thick mud as the girls were pushed backwards.

"That's enough, hold the push!" ordered the ref, after the Hammers had been pushed back the maximum one metre[13]. The ball, tangled up in the mass of legs, was just about visible in front of Fi's feet on the Hammers' side. As ordered, Fi had picked it up and hurtled towards the opposition no.14[14], while the Scrum Half dived to stop her but only grasped air and mud.

As Fi carried on her charge up the wing, leaving in her wake a very dazed and hurting pile of young lady formally known as Amanda Pryce-Edwards, she could make out, from the corner of her vision, the opposition Fullback running at great speed towards her. Fi was already well ahead of virtually all of her own supporting teammates, but her Winger Katia (tall, very thin, German, whippet fast and going out with Josh: the boys 1st team captain, no less!) had been only a couple of yards behind her. The pass to the faster girl was the obvious thing to do, so as not to get run down by the St Pete's Fullback who, being a back, was clearly faster than Fi.

However...

There is a certain medical condition, which normally only affects forwards but can also be found amongst anyone who never usually gets anywhere near the opposition try-line, known as White Line Fever.

The symptoms include the following:

1) *Hallucinations. Visions of glory as the afflicted imagines being carried shoulder-high by ecstatic team mates, holding aloft the coveted trophy, in something like a Bobby Moore '66 pose while cheering crowds line the route to the changing rooms in reverential homage*

2) *Huge increase in adrenalin levels leading to all-encompassing, single-minded determination*

3) *Lack of feeling in one arm, usually the right, resulting in the ball being tucked under the remaining "good" arm in an emu's wing pose*

4) *Inability to pass (please see previous symptom)*

5) *Disorientation: an inability to run in any direction other than the most easily intercept-able of straight lines*

6) *A complete breakdown in the normal decision-making process (i.e. they fast/ big, me slow/ small, maybe NOT good idea to try to outpace/ run through them)*

7) *Total obliviousness towards better-placed colleagues and enemy defences, especially rapidly approaching Fullbacks, who may just have lined the patient up in their sights and be preparing to bring them down in a crashing heap of frustrated ambition, irrespective as to whether or not said, Fullback had been seen immediately before the onset of the condition.*

This condition is usually followed very shortly by screaming, livid team-mates and a "Dick of the Day" award.

Fi didn't even remember how she lost her footing. The 15's ankle tap was so subtle that one minute, the reverential homage was a done deal, the next, almost in slow-motion[15], Fi was stumbling forward, only inches in front of the try-line. She fell flat on her face, the ball hitting the ground beneath her and dislodging itself to bobble agonisingly forward, just over the white line and into the in-goal area. Katia arrived moments later to dive on the ball and Estelle, who had managed to emerge from the scrum and had been running after Fi, along with the rest of the Hammers pack, had called a meek "Try Sir" to the referee, but this was more in hope than any real belief.

"Knock on red, scrum 5, white ball." Then a quick look at the watch and two short and one long whistle blast signalled the game was over; the Mighty Hammers had lost: again.

"Fucking fuck fuck FUCK!" cried Stell. In her sleep, the words escaped again.

Fi had rolled on the ground clutching her ankle, making a: "I think I've done something to it" face, but a livid Stell and the rest of the team didn't even look in her direction as they left the field to form the Winners' Tunnel.

Then, this is the bit Stell could not be sure actually happened or if the dream had decided to insert for dramatic effect:

The small group of boys in the crowd from the men's team exchanged knowing looks. If they were to put into words what they actually felt, they may have said something like: "My God they are terrible! God only knows why they want to play this game in the first place; it's so absolutely typical of girls to not do the obvious and sensible thing and make the simple pass," but instead, Josh, the 1ˢᵗ Team Captain quipped, with exaggerated grace, "Gentlemen, may I interest you in liquid refreshment of the mildly alcoholic nature back at the 'Sheaf?"

"Josh, you're a gentleman and a scholar," came the reply.

The boys all trooped the few hundred yards back to the rugby club, reliving the highs and lows of their games the previous day, as well as making jokes about last night's post-game entertainment of which Gwen, once they had left the rugby club, the night club and then the impromptu early morning drinking after-party at one of their flats, had again been the "star". As the "Three cheers for St Peters" trailed off in the distance, the departing male rugby players didn't even spare a thought for the exhausted and upset young women who were now slouching off towards the changing rooms in the opposite direction.

All except for Carlton...

Having recently retired from playing due to injury, as well as being an old git the wrong side of 40, Caz was a former Premier League player who had joined the Hammers after being sidelined with injury for a number of years, in a vain attempt to "give it one last go" before finally hanging up his boots. His West Indian parents had struggled to send him to a good school, but were horrified to discover that the violent and dangerous game of rugby was part of the curriculum. They were thus dead set against him playing and so, as a result of enormous stubbornness (from Caz' Dad's Guyanese side of the family) Caz went on to excel at it, picking up accolades, trophies and a fair amount of female attention along the way. Now though, his knee surgeon[16] had given him a firm ultimatum: "Stop playing rugby right now and you may need a knee replacement in 20 years time, or keep on playing and I can book you in for next week!"

Consequently and feeling at a bit of a loss, Caz had recently started a rugby coaching course, not so that he could remain a rugger bugger and still be in contact with the sport that had filled so much of his time over the years, but to, "You know, give something back" to the game.

"You know," he thought to himself as he trudged along behind the others, "they're a lot better than I thought they would be. In fact, with a bit of tinkering about, they could actually be not bad at all..."

Stell rolled onto her back and her eyes snapped open. Suddenly, it was all clear:

"I know what I've got to do!" she exclaimed. Her brain buzzed with excitement.

Chapter 4: Fiona Stanley

"..and our Dick of the Day has simply got to go to our no.7, for committing the most heinous crime of the dreaded White Line Fever. Come on Fi, get up and take your medicine!" boomed Stell.

The Wheatsheaf on Fulham Road was one of the new types of "gastro pubs". This meant that the food was significantly more edible than what one had come to expect from the Great British Public House and a lot more expensive. Ultra-modern in design, it had the almost compulsory ubiquitous large screens for sporting events and, due to its convenience to the rugby pitches at Hurlingham Park, doubled up as the home of the Hammersmith and Fulham Rugby Club and its university-educated players and followers. It was also one of the closest pubs to the local Premier League football team, historically supported by the traditional blue-collar locals but more recently with a smattering of young, more affluent city workers priced out of central London, so on big game days, it would be packed to the rafters with both blue-shirted Chelsea fans and club-tied, burly rugby players. There was always a bit of tension when the two completely different tribes occupied the same space at the same time but, in general, things passed off fairly smoothly.

Sunday afternoons, however, were times when one could enjoy a pleasant family meal, in a relaxed and friendly atmosphere, with usually no sports people in sight. There was though, a corner of the pub where the atmosphere was slightly different.

The six selected ladies after the Hammers v St Peter's game stood on the tables in the lounge area, "dirty" pints in hand (i.e. full of the most potent and random cocktail of spirits and beer) so that they could be seen above the thirty or so bruised, wet-haired and occasionally bandaged female rugby players. A few of the rain-drenched supporters from earlier, one or two onlookers who had joined the group out of sheer curiosity, as well as a few of the boys from the men's teams who sort of just hung around the club, swelled the numbers, amidst the mini-mountains of sports bags piled in various corners. "Rhiancé," the Hammers' tried and tested chunder bucket, was in attendance just behind the Awards Table.

Stell, as the home Captain, had begun the countdown. "Three, two, one...." and all joined in with a rousing chorus of "Get it down, you Zulu warrior!" while the six Award Winners (Men of the Match, Opposition Men of the Match and Dicks of the Day from both teams) raced to see who would be the last to drink their pints and thus be prescribed some more medicine. Fi had been the first to turn her glass upside down and place it on her head, to indicate that she'd finished. There were a few drops of concoction left at the bottom though, which dripped down her blonde hair in a sticky, dark gloop. The urge to be sick was quickly quelled by a deep intake of air through the nostrils; it always worked. One of the St Pete's girls was not so skilled in the art of chunder-avoidance and jumped off the back of the table in order to make use of Rhiancé. The sound of her retching was mostly drowned out by the cacophony of cheers and the collective female voices giving a hearty rendition of "Why was she born so beautiful..?"

Leafy, bobble hat, vest, exceptionally baggy jeans falling off her slender, ripped body, new to the team and indeed to rugby, the sport of choice in her parents' native Ghana being football, had been voted Man of the Match by the opposition. She was renowned as the Hammers' fastest runner but paradoxically slowest drinker and, to no-one's general surprise, struggled to finish the last few mouthfuls of her concoction. She came in a completely expected last place and calmly got down from the table and sedately walked towards the toilets.

"She's gonna blow!" someone shouted and again, to the accompaniment of general laughter and another chorus of "Why was she born so beautiful?" to recognise her status as Worst Drinker of the Award Winners, Leafy turned and graciously waved acknowledgement. Once Leafy had vomited, she would come back to the bar where another dirty pint would be waiting for her.

After a further hour or so of similar entertainment, a very merry and inebriated St Peter's Ladies' Rugby team hauled oversized bags onto bruised shoulders and shuffled towards the exits. Stell began the customary song, joined by the rest of the team:

"Bye bye, St Pete's,

Bye bye St Pete's,

Bye bye St Pete's,

We're sad to see you go,

Fuck Off!"

Fiona Stanley made the short walk to her live-in nanny house a happy woman. The bruises from the game were normally anaesthetised by the alcohol until the next morning and the slight swelling in her ankle was nothing a good ice bath wouldn't sort out. Even though all it meant to most people was the unwelcome obligation to drink alcohol at a much faster rate than they would have ideally liked, she was slightly peeved at narrowly missing out on being voted Man-of-the-Match by the oppo', (not to mention Dick of the Day from her own team), for some of the most fearsome tackles she'd ever put in. The throbbing in her right shoulder and chest bone was worth it as everyone would have *definitely* noticed that she was almost always up on the award winners' table.

"Definitely."

She'd won the drinking competition as well, so all in all, she was satisfied with the day's achievements.

Fi was jolted from her thoughts by a sudden panic. "Oh shit," she thought, "I almost missed it." She hurriedly made the three backwards steps to bring herself directly in front of the full sized, mock 17th century mirror, standing slightly to one side of the "Provincial French Bedroom" display of the local furniture shop. This mirror was relatively new on Fi's list and she thought that it *must* have been a genuine antique as the glass towards the bottom seemed thicker than at the top, making her legs appear stubbier but her midriff longer. The first time she saw it, a mental note "Abs mirror" checked in her head. Fi gave a furtive glance in both directions checking the coast was clear, then lifted up her t-shirt to just below the level of her breasts. She stood as straight as she could, thrusting her chest out in front of her, shoulders back, tightening her abs, with arms at her side, palms pointing inwards, middle fingers touching thumbs. A quick turn to the left, swivelling her head so she could see her side-on view - same pose - a half turn to the right to see the other side view - pose - then a quarter turn to the right while twisting her head so she could see her back. She rolled her t-shirt back down, another quick glance around to see if anyone had noticed her routine and then carried on towards home, almost without breaking stride. The whole procedure had taken less than ten seconds.

Fi couldn't help feeling a little disappointed. Last time she'd checked that mirror; her abs had seemed more defined, with the linea alba as clear as day. Admittedly, she hadn't been to the gym all day, it *was* evening, she'd drunk all that beer and she desperately needed to pee, which she virtually always did nowadays. Also, it wasn't *her* mirror so it didn't really count. "When I get back in front of my mirror tomorrow morning, then we'll see," she thought brightly and with that, skipped the remaining twenty metres to her house, which certainly didn't help her swollen bladder or her ankle.

"Fi, ma chère, is that you?" called the charmingly accented but very flustered voice of Mme Leprince from the upstairs landing. Chloe had obviously had a hard day with the twins and sounded as if she needed a break, even though in theory, it was Fi's day off.

"Hi Chloe!" came the mock-cheery reply, as Fi closed the door, whilst in the process of kicking off her trainers in the hall in an unfortunately already pointless attempt to sneak unnoticed up the staircase. If she could disappear into the bathroom before Chloe could intercept.....

Plan foiled, there was no option other than to engage. "Ah well....

"We lost again and I got injured," she said matter-of-factly, while exaggerating the hobble on her way up the stairs. "Ow, it really actually does hurt," she thought. "It's nothing serious though. How's your day been?"

"Oh, you would not believe what those two got up to today" answered Mme Leprince as she emerged from one of the boys' bedrooms. She was short, shoulder-length chestnut ringlets surrounding a round, pretty, very tired, red-cheeked face. "It was like Victor was possessed by the Devil, he wouldn't stop...." and she continued with an in-depth account of her children's antics.

"If you were more of a parent and less of a child yourself, you wouldn't always have so much hassle with them, you idiot!" thought Fi, the words, like bus passengers about to disembark, forming a disorderly queue on the tip of her tongue, just waiting for Fi's mouth to open so they could tumble out onto the nice carpets of the Leprince household and ruin Fi's cosy (and cheap!) living arrangements. Fi stayed silent.

"Why do I always have to look after everyone?" she thought, while turning to the left at the top of the stairs, away from Mme Leprince, "Oh, I gotta go to the bathroom to run my foot under the tap. Is there some strapping in there and could you get me some ice?"

"Er, I don't know where the bandages are. Maybe in the bathroom," came the slightly disorientated voice of Mme Leprince. Wasn't *she* supposed to be telling *Fi* what to do?

The invitation to visit the bathroom was all Fi needed as licence to escape from having to make conversation and she zipped away from Mme Leprince who clearly wanted to talk but, fearful of arousing even the most infinitesimal displeasure in her Super Nanny, fell silent. After all, nannies, even not very good ones, were hard to find. Super ones, like Fiona, were like valuable plots in a goldrush town: frequently the object of bitter disputes between otherwise life-long friends, the enmity lasting for generations. Or at least until the next latest scandal on the Fulham Mum circuit. The merest sniff of a good nanny's potential disquiet would be picked up in the ether and within moments be communicated via the jungle drums to the deepest, darkest renovated kitchens (with side-return extensions) of every Fulham household. By tomorrow morning's post-Wayne's Class[17] coffee at the gym, the opening shots amongst the Mums in the battle for Fi would have already been fired and even if la famille Leprince were to emerge as victors in retaining the services of Fiona Stanley, it would be at the cost of a huge salary increase, which despite their obvious affluence, they couldn't really afford.

But it was worth it. Since Fiona had come to the Leprince residence a year and a half before, life had been so much more bearable. Victor and Olivier now slept through the night and didn't always find their way into the marital bed, where a very annoyed and frustrated M Leprince would huffily roll over, perch on his side on the edge of the bed as if he were on the verge of rolling off into the sea of shag pile, and pretend to be asleep. She also thought that, like their father, the boys had a bit of a crush on Fi, which while highly undesirable in her husband, was probably a good thing for boys that age. Watching Pascal trying exceptionally hard not to ogle that young, taut, impossibly golden body over breakfast was a fair trade for, after almost five years, the luxury of a bloody good night's sleep.

Once on the loo behind the safety of the locked bathroom door, a tiny surge of excitement sparked in Fi's chest, not quite reaching her stomach yet. She looked across the room towards *her* mirror on the back of the bathroom door. "Ok, I know it's not morning, but after I've "been", I'll look a lot better. Then we'll see...."[18]

As she lay in the bath, semi-filled with the ice that Chloe had brought up and left outside the door, knocking timidly so as not to upset her sons' principal carer, "satisfactory" post-poo abs' examination in her favourite mirror complete, Fi allowed herself a little smile. The funny thing was that she really hadn't a clue what she was doing on the rugby field: she just picked up the ball and ran with it! She had only taken up the game two seasons before when it was introduced at College during the final trimester and really didn't understand tactics, positional play, phases, themes and the point of Backs. If you ran straight at people and you were bigger, stronger and fitter, you would normally run right through them. Sometimes they half stopped you, in which case you could pass on to Sib or Mands: if they could keep up. Very, very rarely though, the girl in front of you knew how to tackle and could get down low enough to really waste you. In fact, Fi was convinced that most of the girls she played against were just fat lumps more interested in the rugby club atmosphere and beers after than the mud and blood of the game.

Defence though, was what she lived for. Her idea of heaven, or as close to it as you can get on a sports field, was when one of these Lager Lumps ran at you, ball in hand. Being much fitter and stronger than them and thus able to get really low in the tackle, if she hit them just right, with her shoulder, at a precise spot to the side and just below the middle of the thigh, with her full weight and momentum behind her, she could actually get them to squeal in pain as they crashed to the floor, spilling ball, the team's attack and all thoughts of post-match beers into the mud.

This is the moment that she loved, possibly even more than scoring tries: not the pain of the upended foe, but the audible "Ooohs!" and almost tangible screwed-up faced, half-closed eyed wincing of the crowd as they physically recoiled, shying personally away from the contact but virtually drooling for it at the same time. She loved it when the opposition called her a "fearsome" tackler and random people in the crowd patted her on the back and confessed to being pleased they were not on the end of one of her trade mark "hits".

Until that first trimester, she'd participated in every sport there was, excelling at netball, hockey, cheerleading (by far the most dangerous female sport, bar none) and track and field. Her mother and sister Susie were often on the sidelines, Susie hanging out with some of the other siblings, her mother on her own just staring blankly. Her father would make games sometimes when her mum had one of "her bad days". After her mother left though, the new Stepmom, or ""The Witch", to give her, her proper name," Fi thought, would come along to EVERY–SINGLE–MOMENT-OF-EVERY-SINGLE-GAME, sometimes even coming to practice nights when Fi was perfectly capable of driving herself, and would merrily expel to all and sundry the dumbest and most embarrassing comments Fi was sure would have been odds-on favourites to win a prize at the "Spectators Who Know Nothing Dumbest Comments of the Year" awards.

"She just tries too hard. Doesn't she realise that I am *never* going to love her." She continued her train of thought, "Besides, she's probably just after Daddy's money..."

Fi knew this probably wasn't true though, so she momentarily submerged herself in the icy water to freeze out that particular subject.

It was only after Fi had started playing rugby that things changed. Her father became a regular feature on the sidelines, making a point of being at all the big games, with an almost permanent Rhodie entourage in attendance[19] whilst beaming with pride and letting people know that the star of the show was his daughter.

"Did he ever mention he was a former international?" he would always add. "Seven caps in total but," according to James Stanley, "it should have been more....."

Now that Fi was in London, her father would arrange his business trips so that by sheer coincidence, he would be in Fulham, or wherever else in the south-east of England the mighty Hammers were playing, on Sunday afternoons.

The freezing water was having the desired effect and the aching in her shoulder began to ease. The ankle was still throbbing though, much to Fi's annoyance. Yes, she *did* work her body hard, but if you're going to win, if you're going to be *perfect*, there really is no other choice. "Injuries happen and they are a pain, but I will not be lazy! Besides, if I can walk, I can still get to the gym."

As she slipped deeper into the water, ignoring the ice daggers attacking the bruised muscles, the idea of missing the next morning's Wayne's aerobics class with would-be clone Chloe - whilst the boys were at school - made a half-hearted attempt to enter her head, claiming that it had friends inside who were having a party and so should be on the guest list. Realistically though, it never stood a chance.

She closed her eyes and just before falling asleep, her lips parted and the half-whispered words slipped out, repeated again and again: "Gym is a lifestyle, not a chore; my body, my rules....."

Chapter 5: Stell Aged 5 ¾

Milesborough was such a pretty village. Like the idyllic scenes of a Constable, with cycling Nuns and tepid beer, the cricket pitches were *actually* on the green in the main square, next to the bowls club and the medieval cathedral (complete with tiny nunnery; no cycles though, Milesborough just wasn't big enough). The Olde Swan Pub, right by the lake and named after the white swans which regularly begged at the farthest tables from the main building of the pub's garden, sold warm, locally produced bitter and large servings of home-cooked, traditional food. Apart from the traffic on Wednesday and Saturday market days, the only sound you could hear, over and above the crack of leather on willow of the cricket, was the general low, contented hum of a rather affluent English countryside town ambling along in its own world.

The rugby club was slightly out of the centre of town, just after you came off the main road into Milesborough, but even this was only a ten-minute walk away. Set in its own lush green grounds and possessing a large, well stocked bar with a very liberal interpretation of the licensing laws, as well as having the biggest hall in town, the rugby club was where most of the town's social events were either held or ended up.

On a lovely spring afternoon such as this, you could spend ages wandering through the very well-maintained gardens at one end, or sit by the paddling pools at the other, with only the excited screams of the children to disturb the general peace. If you left your little monsters completely on their own, there wasn't much mischief they could get up to; the car park and only exit was in easy view and besides, one of the other parents was always there to keep an eye on them if necessary. You could even watch the Milesborough Old Boys Men's 1st Team (Rugby Union) take on the local adversaries if you really wanted to, but in general, this was simply a lovely and relaxing part of the world to come to: a perfect place to bring up children.

"Estelle, Estelle, you need to come now! The game's almost over and you know how Daddy likes you all there when he comes off the pitch."

Stell heard her mother's voice - and it did register - but she knew that Mummy was bound to call again and besides, she was having too much fun!

She turned once more towards Matt, a look of feigned determination on her face. She knew that Matt just hadn't understood what a side-step was all about and that getting past him this time would be just as easy as the previous four. However, if she made it look too easy, she'd probably get a Chinese burn anyway, just for good measure. Her brothers Jake, who was 2 years older and little Huggy, the baby of the family, looked on, Jake partly secretly hoping that this time, his best friend wouldn't be humiliated again and partly in general pride for his little sis'. Huggy just beamed in fascination.

"If I get past you this time, again without you touching me, you have to eat mud. Agreed?"

"And if I do stop you, no crying when I give you a Chinese burn. Agreed?"

"As if...."

Stell simply loved rugby. She remembered being dragged down to see her father play ever since she was tiny and when Jake started playing tag rugby three years ago at the tender age of five, she couldn't wait to have a go. You see, it was sort of easy. The boys tended to like running into people and wouldn't stop when they were told: not that you could tell them anything as they just didn't listen. They had to prove they were bigger and tougher than the other boys, which when you play tag rugby and are not actually supposed to even touch anyone, bigger and tougher just didn't enter into it. Now that Jake and Matty were old enough to start doing "contact", such as tackling and crashing through tackles, all thoughts of running round people, and how to stop people running round you, seemed to have completely left their heads.

It was an unusually warm day for this time of year and Stell's pretty pale blue dress was starting to feel really annoying. If she had taken it off though and just left it lying on the grass, Mummy would be really cross: again. She had already dispensed with those ridiculous shoes with the cutesy bow things - where had she put them again? – and the grass felt cool between her toes. The back of her neck was starting to feel clammy under all that hair and she could do with a nice, cold, fizzy drink, but there was some important business to attend to first.

Stell put the ball down onto the long grass behind the rugby clubhouse and wiped her sticky hands down the front of her dress, leaving two parallel lines of faint, sweaty smears, so she could get a better grip on the ball. Preparation complete, she picked up the ball again and tucked it into the bend of her right arm, while swaying her hips from side to side, as she'd seen some of the big girls at school do. The idea occurred to her to say something like, "You wanna piece of me?" as the big girls also did, but firstly, she didn't know what it meant and secondly, she sort of liked Matty and didn't want to upset him too much or he wouldn't hold hands with her again, or even worse, not show her his willy again: not that she'd let on to anyone that they did or he had! He'd also sort of promised that next time, she could even watch him pee...

Matt crouched in a "tackle position", or as close to what he remembered some of the England players doing on television, determined to bring this blonde-ringleted, angel-faced teaser down. Not only did she look like all the princesses in his sister's books, but she could actually do boy-stuff as well like rugby, which made her so cool compared to the other girls. However, Jake was watching and, even though Matt didn't want to hurt Stell, he had to show his best friend that no girl was better than him. Maximum force was thus required.

"Ok," he said to himself. "Last time she looked like she was going right, and she sort of made the ball look like it was going right too, but then did a little step right and went left. All I have to do is watch in which direction she does the little step and then go in the opposite direction. Easy-peasy." It was a Stell expression, but it had grown on him.

"One, two, three, GO!" yelled Jake.

Stell ran the five metres towards Matt at speed, her stride length pretty much normal for five- and three-quarter year-old legs. She then took a long step with her left leg, followed by a short one with the right.

"Got her!!!" Matt thought and dived, with as much momentum as possible, to his right, arms outstretched ready to "waste" the object of his affection. However Stell, appreciating that after four times of being made to look a bit silly, Matt may have finally "sussed on", took another short step, this time to the right off her left foot and easily rounded Matt's flailing grasp. The snort of derision was perhaps a little unnecessary, but hey, she was having a great time!

"It's not fair it's not fair, you cheated!" he complained, while Huggy clapped his hands with glee and Jake looked towards his shoes, trying hard not to be too impressed. "I'm gonna get you!" he wailed and began the chase after Estelle.

"No chance, you fatso, meanie!" Estelle laughed annoyingly and was just about to break into a sprint to evade the angry lunges when, without any warning, she ran smack bang into a slightly reddened but very stern-faced Mrs T.

"Mummy," she panted, "I was just coming," she lied.

Matt had been practising running at pace and then stopping suddenly for weeks now but again, had just not been able to "get it". This time though, the execution was perfect as he drew to a dead halt inches behind Stell under the piercing gaze of Mrs T. It was obvious where Stell got her looks from, but whereas Stell was a Goldilocks or a Cinderella (post-magical transformation), Mrs T was scary Stepmother Ice Queen person, come to eat your children, or at least make you want to look at your shoes and squirm away thoroughly chastened.

He couldn't help a smallish lump forming in his throat though and something in his chest was definitely beating faster.

"Hello Mrs Theakston," he managed to mumble and took a few steps backwards, so that Stell remained between them like the first line of defence.

"Not another word," she said in a quiet but sharp voice, ignoring Matty altogether. "Stell, boys...." Mrs T gripped Stell firmly by the arm and frog-marched her towards the 1st Team pitch. "Boys!" she rasped, this time louder, and Jake and Huggy fell in line, trotting dutifully along in the direction of the crowd about a hundred or so yards away.

"Stell, Stell," called Matty running after them, carrying a pair of slightly mud-soiled, pale blue girls' shoes, with little bows on the front.

Chapter 6: Mrs T

A former high fashion model in the mid'70s and Milesborough's most famous bad-girl during her London years, Anna Theakston (née Kominsky) had suddenly left the London party scene and come back home to Milesborough, shortly after her mother died. The only child of a German Jewish father and Dutch mother who had come to middle England during the war, Anna had left her rather staid and unexciting home life in Milesborough as soon as she could. After a number of bar and shop jobs in London, Anna was spotted whilst working at an "in"-at-the-time coffee bar in Oxford Circus by Serge (né Kevin Baxter from Hartlepool), an up and coming designer from the fashion college across the road. They worked and lived together on and off for a number of years, often consoling each other over huge quantities of red wine during the more turbulent moments of their relationships with their respective, almost constant, stream of ever-changing boyfriends. When Serge died though, at a time when the excesses of their lifestyle were taking such a tremendous toll on many of the people they had worked and played with, and when work became less and less regular once she'd hit twenty-five, it just seemed like the right time to come home.

Anna had rented a small flat near the square, having no other family and retrained as a makeup artist, eventually setting up her own one-woman fashion make-over service. She had met Roger Theakston, a Banker also known at school as FEC (Future England Captain) after his brief flirtation with Premier League Rugby (did summer training at two bigger clubs, midway through the summer was told to "Sod off back to Old Rubberduckians". Twice.), come to the salon to arrange a make-over for his then girlfriend. Roger had just been elected captain of Milesborough Old Boys Rugby Club and was a bit of a local celebrity. Anna and Roger were married within six months of meeting and the three children came swiftly afterwards, the last of whom, Hugh, arrived days after Anna's 30th birthday.

After so many years of drama (and wine), mad, passionate sex with *all* the wrong people (plus wine), illicit substances and wild parties (including even more wine!), Anna had finally found her security.

Chapter 7: Roger Theakston

There were between fifty and a hundred people milling around the side of the pitch, more or less at the halfway line. The thirty, large, bruised, grazed, sweating men were in high spirits. Those wearing maroon and yellow hoops, lead by Roger Theakston, formed themselves into two lines facing each other and began clapping.

"Three Cheers for Ambleton," shouted Roger and the whole team joined in with a very loud "Hip hip, hooray, hip hip, hooray, hip hip, hooray!"

"...and one for the Ref!"

"One!!!!" came the well-rehearsed reply. Even though this joke was not new, the good humouredness of the situation meant that everyone laughed anyway.

After they passed through the Milesborough lines, Ambleton formed their own green and white Winner's Tunnel and began their cheers to Milesborough. As Roger passed through, Estelle broke free of her mother's loosened grip and ran straight at her father.

"Woah, slow down Munch!" he said to the 5 and ¾ year-old Stell, catching her in mid-headlong dive and sweeping her into his arms. "I'm an old man now."

"You're not kidding there, you, old bastard," came a voice from behind. It was Sean, the Scrum Half. Known as Half Pint for obvious reasons, he and a few of the other players had known each other ever since they had attended Milesborough Preparatory School for Boys. Even though the rugby team was now "open", meaning that you did not have to have been a pupil at the school to play, there was still a nucleus of players who were. They tended to stick together both on and off the pitch and probably would do for the rest of their lives.

If there had been a Milesborough Prep yearbook and they had had a page entitled, "Pupils Likely to Succeed", the name of Roger Theakston would have been towards the top. Good looking, sporty, relatively intelligent, Roger was Mr Popular at school. His parents had made some money in the City and had moved to Milesborough to raise a family. The older Milesborough families had quickly come to accept Jeremy and Sally Theakston, not least because they "really played their part" in the running of the town, actively participating in fun runs, fetes, baking cakes for "Guess the Weight competitions" and contributing hugely to the restoration of the cathedral clock tower. It also helped that the local MP and Jeremy Theakston were at University together and they had sons of the same age.

During his whole early life, Roger could have the pick of whatever he wanted. Be it bikes then later cars, clothes (not interested really, but the occasional "must have" item like a WWII British Army Battledress Blouse!) and then girls, Roger normally came through, without any need for force or brashness, by basically being confident enough to believe that he should. He had played rugby since going to Milesborough

Prep and wasn't bad at all, starting off as Fly-Half (clever people, very skilful, can kick) then, due to his height and strength, moving on to Second Row (tall people who do lots of jumping and crashing into others without the ball). He could also side-step, which for someone his size could make him virtually unstoppable.

It was before going to University that a friend of a friend had been invited to attend summer training with one of the most famous clubs in the country and, always on the look out for recruits of the right calibre, the F-O-A-F could bring along one other person whom he considered good enough as well. After much pleading (and the exchange of a few small sums), Roger went along to summer training at Troubadours Football Club (Rugby Union), starting at the end of June, every Monday and Thursday night, until the start of the season in September.

Compared to the life of the average British citizen, Roger enjoyed enormous amounts of privilege but, in his peer group and as instilled in him by his father Jeremy Theakston (or J, as he liked to be called), he considered his life as normal. J was blessed, through years of working at it, with the gentleman's affability to naturally set all around him at ease. Roger tried to emulate his father in everything he did, being as polite, charming and friendly as possible - to the right people of course - so that he could glide through the world and all it had to offer as smoothly and effortlessly as did his father. He also had the firm belief that for him, everything was possible as, up to that point, it had always been.

It is not often that one comes across the very limits of one's abilities. Roger's experience at Troubadours would thrust him right up to the very edge of those limits. And beyond.

Don't Let Them See You Cry

The club ran three senior men's teams, which, with reserves, would mean a total of approximately 60 players. Every year, at least 250 people would attend the first training session. Most of these would have been playing rugby for a while and were the Big Fish in the Small Sea of whichever club they had come from. The aim of the Troubs Coaches was thus to ascertain which of the fish should never have left the shallower waters, then amongst those still able to swim, physically and mentally break them to see who had "the right stuff" in them: the inner strength; the character; the ability and willingness to push themselves to breaking point. If the player survived the examination, they would then try to see if what was left could be moulded into the sort of player that the club wanted.

Roger took one look around at his future potential teammates and his heart sank. Everybody looked as if they had stepped out of a magazine ad for the Perfect Male Specimen. Admittedly there were short ones, preposterously tall ones, Supermen-lookalikes and skinny ones (if you can call ripped, glistening muscles "skinny"), but the collection of males in front of and all around him made Roger, for the first time in his life, feel out of his depth. Unbeknownst to him at the time, this sense of disorientation, of being not in control, adrift in a hostile environment, was one of two feelings that would stay with him for the rest of his life.

Within the first 5 minutes of the very first session, Roger was made to sprint 300 metres, round three sides of a pitch, and his time was taken. If Roger took longer than a certain time, he would be told to leave: immediately, no questions, no second chances. Roger ran faster than he ever had, faster than he ever thought his legs could.

This, however, was just a trick. He and all the others were then told that the time they had just obtained was their "benchmark time". They were then instructed that in all, they would be required to run the distance six times, with a 2-minute recovery between each lap. If any of the runs took longer than the first run, they would be asked to leave: immediately, no questions, no second chances. The last few seconds of the 2-minute recovery period filled Roger with more fear than he had ever known possible.

By the end of the exercise, there were those who gave up, there were those who simply failed and there were those whose legs, lungs, heads and hearts were on fire but had succeeded. Roger was one of these; the others were not heard from again, including the friend of a friend. By the end of the first week, the smell of freshly cut grass in mid-summer made Roger feel he was going to puke, a smell that he didn't know at the time would induce that reflex, which would be the second legacy of his time at Troubadours, for the rest of his life.

His body fat had halved as he was scared to eat, knowing that any excess weight would make him less likely to be able to finish any one of the extremely punishing exercises that you could guarantee the club would have in store for them, specially designed to make them fail. The short train ride on the way to training took on the proportions of the dreaded silence he had read about from the Great War veterans, the terrifying few seconds between the end of the bombardment and the screech of the whistle ordering them over the top, so much so that his body simply shut down and he would fall asleep, his whole being trying to conserve as much energy as possible for the ordeal to come.

By the end of the third week, Roger was almost relieved when he was told to "Fuck off into the darkness and never come back." They hadn't even seen him play.

When he went back to Milesborough Old Boys to complete their summer training and was asked how things had gone at Troubs, he simply said that it had been too far to travel. He went off to University at the start of October that year, a different person to the one who had believed that one could achieve anything if one put one's mind to it and that charm, money and the right sort of background were guarantees of success. He graduated from Oxford with Half Pint and after another half-hearted attempt to play for a Second Division team, something in Roger resigned itself to the fact that that particular dream was just not going to happen. After a year of travel, he joined J's old bank in the City.

"If I remember rightly, Half Pint, you are twelve days my senior, which should mean that you'll be first to the Zimmer Frame!"

Roger Theakston's body felt hot and sticky through the coarse cotton of his rugby shirt. He smelled of a particular combination of sweat, Deep Heat and freshly cut grass ("Oh God," he thought, "I think I'm going to be sick!") and Stell nuzzled her head into his muscular chest so she could fill her lungs with the pungent mixture.

"Daddy, when I grow up I want to be just like you," she mumbled into his shirt.

"What, a big, sweaty bloke, Munchkin?" he laughed.

"No, a ball-playing Second Row forward like you."

"Munchkin, Munchkin, Munchkin," Roger tutted. "You'll get your dresses dirty," he said beaming at her. A few chuckles could be heard just behind them. Collectively, they all were in unspoken agreement that rugby just wasn't for the fairer sex.

"But that's not fair," thought Stell. "The boys do something on the rugby pitch and they're heroes, I do something and all you do is laugh about it and tell me to go play with my dolls. And Jake's not even very good and Matty's hopeless!"

Before she could put her thoughts into words though, Half Pint chipped in, "You certainly wouldn't want to hang around with a bunch of reprobates like us!"

"He knows of what he speaks," came another voice.

Stell's "But, but but..." protests were drowned out by a familiar "Tackle!" yelled loudly by her two brothers and she turned in time to see Jake and Huggy, flying towards her and her father, in full attack mode.

Stell felt herself being swivelled round at speed and hoisted onto her father's shoulders in one deft movement. Roger readjusted his position to leave his hands free to catch, in each arm, the leaping figures of his two sons.

"Good attacking skills boys, but I'm too bad for ya'!" he said with a false American accent as he squeezed his sons tightly to him. Jake and Huggy giggled wildly and Stell smiled, through clenched teeth, but said nothing. With three children clinging onto any available space on him, Stell's dress partly covering his head almost down to his protective ear tape, Roger looked the ideal dad-like climbing frame. Some of the crowd smiled approvingly at the spectacle and Mrs T, ten metres in front and slightly to one side, gave herself a small, internal pat on the back. Some of the other summer-dressed ladies watching this little scene, including one or two of the wives and partners, felt a tiny bit of an appreciative chest-flutter and either looked away as demurely as they thought they should or indeed stared directly into Roger's eyes, hoping to register his interest and thus give him a reason to talk to them when back at the clubhouse.

"Funny that," said Rick, the Hooker and "thrower in" to the line-out, "five minutes ago you couldn't catch for love nor money, now you're juggling three rug-rats!" There was general laughter at this, including from the Ambleton players, who also had wives, girlfriends and children in the crowd coming to congratulate or commiserate with them. Apart from the few children remaining on the pitch kicking whatever balls they could find over the posts at the clubhouse end, all marched off towards the beer, food and showers. The sounds of good-natured banter, laughter, in-depth post match analysis of the self-deprecative kind and general ribbing filled the bright, late afternoon.

As Stell rocked gently from side to side, still perched on her father's shoulders as they reached the clubhouse, where he shooed the children in before turning towards the changing rooms, something in her, and she didn't know what or why, felt a little crushed.

Chapter 8: Fi's Dad

During the Bush War, or the Second Chimurenga depending on your point of view, and for a time afterwards, James Stanley's family suffered.

The middle son of three (plus a girl), James was born almost nine months to the day after his father returned home to Mashonaland, Rhodesia at the end of the Second World War, a piece of Italian shrapnel lodged in his upper thigh. The farm had survived the war well and it didn't take long before it was producing even more tobacco than it had in its most prosperous months.

One of the strongest memories Jimmy had of the Olde Country was the long cycle rides to school, across open field, round the stables with the free ranging horses accompanying him some of the way, the cheeky short-cut across the bottom of Old Man Johnston's farm and then the winding dirt road which led past the dairy, with its straw-roofed workers huts and then through one of the many large gaps in the school's highly porous hedge border to enter the grounds at the foot of the playing fields.

Fluent in Shona and Ndebele, the locals always called out to him on his journey and he always replied, as politely as he had been taught, exchanging the odd joke and pleasantries while his legs pumped away as fast as he could on his rickety old bike.

A natural front row forward in terms of size and shape, Jimmy was short for his age and quite stocky, with a good deal of raw strength, enhanced as early as was allowed by his father's specially equipped gym (imported from the US at outrageous cost). He represented the school rugby team in every year of his attendance, first at Tight Head Prop and then as the other boys shot up and his height remained the same, at Hooker, right up until international selection at the age of 18. He was twenty when UDI was declared and the initial euphoria of independence gave way to total despair when he realised that the impending sanctions spelt the end of his international rugby career.

Jimmy would never again experience the thrill of pulling on the green and white Sables jersey, feel the lump in the throat and the hair-bristling jolt of electricity of the national anthem, sung heartily at the tops of the lungs of 50,000 fellow Rhodesians at Rufaro Stadium, proving a major triumph of optimism over reality as they would invariably lose, but it didn't matter as you were doing the thing you loved, lining up against the biggest and the best the world had to offer, at the highest level possible. He was only 21, but already Jimmy felt that the best part of his life was over. The future that he could have had was being robbed from him and there was nothing he could do about it.

Nobody knows for sure the exact day the Bush War began. It was sometime in 1972 that Jimmy noticed that some of the local boys just weren't there anymore. Even though most families still smiled at him, the warmth and familiarity seemed to have also departed.

By the time relative peace came some seven years later, Jimmy had lost his father, two brothers, a sister and his mother was stricken by cholera through poisoned drinking water. Zimbabwe was formed the next year and the newly elected President appealed to the whites to stay and help build the new country. On demobilisation, Jimmy moved back to Mashonaland to nurse his mother in her final days, quickly marrying Penny Johnston, the sole surviving member of the family of the neighbouring farm, more through duty and shared loss than love. He couldn't have known at the time that her experiences through the war had left her as dead, cold and lifeless inside as her destroyed home.

Jimmy knew he had to try to bury deep inside himself the anger and the barbarism of the war, annexed the two farms and through extreme hard work and single-minded determination, was able to not only rebuild his shattered life but those of the people around him. He successfully traded with the States and built up a stash of US Dollars in offshore accounts, to be used "for a rainy day" if the climate in the country changed. During this time, Penny gave birth to first Fiona and two years later to Susan. In 1987, just before the farm expulsions began, Jimmy sensed that the rainy day was approaching and sold the enlarged and prosperous farm to his loyal foreman for a good price. With the help of business contacts, Jimmy bought four one-way tickets to California.

The investment into run-down buildings close to the famous beaches, then their subsequent conversions into gyms, paid dividends almost immediately. Despite the new-found wealth though, Jimmy felt as if he were stateless, his country gone and his love for the game of rugby twisted into an empty bitterness for what might have been.

Being wealthy and a former international, he soon found himself very firmly at the centre of the sun-seeking West Coast Rhodie community and enjoyed a lifestyle similar to back in the Olde Country. Many nights among his countryman, drinking tankards of rum and coke, filled with so much ice that the first few sips numbed the bottom half of your face, often resulted in heated and probably wildly inaccurate reminiscences on Rhodesia ("God's own country"), the state of the new nation of Zimbabwe ("Communists running the place to the dogs") and the lack of virtually any good rugby in the States. These evenings were often followed by enormous hangovers and ill-tempered contrition the next morning.

Fi's mother Penny did not survive the transition well. She missed the feeling of space, the smells, the sounds, the evening skies of the bush of her homeland. In America, you could hear neighbours, traffic, police sirens, people! After the divorce, Penny Stanley moved to South Africa to stay with cousins.

Within virtually days of her departure, a new, younger, plucked and painted American-peroxide Mrs Stanley was seen in tow. Fifteen years Jimmy's junior, Cheryl ("Just call me Cherry", or "the Witch" according to Fi), who had worked her way up from Receptionist in the gym to General Manager in a remarkably short space of time, had completely captivated Jimmy and restricted his Rhodie nights to only one or two a week. The ten-year-old Fi and the younger Susie became projects that "Call Me Cherry" was going to mould into proper American young ladies: well at least until Fi and Susie had a new brother or sister.

The first thing to go though would be what "Call Me Cherry" referred to as, "those ridiculous accents…"

Chapter 9: Milesborough Old Boys Minis Under 9s

Stell closed her eyes for the third time, clenching her fists simultaneously. Rocking gently backwards on the balls of her feet, she looked up. The posts seemed to stretch up into the heavens, staring down on to the head of the precocious 8-year-old with a mixture of complete contempt and disbelief. Surely this little blonde girl wasn't going to attempt a penalty from what, a full 20 metres out? No, absolutely no chance. The late September sun shone low over Milesborough that particular Sunday morning, casting warm, dappled light through the still green trees that bordered the rugby club by the clubhouse. Stell winced.

"Whassamatter, Girly, lost ya' bottle?"

Huggy shot a glance towards Darren that was heavily laden with malevolence. He had followed his older brother and sister into playing rugby and was showing all the promise of a natural Scrum Half: small, fast, quick-witted, a good pass, even at the age of 6 and, most importantly, an almost suicidal naked aggression, lurking just below the surface. For years he had known that he could get up to all sorts of trouble, being little and quite cute and Jake and Stell would normally either cover for him with Mum or fight on his behalf when it came to disagreements with their peer group. It was only recently though that he realised that it was much more fun actually doing the fighting himself!

At the age of 5 and 6, despite what they may actually get up to, boys (and girls for that matter), don't like fighting. Physical pain, or rather the thought of it, frightens them as even parents seem not to know how to make it stop. The reason they still fight though is because they actually really enjoy the hitting!

Huggy thus worked out that if you could launch an attack first and inflict pain, irrespective of the size of your opponent, after the initial swift and violent assault the enemy would normally burst into floods of tears and beat a loud, wailing retreat back to the arms of their respective Mummies. And if that didn't work, there was always Jake and Stell as back-up…

"Perfect psychometric profile for a Scrum Half!" future Games Masters would eventually discover.

Now that Huggy hadn't needed Stell to bail him out for weeks, he felt that he was The Appointed Defender of the Theakston Honour and any perceived insult to the family, especially to his adorable sister, should be dealt with with extreme prejudice.

Darren didn't "get" the Theakstons. They were undoubtedly Posh Kids from the Posh Houses in the "Lanes" and it was quite clear that their family had loads of money, but they were actually all really nice. Unlike some of the other kids at the public school he attended, Jake and his mate Matty talked to him and had even invited him to the rugby club ("Did you know my Dad used to be the captain and runs the Minis now?") in order to save him from the terrible stigma of always being the Last One Picked At Games.

It was just as well really as he had been hopeless at rugby when he first came to the school. Darren, his Mum and little sister had moved up to Milesborough at the beginning of the school year, from one of the only moderately-disastrous London Council estates. For about a year before the move, he had been hanging around with some of the older boys from the estates and although he hadn't personally gotten into any trouble - apart from that time he'd brought a "new" bike home one evening that his Mum made him leave outside the local police station - according to his Nanna, it was really only a matter of time. A small inheritance from his Aunt Jean, along with the insurance money from his Dad's compensation had allowed his Mum to move the family closer to Nanna up in Milesborough, rent a small cottage where he could have his own room and enrol him into Milesborough Preparatory School for Boys.

Before coming to Milesborough, the only sport Darren had ever played was football. Lack of money had also meant that his staple diet had consisted of chips with everything, washed down with various colours of fizzy, deathly sweet, carbonated water. Being at a rugby-playing school and having no clue about rugby, plus having a waistline as living testament to his eating habits was tantamount to having a sign on his forehead stating: "Little fat misfit last to be picked for anything: please ostracise with care." He was in real danger of that particular label having an effect on not only how he was perceived in all other aspects of his school life but, according to various sociological theories, probably for the rest of his life as well. Matty had taken pity when the new boy had arrived and with Jake, who was always one of the "pickers", being captain in virtually everything and thus a relative authority in the classroom, they had offered him a modicum of protection from the merciless pillorying of which little boys can be so capable.

The Theakstons had a knack of making people feel welcome and at ease and had seemed the perfect family: Dad: Mr Popular; Mum: beautiful (even though very definitely scary); Jake: the sort of boy you wished you were and Stell: absolutely marriable. The only one to worry about was Huggy though, who definitely had the makings of a miniature psychopath. Darren looked over towards Huggy glowering just behind his right shoulder and decided it probably wasn't a good idea to try to goad Stell anymore.

Stell completed her pre-kick ritual (turning side on to the posts, arms cradled together in front of her) and struck the ball with her right foot. It limped onto the bar, stumbled against one post and flopped over to score the penalty.

"Three points to England with the last kick of the game and the Twickenham crowd is going wild!" shouted Matty, appearing at the side of the pitch precisely when the kick went over. He and Jake had just finished the serious rugby (Milesborough Minis under 11s, with full tackling and Roger Theakston as Head Coach) and even though tired and bruised, were beaming away at their earlier performances. Darren had injured his shoulder playing at prop for school the previous week so had been designated "baby-sitting" duties by Mrs T, which involved looking after the young ones who finished half an hour earlier than the under 11s. Mrs T only very rarely attended the Minis sessions on Sunday mornings now, preferring to spend some time on her own for once, pottering around the house and listening to the radio.

"Well done Sis," said Jake. "Are you guys in some sort of competition then?"

"Yep," interjected Huggy, "And Dazza-boy got whipped by Stell. Again. These people just don't know when they're beaten." Huggy especially liked the "these people" remark, as he was determined to let Darren know that he wasn't like them, he wasn't liked and he wasn't welcome. He also had this annoying habit of just staring at his sis' with his mouth open like a drooling idiot that made Huggy simply want to kill him.

Darren was furious. "I'm a bleedin' Prop, what do I need to kick for anyway?"

"He's right," said Matty, feeling solidarity with his friend at having lost out to Stell. He was officially no longer in love with Stell, so was able to defend his mate without feeling a pang of disloyalty. Well, almost... "And he's one of the best Props the school has ever had. Some of the Masters believe he has the potential to go all the way."

"Yeah, all the way back to the Council Estate in London," added Stell. She really didn't mean it: she had never been to a Council Estate, but she'd heard Darren talk about it with a mixture of fondness and fear and so was sure that referring to it would get under his skin. Deep down inside, she actually quite liked him as he seemed so genuine. His puppy dog devotion made her feel safe and even the way he constantly tried to suck up to Jake and Matty was endearing. The fact that neither Darren or Matty would admit that they both really liked her made for hours of good clean fun, as it was brilliant watching them struggle to maintain their friendship when they were so obviously rivals in love. For Stell, it was great to be a girl sometimes!

Darren, honour slighted, felt the need to defend himself. "My Dad came from a Council Estate and he was a Para. He told me all about Norvern Eyeland and the Nazis and that. He's done more for this country than your Dad ever did."

A pang of retaliatory anger shot through Huggy.

"Depends what you mean by "more for this country"," said Jake. "Everyone recognises the contributions that people such as your father have made Darren, but I tend to believe that war occurs when civilised systems fail. Maintaining peace is surely preferable to war and my family, through helping to build civilised systems, do just as much."

Nobody understood a word of what Jake had said and even Jake, having heard such a speech from his father a million times, had only a vague idea. It did sound mightily impressive though and Darren, sensing an attempt was being made to placate him, as well as realising that the look in Huggy's eye showed an attack was imminent, decided to try to diffuse the situation.

"So, what's your favourite war then?" he asked everyone in general.

"Trojan," said Matty in all innocence. Stell, realising that the classical conflicts of thousands of years ago would probably not have been at the forefront of Dazza's conscious, sniggered. Huggy clocked on that fun was being taken out of his favourite victim and, even though he didn't know what they were talking about, decided that this was the funniest thing he'd ever heard. He fell to the floor in fits of hysterical, forced laughter and rolled over and over in the grass. The other boys and parents now leaving the club house and making their respective ways towards their cars turned their heads to see what all the fuss was about.

Feeling the eyes of all those other boys, Stell, Matty, Jake and that demented dwarf Huggy boring into him, Darren suddenly snapped.

"You lot fink you're all so special dontcha, like you got this perfect family and nobody else is worff nuffin'. Well you're not as bleedin' special as you fink! Your Dad's nowhere near as special as you lot fink! The bleedin' cheater!"

Huggy was immediately dragged back from his play-acting by the blatant attack on his Fantastic Father. He scrambled to his feet and dived at Darren, hitting him square in the chest with full force. Darren fell to the floor and the two rolled around in the grass, Huggy desperately trying to claw at his face. Eventually Darren managed to grab hold of Huggy's hands and threw him off so he landed two feet away on his back. Stell was immediately on to him though and pressed him to the grass. Darren felt his strength desert him as Stell rasped into his face from two inches away, "What the Hell do you mean?"

"I don't mean nuffin', honest, I don't mean nuffin! Get her off me!"

Matty, in shock, and Jake, eerily calm, gently eased Stell off of their distraught friend. Once Darren was sitting down on the grass, sobbing, and the little crowd of parents and their sons had dispersed, Jake said in a very calm, measured voice, "I think you'd better tell us what you know." Darren knew that in this ice-cold, determined mood, Jake was not someone to mess about with. He made up his mind to tell all, the words coming out in a breathless rush.

"Last Sunday yeah, I had to stay behind to see the physio because of my shoulder, yeah. Well I was waitin' outside, it was about one o'clock, and there was no-one else about, apart from one of the under 14s who was in the physio room. Well, Mum was waiting wiv' me and then she went into the club house for some water. I got bored waitin' and went to get her, but I went the back way through the car park."

"Get to the point," hissed Jake.

"Well, I saw 'em," continued Darren. The looks of incomprehension that greeted him suggested that further clarification was likely to be needed.

"What, you saw Dad and your Mum together?" asked Jake.

"Nah, I saw your Dad and Rob's Mum Mrs Pearce in her car. She had her boobies out and everyfing. He was all over her he was!" Of course he couldn't be sure of the sighting of "boobies", but he thought he'd add that salacious detail for good effect.

Huggy burst into tears, Stell just sat there trembling. Matty stared at the grass and was also shaking. "Go on," pressed Jake.

"That's when my Mum came out. She had obviously been lookin' for your Dad and when she looked at where I was looking, into Rob's Mum's car, and she saw what they was gettin' up to, she completely lost it! She was banging on the car window and shouting and swearing. Rob's Mum drove off like she was at Brands Hatch. Then the physio was calling me and Mum said I had to go. She's never said a word about it since then, but every now and then I hear her cryin'."

"But, I don't get it," said Matty. "Why was your Mum acting like that, Darren?"

"Because he's been seeing her as well, you idiot!" rasped Stell.

"Darren?" asked Jake firmly.

Darren nodded his head. "He's been coming round our 'ouse for the last few months now. At first, it was to see me to give me rugby tips and that, plus help a bit wiv' school work and that."

"Eh," Stell reflected, "he didn't do that with me!"

Darren continued, "Then, I've seen 'im coming in late at night and leave sometimes in the morning."

"So that explains all those meetings in London over the last few months then?" thought Stell.

Darren looked at the faces of his three friends, plus Huggy. They were disconsolate, their pain twisting in his heart like a knife. He even felt sorry for Huggy, whose bottom lip was trembling.

Stell felt numb and couldn't bring herself to cry. Huggy burst into tears though and Stell hugged her little brother tightly to her.

Trying to ease the pain, Darren added, "'Ee don't come round no more though, and all Mum does is cry."

"That's because he's too busy seeing everyone else!" Stell thought, who over the last few weeks had noticed, but hadn't really given much thought to, the much greater number of Mums than normal during what should have been their coveted "time off" from the kids, in full make up on a Sunday morning, lurking around the u11s rugby pitch. "They can't all be interested in getting their boys to play rugby?" she'd wondered. Well, she was right.

"The dirty bastard. The dirty, dirty bastard."

"What are you chaps all scheming about then?" came the pleasant voice of Roger Theakston, who had just finished tidying away the kit from the u11s rugby session.

Chapter 10: A not so fond farewell

Stell and Huggy sat on the floor in her room, hugging each other tightly while gently rocking from side to side. Jake had gone to his room and was probably playing on his computer or something. He'd been deadly quiet in the car, in fact they all had apart from Huggy who wouldn't stop crying. After dropping Matty off at his home, the silence seemed to have taken Matty's place: an uncomfortable and unwelcome guest who insisted that nobody speak. All her father had said when he saw their collective grief-stricken faces at the rugby ground was, "Oh God, oh God...." and for a moment his face became a mask of horror. He then started issuing commander-like orders, as he had been doing a lot recently, telling Darren to go into the club house to wait for his Mum and the other children to follow him to the car. Stell so wanted to shout how much she hated him, but you just didn't speak to Daddy like that.

When they got to the house, Mrs T knew instantly there was something wrong. The children had been sent upstairs and all Stell could hear, before she shut her bedroom door, was "Anna, I think we need to talk..."

They had expected shouting, banging of doors, throwing of plates etc as should have been standard procedure in such situations according to all the television films they'd seen. This silence, in contrast, was eerie. So this is the noise a dying family made? Almost nothing, except for the occasional shut drawer, the opening and closing of a few doors, a few phone calls, the bump and scrape of a few suitcases being taken downstairs. Stell felt empty inside. Ok, she knew that Mum maybe wasn't perhaps the most fun parent in the world and when she was not happy with you, those icy, accusing looks could make you want to confess even to things you hadn't done. But what on earth was Daddy doing with Darren's Mum! And Mrs Pearce as well! What was Daddy thinking?! There must be some reason behind it: Dad wouldn't do anything like that if there weren't some sensible explanation.

"That's it," she thought, "it was all some mistake." She knew Dad wouldn't cheat on Mum and certainly wouldn't cheat on her. She was his lovely little Munchkin, whom he loved – he did love her 'cos he used to say it so often – it must have been Darren's Mum's fault.

She concluded that, "You just can't trust those people...."

But then there was Mrs Pearce. And, come to think of it, a whole gaggle of them trailing after him on a Sunday morning that if her Dad were to turn around suddenly, they'd probably all run smack bang into him! "I bet they'd love that..."

Stell's thoughts were interrupted by the doorbell. She let go of Huggy who tried to cling on to her, but when she brushed off his feeble grasp, his arms just flopped to his sides. Making her way carefully to her bedroom door, she opened it to see her father downstairs in the hallway, with a large suitcase, just about to go out the front door. A taxi driver was waiting on the path outside. Mum stood in the hallway at the foot of the stairs, stern-faced, eyes red-rimmed but make-up still perfectly in place. It was obvious she'd been crying, but she'd still found the time to look almost flawless.

The realisation that her father was leaving her, possibly forever, suddenly hit Stell. She threw herself downstairs in panic.

"Daddy, Daddy, don't go!" she wailed as she bounded towards him. Hearing the rushing footsteps down the stairs, Roger Theakston turned around just as she flung herself onto his legs, hugging them tightly to her.

"Munch, let go," Roger said as firmly as he could, a little tremor in his voice.

"Daddy, don't leave me, don't leave me, I'll be good, I won't fight anymore nor play rugby, I'll eat my breakfast and get up when you tell me and do as you say and wear dresses and do everything you want, I promise I promise!" The words and tears spilled out of her as she squeezed her father's legs, pressing her head into the rugby shirt taut over his still flat stomach. He smelt of the sweat of the morning's training.

"Get OFF me!" Roger shouted, his voice louder than she could ever remember it being. He grabbed Stell's arms and tried to forcibly drag her from him. She refused to give up so easily though and using all her 8-year-old strength, held on for dear life. If she let go now, she'd lose him forever.

"FUCKING LET GO!" he screamed. Roger seized Stell's upper arms and peeled them from him, while sweeping her up and throwing her to the floor. Stell crashed into a heap on the hallway carpet and her mother rushed towards her. Jake, brought out of his room by the sobbing and shouting and Huggy, tiny face streaked by tears, peered down at the scene from in between the spindles of the upper landing. Partly in shock at hearing her father swear for the first time EVER, and being partly asphyxiated by her mother's crushing embrace, with the pain in her throbbing arms mounting with every second, Stell's world collapsed. She heard the door slam shut.

Through the hysterical, loud sobs, she managed to cry out as loudly as her voice could stretch to, "I hate you, I hate you..."

Chapter 11: Roger Theakston: Dirty Bastard

"Oh my God, what have I done?" Roger thought as the taxi meandered through the Lanes back towards the centre of town. The image of Stell's little angel face, tears streaming down her cheeks and the words, "I hate you" ringing in his ears brought home to him the enormity of what had just transpired. A good, stiff single malt whisky (aged at least 10 years) down at the Olde Swan would help him think things through.

So as not to dwell too much on emotions, Roger turned his mind to the practical. "One of Half-Pint's partners from his law firm should be able to thrash out some sort of deal in the divorce. Good job this isn't America as I wouldn't have a hope! Anna will obviously go for the jugular – no wonder hurricanes were named after women," he thought. "When they arrive they're all hot, wet and wild, when they leave they take the car and half the house!"

But then, Anna had never really been all hot, wet and wild.

He remembered when he first met her, in that ladies' salon in what seemed like a lifetime ago. What was the name of the girlfriend at the time that he was smitten by? "Doesn't matter really." Anna just looked stunning. She had the longest legs, clad in those white high-heeled boots, her long blonde hair was piled up on top of her head and miraculously all held in place by a single long chopstick type thing in a way that looked like she'd either just chucked it all together in seconds or that someone had spent a good part of the morning arranging every last strand of. Either way, it looked fantastic.

Then there was the face. Reminiscent of one of those porcelain dolls – absolutely flawless (being a bloke, Roger wasn't familiar with the concept of foundation, especially not so expertly applied) - that little, pointy chin, snooty nose, thick, dark eye-shadow and mascara enhancing those unfeasibly long lashes. What had really captivated him though, and captivated is no exaggeration because he literally could not move for a few seconds after seeing her, was her eyes. Large, round, steely blue, incredibly sad, they seemed as if tears were on the point of seeping out, ever so quietly, as if an inner pain was attempting to leave her body, but in a way so as to not make too much of a fuss.

Of course Roger recognised the face and instantly remembered who she was – all the half-heard stories of London-based indiscretions where nobody seemed to know any detail but everyone was sure something naughty had happened – none of it mattered. He felt that he could coax that sadness out of this amazing looking woman and replace it with happiness and light and life. He could make those eyes sparkle and laugh, he could make that slightly emaciated body dance and jump and clap its hands and wriggle and writhe with pleasure and...

"Steady, steady!" he interrupted himself, suddenly becoming aware of certain parts of his anatomy enthusiastically rising to the theme. Regaining composure, he half-whispered, "Roger Theakston, pleased to meet you."

Over the course of his dating years (13 – 30 approx: he started young, his mother had a friend who'd always found him cute and tried to slip her middle-aged tongue in once or twice, when his Mum wasn't looking....), Roger had, as a result of rather a lot of empirical research in the field, established a theory, that he never tired of sharing with Half-Pint and the boys, with regards to Risk (looking like a berk after being told to sod off) and Reward (getting totty as high up the food chain as possible).

Women came in three categories: the Securities (as in, "I know I can go home with her if all else fails during the course of the evening, so she will be my fall-back option"), the Oh My God She's Fantastic (no explanation necessary) and the Others, who, in terms of attractiveness resided somewhere in between the two. Now, so many men spend so much effort on the Others, wining and dining and investing time and money etc when what they really wanted was an OMGSF but didn't have the bottle to approach one. Unless of course they were exceedingly drunk.

It was only after a sufficient quantity of alcohol had been consumed that one would attempt to talk to an OMGSF, but by then, coherent speech, wit, charm and most of all just being nice (that last pearl of wisdom was only acquired by Roger after copious amounts of research) was something that *other* people did. So, OMGSFs were normally only accosted by sad, pissed, spineless individuals and so they spent lots of time looking good but being bored. And lonely.

Rather than invest time and energy in one of the Others (or go for the default Security option), why not simply approach an OMGSF, whilst still sober of course, and see what happens?

If you win, you've struck gold and all your mates will pay eternal homage; if you lose and you're told to exit stage right, it makes no difference how attractive (or not) the young lady is who's issued said marching orders.

Taking all muster-able courage in both hands, Roger continued, "I wonder if you could help? My, er, Mother's birthday's coming up and I was thinking of doing something a bit special this year."

The dead eyes only half-registered interest.

"I say, nice boots!" Roger blurted out (staged blurt for "sincere" effect)." Now she'll have to respond," he schemed. If your initial approach doesn't work, an alternate one is to compliment a girl on something that she normally never gets complimented on. Like her boots, for example. Saying, "You're beautiful" to a woman who is beautiful is probably not the most original thing they've ever heard, but saying, "Are those Jimmy Choos?!" to beautiful women will at least get you noticed. Even if she does think you're gay.

"Er, erm, thank you," Anna replied. Then, feeling something more was required from her side after a rather unexpected compliment from someone who looked the least likely person in the world to be interested in ladies' boots - expensive suit, even though a little too conservative, light blue lining (nice), plumby, confident voice, blonde floppy hair, fairly good looking in a Little Posh Boy sort of way - added, "I got them in London. Carnaby Street."

"I love it there," Roger went on, possibly slightly too enthusiastically ("Slight slip, will have to play it a bit cooler," he thought).

"Do you go there often?" he said, trying not to groan at the use of the tired and overworked, but nevertheless effective, classic chat-up line. He pressed on regardless.

And so conversation was joined. They talked about fashion and trips to London, Roger pretending he didn't know who she was, or had been and Anna pleased to be able to speak to someone who seemed quite nice about things she found interesting. They ended up arranging for Anna to come to the house to meet Mrs Theakston for the phantom makeover (his Mother Sally was initially furious but secretly admired the scheming, as well as obtaining an inside track to one of Milesborough's favourite talking points of the moment: how envious her friends would be!), and after hours chatting with Anna about makeup and modelling and eventually her life in London, Sally and Anna became firm friends. Anna's role changed over a very short space of time from Roger's friend to confidante to virtually part of the family.

It was more or less taken for granted that, after a relatively brief courtship, full of introductions to a dizzying array of family members (on Roger's side), family friends and assorted others that Sally Theakston wanted to impress, (one of) Milesborough's Most Eligible Batchelors and its Most Attractive (and infamous) Young Ladies would soon be married in a blaze of paparazzi. Even some of the London journos would put in an appearance, keen to make the short trip down the M4 to cover what would be Milesborough's picture wedding of the year. A surge of pride rose up in Roger at the memory of those pre-wedding months. He'd scored such a hotty, even his father J was impressed.

But, old habits die hard. After spending most of his adult life perfecting the skill of seduction (no skill really, just being nice and having the guts to make the initial approach; being attractive, rich and successful had nothing to do with it!), it would sort of be rude not to use it.

Stories emerged about what happened on the Stag Do to Amsterdam. However, with the old mantra of "what goes on on tour stays on tour" being employed to the maximum, none of the rugby boys would go into any detail about Roger pulling in the lap-dancing clubs ("No-one pulls in a lap-dancing club, the man's a legend!")

"Besides, like calories consumed at the cinema, indiscretions committed at away fixtures don't count."

In the first few months after the picture-book wedding, Roger was ecstatic. He was working hard and training harder and apart from a few "shenanigans" that had started before he met Anna, to which he was *definitely* in the process of putting an end, he was mainly faithful. When patchy news of Roger's extra-curricular activities filtered through to Anna via the wives and girlfriends' network, Anna chose to ignore it, putting it down to over-active imaginations, misunderstandings and eventually jealousy. She'd scored the big fish in the little Milesborough sea, why wouldn't there be some residue envy floating around?

Suspicions though, at first so infinitesimally small that they were no more than the suggestions of whispers, seemed to linger. Was her loving husband really at a meeting until that time? Did he really have to go away for work that weekend? Did he really smell of that other perfume because he was sprayed by one of the fragrance girls at Harvey Nics? The long, auburn, obviously female hair in his boxer shorts could so easily have been as a result of the shared laundry at work.....

It seemed silly to question Roger as he in general was quite lovely but, little by little, Anna began imagining a wild and torrid alternative life for her husband, in which he entertained bevies of buxom page 3 beauties, wearing extraordinarily kinky clothes (him, not them), drinking champagne from patent leather stilettos in lust-crazed orgies of debauched pleasure!

A bit like her London days....

Anna found herself increasingly distracted, not able to concentrate on anything she was doing and thoughts of Serge and other dead friends from her previous existence began to flood back. The distance between her and Roger started to grow and she felt that her perfect, normal life, that she was so lucky to have found after her wild and ultimately self-destructive last few years, was slipping away from her. There was only one thing to do.....

The quick-fire birth of Jake and then later Estelle had a deep effect on Roger. Staring into their little faces in their cots, seeing his Mother's chin, J's nose, feeling the strong grip when he put his finger in Stell's tiny, proud fist ("Er, that's not right, I mean in Jake's tiny fist!" he corrected himself), Roger vowed that he would be the sort of man they would be proud of. Jake and Stell would view him as he saw J: strong, powerful, a great laugh, limitless wisdom, caring, kind, devoted. Jake would be a mini Roger Theakston: great sportsman, good with the ladies, an all-round good bloke; Stell: a striking, porcelain beauty, just like the woman he'd married. From the moment he left the Milesborough General Hospital (Private Wards), hours after the birth of his son, he would be a changed man.

After the birth of Estelle, the Theakston marriage enjoyed 3 years of relative bliss. Mrs T, who was now a Full Time Mum, was kept busy by the endless drop-offs and pick-ups to schools, Nannies, childminders and after school clubs ("but it's important that Stell does Baby Pilates – it's good for her biorhythmic karma"). There was also the gym, coffee mornings, Mother and Baby groups and visits to Other People Who Have Children That Age, even if that was all there was in common. Roger was moving up the greasy City pole, having been made FX Director the previous year and was now Milesborough Old Boys' (Rugby Union) 1st Team Captain.

Dilemma: Stell was in full time private nursery ("Oh how her Spanish is improving as her teacher Raimonda from Colombia hardly speaks any English you know!") and Jake was in school, how was Anna going to now spend her time? Should she venture out into the world to seek respectable, paid employment and do her bit for the financial welfare of the family or should she have a third child?

Hugh Aloisius Theakston was born 9 months, 3 weeks and one day after Stell began full time nursery, just after Anna turned thirty. Roger thought, after five years of nappies, sleepless nights, blended mush for food, a wife who dressed in perma-track suit (complete with indiscernible dried food attachment in full view) and looked like sleep-deprived death, plus crying, crying, CRYING, it was all going to start again....

Chapter 12: Dinner Dance

The end of the season couldn't come quickly enough. Results for the Mighty Hammers had been less than impressive, but at least they had warded off the threat of relegation for another year which, after their meteoric rise up the league structure following their inception four years previously, could have spelt disaster. When the Ladies team started, not many of the girls had played rugby before as normally, even if you had dabbled at tag rugby when you were little, as soon as you had to tackle and be tackled at age 9, virtually all the girls stopped playing.

Hardly any facilities existed at all for ladies' rugby until Uni age, when those who may have played before pre-age 9, as well as complete newcomers to the sport (what other sport can you join as a complete newbie at age 18 and still be no worse than anyone else?) could enter into the surreptitious world of mud, blood, bawdy songs and hard drinking. Unlike the boys, most of whom had no choice in the decision whether or not to risk life and limb on the rugby pitch but were made to play by cither, fathers who had played themselves or by their good schools, rugby for a young lady in England is a personal decision, often taken in the face of enormous hostility. Friends, family, former teachers, boyfriends (past and present) the milkman and even passing stray neighbourhood dogs all thought that they were allowed to express their opinion on whether rugby was a fitting activity for dear sweet Penelope or Felicity or Samantha. And why shouldn't Rover have a say; everyone else seemed to?

The scandal and universal disapproval in which Penny/ Flicker/ Sam would now find herself when she went back home, usually during the first couple of terms of Freshers' Year, would produce an unusual effect. Some young ladies, deafened by the mounting whispering campaign and insinuations about their sexuality from so-called "friends" back home would simply just stop: it was just too much hassle. What made things even more confusing though was that friends and family who only a few years previous, and even now, feted and celebrated the achievements of fathers, brothers and boyfriends on the rugby pitch now seemed to be the most ardent in their disapproval when it came to poor Pen playing. Penny would simply slip back into the world of "Other People's (even though well-meaning) Expectations" and a little bit of her: her independence, her desire to choose, her belief that anything was possible and achievable, would wither.

The young ladies though who decided that, despite all the hostility, they would continue, adopted an "Everyone Hates Us, We Don't Care" entrenched mentality and seemed to be driven closer together as Rugby Girls rather than, as the collective disapproval had probably intended, be driven apart. Being a Rugby Player now became a defining characteristic – a stand against people's conception of who they were, a way of saying to Mum and Dad and weedy, macho-man boyfriends and the prissy, bitchy girls back at school "Fuck you! This is me, deal with it."

There was only one small problem though.....

The girls had no idea how the game should be played!

Oh there was always the one or two who had more of a clue than the others, which wasn't really hard, but in general, the only reference points they had were their local men's teams or the rugby they saw on television, in the days when some international teams believed that large men running not particularly quickly right at other large men waiting for them ("Big men running straight!") was the most effective way of scoring a try. It was no surprise then that a good proportion of the ladies playing rugby tended to adopt that particular tactic. Being big, strong and harder than the rugby boys were prized attributes, to the detriment of speed and skill, so the general school of thought in ladies' rugby was that the larger and less fit you were, the more suited you were to being a rugby player.

It also meant that you had an excuse to indulge in all sorts of behaviour that would otherwise be assured to get you arrested but, for some strange reason, because you were a rugby player, all seemed to be perfectly acceptable. Thus, in any given town centre on any given night, being found handcuffed to a lamp post, whilst scandalously, paralytically drunk, covered in a combination of the regurgitated remains of last night's curry and a weird, unrecognisable sticky substance, wearing underwear of the opposite sex and singing the most outrageously lewd and tasteless songs is all totally acceptable and almost unremarkable if the Counsel for the Defence can make a credible claim that you do in fact, play rugby.

"Oh, that makes all the difference then! Officer, why on earth didn't you say so before? Which team do you play for?

Troubadours, you say? I knew a Second Row there, back in '65, by the name of..."

"So, Mr Idi Amin Dada, what position do you play? Hooker for Sandhurst?[20] Oh, that's alright then! Officer, release this man at once! I played there myself when I was a lad....."

"So, Mr Hussein, is there anything you wish to say before I pass sentence? What, Fly-half for Baghdad Old Boys? Why didn't you say so before?"

At the lower levels of the WRFU South East West League structure, as many of the players had never seen a rugby ball up close before, the standard of play was not high. In fact, it was only after the Hammers had been promoted two seasons in a row, they could more or less guarantee that the opposition would have enough players to fill all the positions on the field. To be relegated from WRFU South East West League 2 would mean a return to the local leagues and thus a drop in standard so great, most of the best players would have no choice other than to leave. To get back up from this mire of mud-caked large people, who really were only there for the beer and comraderie and had little knowledge or interest in playing the game as it could be played – a game of movement, space, fluidity, skill, attack, counter-attack, last ditch defence, power, commitment and heart - without the best players, would be so much work that the future of the ladies team would be put in doubt.

Stell was in pensive mode as she readjusted that silly frock for the 700th time. Empire lines were only ever a good idea if you had no boobs and a fat belly that needed disguising. If you had the curves, and she had, and had no need to hide the belly (er, no comment), then she should have gone out and bought something new, as opposed to simply borrowing something from Huggy's girlfriend. Lucinda was so sweet, but knowing that a special bond existed between Stell and Huggy, just tried a little *too* hard to be mates. Still, it meant Stell didn't have to go out and buy a new frock which would be used exactly once.

"Stell, we need to go or we'll be late," called Gwen's voice on the other side of the bathroom door. "I mean, we're late already, but we'll be *really* late."

"I can't get my tits into this stupid dress. Will you help?" she said, sliding over to unlock the bathroom door.

Gwen, in a shimmering jade green silken dress (a change from her normal colour choice so as not to clash), with not strictly matching lilac fake flowers and trimmings, entered and immediately set to work on adjusting the fastenings at the back of Stell's ballgown. The peach taffeta, set against the pale, lightly-freckled skin on Stell's arms and back, along with the mountains of blondish, thick, wild locks, untidily piled on top of her head, gave Stell a pastel glow.

"Gorgeous," Gwen whispered, and Stell felt a little flush of embarrassment. "Bloody hate dresses," she thought.

Adjustments done and after a quick swig of Cava from the glasses still on the dining table, the two rushed out the front door of the Mansion and into the waiting taxi, the driver of which momentarily took his mind off the amount of time he'd wasted sitting around outside the house and to the appearance of the young ladies now entering his cab. He suppressed an appreciative smile and said, in his thick Afghan accent, "Where to, ladies?"

"Queen's Club, please."

The annual dinner dance at Hammersmith and Fulham Rugby Club, normally held in April at the end of the season, is a very formal affair. Black tie, sit down three-course dinner, set speeches, annual awards for performance during the season, it was an opportunity for the club to acknowledge the contributions to its smooth running, both on and off the field of play, of all those who had helped it continue in the traditions of open, fair play, sportsmanship and Corinthian values, on which it had been founded some 25 years previously.

It was also the mother of opportunities to get severely pissed.

The ladies had started early, having a pre-Dinner Dance party at the Theakston Mansion, in which serious quantities of Cava were consumed. By the time the first revellers arrived Stell was still not ready, so conducted the festivities in tracksuit, with a view to changing just before leaving. The mad taxi dash to the Queen's Club, one of London's most prestigious tennis venues and only minutes from the rugby club, was almost an annual ritual in itself.

The taxi arrived at the security gates of the tennis club and, after rummaging around for change in their ridiculously small handbags, Stell and Gwen paid the driver and got out. Passing the immaculately-lawned tennis courts to their left, they headed through the car park, into the club house, following the printed signs marked "HFRC Dinner Dance" and up the stairs towards the Great Hall.

This was the time of year when the Queen's Club was at its best, with the preparations to the annual pre-Wimbledon tennis extravaganza, the Stella Artois tournament, well under way. All the white stands were freshly painted, the grass courts appearing as seas of perfect green, each blade of grass cut precisely to the regulation standard, each line a masterpiece of geometric accuracy.

When Gwen and Stell arrived in the pre-drinks hall, everyone was about to pass into the main hall for the dinner." What time do you call this, Captain?" whispered Fi, so all within ten metres could hear.

"Sorry, wardrobe malfunction," she replied sheepishly. Then, remembering not to appear on the back foot in front of Fi and everyone, added, "Tits too big, I'm afraid."

"That should shut her up," she thought. A ripped, fat free physique is all very well, but bra size is often an unwelcome casualty of the quest for a perfect body.

"Ouch. 15 – Love," came the voice of one of the girls, keeping with the tennis theme, to the accompaniment of a few guffaws. Fi made a mental note of the insult as they filed into the dining hall.

"....and the Player of the Season award goes to Ben O'Connor!"

The slight, popular young Fly Half (no.10, very skilful, very clever, runs the game, the equivalent of the American Football Quarterback - minus the shoulder pads and size though, as his job is to move the ball *without* getting hit) got up, buttoning his jacket, to the general applause of all gathered. All those at the table at which he had been seated, one away from the top table but only a few short yards to where the speaker, Roddy, had made the announcement, rose in a standing ovation, a cue followed by all the other nineteen tables. White and red gladioli, of differing heights, bedecked the centre of each table, a large circle of white cotton, white fairy lights wrapped around their long stems to create small islands of light. The theme was picked up on the walls, with cream fairy lights surrounding red and blue bunting, in the rugby club's colours and the general glow seemed to emanate from the young Irishman as he made his way forward. Ben had only come to the club at the beginning of the season and was already tipped to go on to play at higher levels. County was next and, if the club could withstand the approaches of bigger London outfits, or he didn't return home to Ireland, he would play an important part in taking the Hammers up the league structure.

When all the speeches had been made, Estelle rushing through a rather good effort in optimistic spin and damage limitation (Hammers Ladies 15, Played 14, Won 3, Lost 10, drawn 1) with lots of "bright futures" and "consolidation since the last two promotions," the need to stay sober pre-speech was swiftly replaced by the post-speech opposite. To further add insult to injury, Fi had been awarded the "Best Newcomer to the Ladies' Team", which was probably accurate, but it just rankled.

In a moment of contrition during a training session at the beginning of the season, Stell had tried to point out, in true marketing speak (learned from her boss Patricia at BetNow!, known as Trish for short or, when she was out of earshot as "Patty Platitude" for her original and intellectual sayings – "Why oh why did I ever quote *her?*" she had regretted as soon as the words passed her lips) that, "There's no "me" in "team". Fi pointed out that actually there is, but you have to re-arrange the letters. Sticking with the same theme, she went on to explain that there's also a "meat" in team, which would probably explain why, using Stell's logic, most men's rugby teams were full of such meatheads. The whole training session had descended into farce and unfunny anagrams, with the general conclusion being that Stell had to accept she was made to look rather silly. "I was only trying to help," she thought. "Bitch."

OK, she wasn't the best coach in the world, but this year, she was going to do something different. She hated being 2nd last in the league, avoiding relegation only by the vagaries of the WRFU's points allocation system and, whilst waiting at the bar for hers and Gwen's doubles, after the formal part of the evening just before the dancing began, she vowed that if it meant she had to sleep with an ex-Premier League player in order to get a good Coach, well, there were worse things in life....

Chapter 13: Carlton Edwards

Carlton was sitting behind the Ben O'Connor table, feeling very out of sorts. Here he was, at a rugby club annual awards dinner, with no chance of winning anything as he hadn't played in what, two seasons now? – and on the evidence of his last outing, there was not a hope in hell's chance that he ever would again. "Apart from maybe the One-Legged Vet's team....." he thought.

He wasn't an Allikadoo yet (just still too young, plus his steadily expanding waistline wasn't quite up to the size of the Elder Statesmen's - yet) and he wasn't a player, so why exactly was he here?

His loving wife Britta had done another of those, "I'm going back to Denmark and taking the kids" things again and, this time, he was pretty convinced that this was definitely it. After all those years training, playing and, erm, celebrating, Britta had finally thought that now that he was no longer a rugby player, he would become exactly what she had always hoped: a stay at home, mending the garden fence and washing the car on Sundays, good, Danish husband. Actually, not the "car" car, which was quite a nice Saab convertible, silver, turbo, too flash by half, but a trade-in sensible station wagon, with lots of storage room, a roof rack and four doors. Only problem was, Caz had no clue how to wash the car, apart from driving it to the nice Iraqi people on Hammersmith Grove who would valet it and have it spanking new in under half an hour. Oh, and he wasn't Danish. He did quite like the beer though....

Britta had met Caz on holiday in Brazil, when she was travelling around South America for her Masters with a friend. He seemed a bit bonkers actually, going running every morning just before the temperature really warmed up and when even walking would become a sweltering chore. He would appear at the breakfast table, all taut, sweaty muscle, down a gallon of water and then disappear off to his room to shower. By the time he'd come down again, she'd already finished her breakfast and left. They had eventually got talking in the middle of the Maracana football stadium and he had seemed a nice enough, friendly sort of chap. She hadn't a clue what rugby was and really didn't care until she and her friend Halla became friendly with two other English boys who were staying at the same hotel and had just finished their studies at Oxford University. To tell the truth, she and Halla quite fancied *them*. However, when Caz came along and the two Oxford boys found out who he played for, they almost dropped to their knees in adulation. "Oh," she remembers thinking. "Oh dear."

Caz ripped his knee ligaments at the start of the next season on his return to England and his recuperation resulted in a long-distance relationship which culminated in her moving to London and spending the next fifteen years wishing neither she nor Caz had ever heard of rugby. The first words she ever taught Caz in Danish were "skritepave" and "overfulsom"[21], which seemed to be absolutely accurate. After years of waiting for him to grow up and abandon the game, she'd finally given up.

The only reason Caz was at the dinner was because it was considerably more fun spending time with the rugger buggers than staring at the walls of his already empty house. He had also started coaching Mini Rugby halfway through the season, which sort of entitled him to still hang about the club without seeming too sad. Mostly though, he could really do with a shag.

After the speeches, the drinking and the dancing, people broke up into smaller groups to continue the celebrations at private parties. Caz found himself at a house party at 4 am with some of the guys from various teams, their partners and one or two of the ladies' team, including a very, very drunk Stell and Gwen. They were all holding forth on the best back line formation for the current England squad.

"Go on, you ask him then," urged Gwen.

"Alright, alright, give me a chance." Stell made an inebriated attempt to readjust her dress, shook her wild brown-blonde mane for full effect and sidled over to Caz.

"Caz, you old bastard," she started. Caz broke off from talking about the merits of ball-playing centre partnerships and looked up. "Ooh, she looked nice."

Stell sat down on the floor next to him. "Look Caz, we need a coach and as you're a Cobra (Stell had found out during summer training two seasons before that they had gone to the same university, be it 13 years apart and had both played for the Uni' rugby club) and know a thing about this rugby stuff, well, could you help?"

"Er, no," came the firm answer. He was smarting ever-so-slightly at the "old bastard" bit.

"Please, please, please, please!" carried on Gwen, rushing over and spilling a varied collection of cups in every direction. "Obviously sexual favours will be included and you wouldn't have to pay us too much!" The other boys looked on with interest.

"Gwen darling, I told you after the last time that I wouldn't shag you again." Gwen had a bit of a reputation for not being too withholding with her affections and so assorted ears around the room pricked up for some fresh gossip. Stell came to her defence:

"I've heard it's no bigger than this anyway," she said, crooking her little finger. A few laughs from the boys.

"My nickname at Uni' was Needle Dick the Bug Fucker," added Caz, laughing a little too-confidently. "Either this chap was a good bluffer or maybe there was more to him than met the eye. Hmmm...." Stell thought.

"Go like this," he instructed Stell, pursing his lips to make a tiny circle with his mouth. All eyes turned towards her, Stell, not wishing to appear a bad sport, rolled her lips into a small circle.

"Nah, too big," he said. "There'd be no point in you giving me a blow job – it wouldn't even touch the sides!" to the accompaniment of much laughter. Even Stell had to admit that although enormously crass, he'd got out of the situation quite well. He seemed like a good laugh and obviously knew a thing or two about the game: he was certainly old enough. This could be just what the team needed. She looked over at

Caz, who by now was standing by the kitchen door about to get himself a drink.

"Ah well," she thought, "if at first you don't succeed, there's always plan B."

She drew herself up from the floor, as stealthily as her drunken legs could manage, and crouched in tackle stance in preparation for a full frontal assault. Caz turned round just in time to hear a shouted "Tackle!" as Stell came flying towards him.

Once they had untangled the mass of limbs, furniture, plastic cups and spilt alcohol, and were lying panting on the floor after the mini-wrestling bout, silly, inebriated smiles on their lips, faces leaning only inches from each other, Stell whispered, "Caz, will you coach us next season?"

"No, no chance. Absolutely not."

Chapter 14: The Troubadours Experience

At the tender age of 23, far older than is usually the case, Carlton Edwards went along to attend summer training at Troubadours Football Club (Rugby Union) with a friend from work, who had been invited by an old school friend and existing player.

Up until that point Caz, in probably a similar way to most wannabe Troubs, felt that he was rather good. Not just at rugby, but at everything. He had been in the top stream at school for everything, right from the earliest he could remember and sort of felt that he had a right to be, without necessarily putting in much effort. OK, not-as-good-as expected exam results etc. seemed to suggest that some effort should have been expended, but he still did well enough not to have to worry too much about changing anything in his general demeanour or outlook on life.

Until he went to Troubadours.

Being naturally quick and thus not having to run to his maximum capacity to keep up with the others, the running round three sides of the rugby pitch six times wasn't too difficult at first. In fact, on the fifth lap, he decided that he was going to slaughter his benchmark time and really go round as fast as he could, not really to show off but to let all watching know who was fastest. He tore past all the others in his group of six to finish well ahead of his benchmark time. The old hands in the group, as well as the coaches, exchanged knowing looks.

On the sixth circuit, his legs froze.

Maybe it was the inactivity of the previous off-season months, maybe it was the sudden increase in speed after four rounds of conditioning for a much lower speed, maybe it was all sorts of things, but by the end of the sixth circuit, he felt as if he were running backwards, the burn in his thighs, calves and the backs of his ankles (he didn't know up until that point that the backs of your ankles could hurt!) searing with an internal, constant white-heat. Nobody but he was surprised.

The remaining hour and a half of the training session was an exercise in sheer, unbridled pain. Caz reckoned that the only reason he wasn't told, on that occasion, to "Sod off into the darkness" was because, despite his silly attempt to show off on that first day - a bit like the poor chap at the front of a cavalry charge: "Good bloke!" everyone cries, whilst secretly thinking "Bleeding idiot" – the coaches must have seen something that they could work with and he was given the benefit of the doubt.

From then on, his policy was to stay amongst the crowd, not trying to stand out or show off again, so that he could last the course.

Caz' second major lesson came halfway through the summer, after the numbers attending had been whittled away by half. Caz realised that amongst those still remaining, people whom he had been easily lapping in the first few sessions at the beginning of the summer were now beating him quite comfortably. Realising that he was in danger of being asked to leave, panic set in and he decided to try to find out why. When speaking to other players afterwards in the bar, during the five minutes or so before everyone pushed off, over a nice glass of orange juice and lemonade, Caz was surprised to learn that the two nights a week at Troubadours was only a tiny *fraction* of the training the others were putting in. Every single day was a training day, be it sprint intervals, weights, endurance, sprint simulation all interspersed with endless rowing in the gym. Although he thought he was working hard, he was slipping behind bit by bit as he just had not realised that the vast majority of the training takes place *on your own*. "This is a bit serious," he thought. "But I have to show the people back at Old Rubberduckians that I can do it."

Every aspect of his life changed. He woke up at five thirty so he could get to the gym for six, doing an hour and a half of various strength and speed exercises at his gym in the City before work. Every evening on non-training nights he would do a full three hours, only reducing to two and a half hours when he started cycling from home to the City, in order to not have to waste time doing a warm up. He even did mini-morning sessions on rugby training nights, making sure he didn't overwork his legs as they simply would not be able to cope with the evening's torture. He became conscious of what went into his body as well, majoring on pasta (no sauce), salads (no dressing), chicken, fish, fruit. Alcohol was restricted to wine (no spirits or beer) and after a bit, as his muscles bulged and his waist thinned, Caz even had to throw away all his old work suits as they were simply the wrong shape.

He was super-fit, in probably the best physical condition that he would ever be, and simply felt invincible. When going about his Investment Adviser business in the City, he took to wearing the distinctive Troubadours tie and regularly bumped into other Troubs, often with bursting blue Lloyds of London folders under their muscular arms, also sporting club tie and walking, chests puffed out, arms not quite going down straight at the sides of their bodies, like young, fit Achilles. They exchanged confident nods to each other or sometimes stopped to exchange a few self-deprecating words. Mostly though, words were superfluous as they all knew the hard work that had gone into making them who they were and representing the team they did.

By the start of August, he even began to look forward to the training sessions as they were a chance to demonstrate how fit and fast he was. The slight change in the smell of the freshly cut grass between July and August, an almost imperceptible difference in the dryness in the air, meant that he no longer had the urge to gag. Also now in August, the actual rugby training started.

The Troubs philosophy was ball in hand at all times. The forwards would get quick, ruck ball (falling on the floor when tackled, but making sure your team coming from behind you could get to it easily and the other side couldn't) to the sublimely skilful halfbacks (9 and 10) who would work some bit of magic and get clean ball out to the lightning fast backs (the first phase of an attack). If they ever got half stopped, the Supermen on the team (7, 6 and 8, in that order), would appear out of nowhere and save the backs from being killed by the opposing 7, 6 and 8. Then the forwards would go again (second phase), looking for any potential gaps in the now not-so-organised defence, with a view to going straight at the opposition 9 and 10. If they could make the 9 and 10 commit (try to tackle them), they could then recycle the ball to get it out to their fast boys in the backs again, who would have realigned to attack again where they felt the defence was weakest. The fitness of the forwards was remarkable, the manual dexterity of the halfbacks in particular almost ridiculous in its speed and precision, the running of the backs a cross between will-o-the-wisp and the wind, and the ball moved from hand to hand and around the park so quickly that, even though you knew where it was supposed to end up, it was hard work just following its path.

Caz' head was in a spin. He had thought that he'd played rugby before, but nothing like this. The guys he was playing with and against were, not to put too fine a point on it, simply awesome. On Thursday nights, Troubs played Ones against Twos (the 1st Team against 2nd team). Caz had a better recollection of the sole of his opposite number's boots disappearing off into the distance, as he looked up prostrate from the grass having completely missed his tackle, than the chap's face.

The usual tried and tested way of playing rugby in England was very different to the Troubs way. Big forwards would run into other big forwards, all would pile into a heaving mass of bodies trying to push forward and trying to stop others pushing forward which, after rolling around a few times, would either collapse to the floor or grind to a halt. If the ball emerged, the 9 would pass to the 10 who would kick it off the pitch into touch. The opposition would throw the ball onto the pitch through a lineout, the 9 would pass to the 10 who would then kick it into touch for his team. Or just kick the offending item up in the air and hope your team could catch it first. The hope was that your 10 would kick it into touch closer to the other team's tryline than their 10 had kicked it from. Just like the Battle of the Somme, net ground made was measured in inches. Eventually someone would do something wrong and the referee would allow one of the 10's to kick a penalty between the posts. Every once in a while, especially if a team were losing and there wasn't much time left, a team would dare to pass the ball to the backs, but by this time it was normally too late: the backs were cold and the crowd had lost interest.

To the uninitiated, the Troubs style of play thus seemed to be a devil-may-care, flamboyant, recklessly cavalier approach to the game, which was OK if all you wanted to do was please the crowd but by which you'd never win anything on a cold, rainy, mud-encrusted wet weekend in Wigan.

To Caz though, the road to the Shelton Memorial Ground in south-west London was the road to Damascus. He had found his epiphany, not only in the style of play, but knowing the amount of work and the sheer physical commitment necessary for this apparent "recklessness" to work, a new work ethic. Being "naturally gifted" was not enough and in fact, didn't mean anything past the first few attempts at anything new. What really made the difference between being at the top end of mediocre, which is where, if he were to admit it, he had always been, to being outstanding was sheer hard work: training and practising so hard that to all those watching, playing beautifully and winning seemed "natural", almost effortless. A famous golfer, when once accused of being lucky, answered, "The more I train, the luckier I seem to get!"

It also really wound the opposition up, if you could thrash them and still play the game as beautifully as it should be.

Even when he eventually left Troubs after the third knee op, the impression that the Troubadours' style of play and general ethos had had on him would remain with him for the rest of his life and in everything he did.

When the Sunday afternoon's post-Dinner Dance hangover eventually subsided, Caz could not let his conversation and almost extra-marital clinch moment with Stell go. She was lovely, in a "I'm going to compensate for my excessive female curves by being a bloke" way, but more interestingly, he'd seen the girls play and felt that, with only a few Troub-type pointers, he could change things around for them. He was also going to have far more time on his hands over the coming season, now that it was likely that Britta wasn't coming back.

"I've been relatively successful as a player and captain, but can I do it as a coach?" played and replayed itself in his head. He was in the middle of the RFU coaching courses, sponsored by the Hammers and was teaching the kids tag rugby on a Sunday morning (which his own son, moved to Denmark, would no longer be attending...), but was he doing enough to give something back to the sport that had given him so much (two crumbling knees excepted)?

Two weeks after the Dinner Dance, Caz sent a text message to Stell Theakston. It said simply, "I'm in."

"Oh Christ....."

Chapter 15: Summer Training

Due to coaching course commitments, Caz was not able to start the ladies' team's training until the end of July. The girls had been playing touch rugby for most of June and July and had recently started doing some fitness, with the boys, under the increasingly sadistic tutelage of Ian, the club fitness coach.

During the warm-up exercises, the girls tended to stay in one group, bunched together at the far end of the training pitches.

The rugby pitches were being seeded for the start of the new season, so training could only occur in one corner of the first team pitch and on the funny little bit of space over the fence, used as the ball skills area, where there was barely enough room for the 40 – 50 boys who turned up for training, let alone the girls as well. The ladies had thus traditionally to settle for the bit of sloped ground by the trees, the farthest corners of which the spotlights in winter struggled to reach. A demarcation line between where the boys' training area ended and the girls' began, was a row of cones, which was supposed to start at the second spotlight from the end but was creeping over, ever so gradually since the start of summer training, towards the first spotlight to encroach even further into the girls' space.

After the warm-up and stretch and just before the serious fitness began, Caz called the 12 assembled ladies over to their training area. Slightly confused by the unprecedented order to retreat from the forthcoming punishment that Ian, who had been specially imported at huge cost (travelling expenses and a couple of pints a week), was bound to dish out, the ladies followed him over the fence, not quite knowing what to expect. Caz cleared his throat.

"You've possibly seen me about the club so I'm not going to make a long introduction. For those of you who haven't, my name is Caz and you are lucky enough to have me as your coach for the season." One or two groans could be heard. "Now, none of us is getting paid for this, so above all this season will be fun. We will also play some great rugby and win things. I have various philosophies about how the game will be played though, with which I will no doubt entertain, enthral and bore you throughout the season, but the first one is that I don't believe in fitness."

"Eh?" was the common response.

"Nope, running around a muddy field time and time again is not the way to play rugby. But, enough chat, let's get started with a game of touch."

Caz organised the girls into two teams, with a fairly even split of forwards and backs per team. He had already laid out a grid with cones to emulate a small playing area, which seemed to extend past the second spotlight. "Oh dear, we're going to get in trouble," thought Stell. Halfway along both touchlines though, were two larger traffic bollard cones, which for the time being went unnoticed.

Caz threw the ball to one of the teams and shouted, "Play!"

The rules for the game were simple. Each team had to try to score a try by placing the ball over the other team's try-line. If you were touched with two hands below the waist while in possession of the ball, you had to pass it backwards to a team mate who would then try to score. After each touch, the defending team had to retreat five yards to give the attackers some space. Each team were allowed to be "touch tackled" a maximum of six times before the ball was "turned over" i.e. they had to give the ball to the other side. To all the girls, except those brand new to rugby, "touch rugby" was second nature. After a couple of minutes of neither team making a breakthrough, Caz decided to change things around.

"Right, this new game is called "Bastard Touch". Same rules, but every time you touch-tackle someone, you have to run around the nearest of the two bollards on the sideline." The girls looked up.

"Excuse me," asked Gwen, do you mean the game stops so we can run around the bollard and restarts when we get back?"

"Nope."

"Do all the defending team have to run around the cone?" she persisted.

"No, only the tackler."

"Which cone do we run around?" she continued.

"Gwen, demonstration please," Caz said, calling her out into the middle of the pitch. He asked Ciska to throw him the ball.

"Right," he said, running slowly towards Gwen. "Touch tackle me." Gwen obliged half-heartedly, a look of complete incomprehension and mistrust on her pretty face.

"Now run around the cone." She started off at jogging pace. "No, sprint!" he shouted. Gwen jumped up with a start and sprinted the twenty yards to the cone, rounded it and ran back to her start position in front of Caz.

"Now, while you're doing that, the game continues."

"But that means that while the defender is running round the cone, their team has one player less!" She was determined to make her point, even though she wasn't quite sure what that point was.

"Aha!" said Caz.

"Oh, I get it now!" Gwen cried, a little illuminated light bulb appearing just above her head.

"The attack needs to look to see where the gap is in the defence and *communicate*, the defence needs to communicate to block that gap. Now play," he said, tossing the ball to Gwen.

After five more minutes, with much shouting on both sides as well as tries being scored by players going into spaces, Caz introduced a few more variations (any defender can run round the cone, not only the touch-tackler, only passing to the left, the tackled player having to roll the ball backwards through their legs and a nominated Scrum Half having to pick it up every time) the girls were sweating buckets and panting away like fury.

"OK, go get a drink and meet me over at the next grid."

As the girls trooped over to where their water bottles lay, under the puzzled gaze of the boys' teams which, coming over from their fitness grid to their ball skills practice area, just couldn't work out why they seemed to have a bit less space than the previous week, they seemed tired but in happy mood.

"I thought you said you didn't believe in fitness," came the breathless, almost unanimous chorus from the exhausted young ladies to Caz. "We're shattered!"

"I don't!"

Chapter 16: Post Training

Stell, Fi, Gwen, Mads, Sib and Caz sat in the Wheatsheaf pub after training, at a separate table to the others, to discuss the way forward.

"Excellent sesh by the way Caz," opened Stell. "Have never done touch like that before."

"Thanks, Stell. Would love to say it's all my own work, but the RFU are really trying to change the way rugby is coached and played in this country. As I'm fresh off the coaching production line, I'm really only trying to pass on to you guys what they're teaching me." "Good attempt at modesty Caz," he thought to himself. "Well done."

"I don't think we worked hard enough. I don't think we did enough fitness stuff. I didn't feel tired at the end of the session," said Fi. Was she trying to disagree with Stell just to be difficult, or did she want to demonstrate what a hard bunny she was? "Hard to know just now," Caz thought.

"Correct," said Caz, bringing himself back from his mental aside. "Fitness is not my main function. If I knacker you out running you into the ground, you'll be too tired to take on board new ball skills stuff. Anyone can run you till you puke, but we have so much to get through re: basic skills and game play, you can do the "gym till you drop" stuff, in your own time. Besides, fitness doesn't work," he said firmly.

"Uh oh," everyone thought, "red rag to a bull. Fi won't be best pleased…."

Fi bridled. "Are you saying that fitness isn't important? You'd prefer a bunch of lardy-arses on the team than proper athletes?" Although not directed at Stell, who certainly wasn't the skinniest girl in the world, it still smarted.

"No, what I'm saying is that we've all been in a fitness session, probably the first that you ever attended, when you give 100% at some point because the trainer has told you it was the last exercise. Then, just to be funny and you've nothing left in the tank, the trainer says, "Just one more exercise" and, because we don't want to seem like a lightweight, we've finished the "one more exercise" and felt like death. We've all been there." He looked around at the assembled ladies: more nods of agreement. "From that point on, in fitness sessions, we NEVER give 100% as we always need to leave something in the tank. What do you run at in fitness sessions, 70, 80% tops?"

"I always give 100%," said Fi, rather unconvincingly. If she did that in every exercise for an hour and a half, she'd be dead.

"Well, I know that I never did. The worst thing you could do was to not finish the session, so you simply *had* to gauge yourself. The trouble is, in a game, you NEVER run at 80% capacity. You either have the ball or are chasing someone who has the ball, in which case you go flat out as fast as you can, or you're jogging into position, in which case you go at 20 – 30% of capacity. To my mind, there's just no point in training to run at a speed that you'll never use in a game."

The girls were quiet. Either this man really knew his stuff, or he was full of bullshit.

"There are also certain natural laws that apply, in life as well as in rugby…."

"Go on," the team thought…

"There's the "Law of the well-meaning precedent" to start with. Basically, if you do the right thing once, the next time the same situation comes around, people will think less of you for not matching your original effort, irrespective of the inconvenience and personal cost to you."

A few murmurs of agreement.

"Then there's the law of rucking….." he continued.

"Rucking is one of the parts of the game that the "Powers That Be" were trying to get rid of. Why? Because it's extremely dangerous!"[22]

"…..so, when is it rucking and when is it stamping?"

Fi started with a complicated and probably accurate explanation. Caz interrupted, "It's rucking when your side's doing it. When it's the other side, it's definitely stamping!"

General groans, but at least the girls were smiling.

"And last but not least, there's Cole's Law." Pause.

"What's that?" asked Mads, taking the bait.

"It's chopped up carrots and cabbage, with a little mayonnaise, but that's not important right now..."

"Oh my God, a whole season of this….."

Chapter 17: Crash Baggies

Caz had set up a small grid, about 5 metres wide and 10 metres long. Halfway up the grid, he had constructed a defensive position of two large tackle bags, held by Mands and Mila, a huge Tongan. A roaming defender with a tackle shield and another with a protective body suit were also in attendance. The demarcation line between the boys' and the girls' training area had shifted eastwards so it was now precisely in between the second and third spotlight. This bit of ground-stealing had been noticed by the 1st Team Coach, but he had more than enough space at the moment so wasn't going to call Caz up on it just yet.

The exercise was to try to go through the defensive position manned by the defenders and score the try. If you were half-stopped by the body-suited defender, the tackle-shield defender was instructed to bosh the hell out of you. Everyone would have one go each then the defenders would swap with the attackers. Eager to re-establish dominance after feeling her gym ethic questioned, Fi went first.

Fi crashed into the large tackle bag held by Mila and came to a grinding halt. Undeterred, she crouched low, protecting the ball in her crooked right arm while heaving against Mila's bag, leading with her left arm and shoulder, legs pumping away to give herself more momentum.

"Ok, let her go!" called Caz to Mila, who grudgingly moved to one side so Fi could continue her run. Gwen, in body suit, immediately grabbed hold of Fi before she could get up any speed and Siobhan, with small tackle bag, came flying in from one side at the partially ensnared Fi, knocking her and Gwen to the ground. Fi was still five metres from the tryline.

"Next," called Caz. Stell picked up a ball and charged forward into Mila's bag. One shuddering halt and a huge Sib-generated bosh later, she too was despatched to the sidelines with even less ceremony than Fi. She didn't want to protest that this particular exercise was impossible but the expression on her face spoke for her.

"Ooh, I'm liking this!" Sib tried not to chirp gleefully.

"Change the bag holders please," added Caz, mindful not to use the expression "bag ladies".

"Oh fuck," thought Sib.

The girls were so sharp-witted and so willing to chat, as opposed to actually train, that Caz had to make sure he steered well clear of any of the normal expressions one would use when coaching that could be perceived as having any meaning other than strictly rugby. For example, when instructing a player to offer close support to a ball-carrying colleague, it is perfectly acceptable, under normal circumstances, to shout, "Get right up his arse." Such an expression, if used in a ladies' rugby context, would be the cue for laughter, sexual innuendo and the next five minutes of the session would be of no use to man nor beast.

When describing a switch move, where for example the number 12 (Lara) pretends to pass to the number 13 (Ruth) on her right shoulder to the right, but, because of Ruth's angle of run, actually passes on the right shoulder but to the left i.e. back inside towards the pack, it is highly recommended that you do not say, for example, "Ruth, I want to see you come inside Lara." The verbal faux pas would probably spell the end of the session as a mixture of shock, horror (all feigned to embarrass the Coach) plus exaggerated laughter would be so much more fun than running around a muddy pitch!

The most heinous of potential verbal crimes that a Coach could commit though, when coaching ladies' rugby, is to use the word "fat".

Men and women, according to some of the great psychologists of our times, are allegedly from different planets. They thus respond to criticism differently and require different forms of words in order to be motivated. It is perfectly normal to say to a group of male rugby players, "Get your fat arses in gear" or refer to the forwards as "the ugly fat boys" and the backs as "girls". Allegedly, for men, being shouted at and told they are "a fat bunch of princesses", "utter garbage", "complete shite" etc. makes them want to do their utmost to prove the Coach wrong if, of course, they respect him.

However, the reaction that a Coach may get from a group of tired ladies, if he were to utter the endearing words, "That was complete shite, utter garbage, you fat bunch of princesses. Get your ugly arses into gear," could vary from wailing, banshee-like tears to a punch in the face, with any reaction in between also being a distinct possibility. The reaction that he could be 100% sure that he would *not* get though would be a compliant and motivated team.

After each girl had had a chance to run at the defence and was knocked into touch, they were asked to perform the same exercise but this time in pairs. If they were stopped at the large bags, they were to try to pass the ball to the support player who would then go on to try to score the try. As per normal, Fi went first.

Fi hurtled into Mands' bag this time and actually managed to knock her back slightly. The body-suited Mel though was quickly up onto Fi and wrapped her arms around her, hugging her to Mands' tackle pad in a Fi sandwich. Fi dropped into a low crouch, swivelled round so her back was to the pad and her face was at the level of Mel's, midriff. Stell was running up behind her, a little to the left and Fi, who was now in a fairly secure stance, was just about to pass when something crashed into her from the side with a tremendous, dull thud. The ball was jarred from her grasp as she let out a loud squeal of pain, falling to the floor. Stell flailed unsuccessfully at the ball in an attempt to catch it and continue the attack, as it spilled to ground just inches from where Fi lay.

"Oops, sorry," beamed an exceptionally-pleased-with-herself Sib from behind the small tackle bag. No matter how hard she tried, and she certainly wasn't trying very hard at all, her contrition just didn't seem that believable.

When the group were halfway through the exercise, no-one having managed to score a try, Stell finally piped up.

"This is fucking impossible. How the hell are we supposed to crash through those fucking huge bags? This is bollocks."

Before Caz could answer, Gwen had another light bulb moment.

"Stell, come with me," she said, picking up a ball and barging to the front of the queue. Stell, nonplussed, did as she was told while muttering bad things about Old Cobras under her breath.

With Stell in support, Gwen ran straight at Hannah who was holding a large bag. Just before she got to Hannah, she did a little step and went to Hannah's right, easily rounding her as the bag was too heavy to reposition with any speed at all, and still keeping within the 5-metre line of cones. Siobhan in body-suit and Mads with bosh-bag, slightly taken aback by this unexpected turn of events, hurriedly shuffled over to the extreme right of the grid to stop Gwen, Siobhan just managing to grab onto her before she made it to the tryline. Gwen crouched, turned so her back was towards Siobhan and as Mads arrived preparing for the bosh, slipped the ball to an onrushing Stell who ran the remaining three yards to score a try unopposed. There was a collective cheer.

Even though pleased at having scored, Stell was fuming inside. Why had they spent the last 10 minutes doing the wrong thing when the so-called Coach could have easily told them what they should have been doing?

"Why didn't you say we didn't have to run *into* the bags?" someone asked, putting Stell's thoughts into words.

"What if the bag-holder were a tiny one and you were a big one?" asked Caz. The general air of confusion suggested further explanation was needed. Caz continued. "Given any situation that happens on the pitch, you have to deal with it in the way you see best. Much as I love you, I'm not actually on the pitch with you. When instant decisions are necessary,

I don't want you thinking, "What did Caz say again?" I want you to *think*: read the situation yourself and act upon it."

After a few moments of silent reflection, Caz added, "It's so much more effective to go round people than go through them. I've no idea where people get the idea that bashing into people is what rugby's about."

This was hard to take in. Everything they'd ever seen of rugby, well boys' rugby, was about the bosh: the physical confrontation and proving dominance over the guy (or girl) you'd just smashed into.

In retaliation against the confusion the Coach seemed to be introducing in their well-established philosophies, a voice from somewhere at the back of the small huddle called, "You're such a smug bastard."

Ignoring the comment, probably from Mel, Caz said "Everyone go and get a drink and when you come back we'll progress this. In the meantime, have a think about this."

"Oh God, here we go again..."

"Rugby is a game of contact or of contact avoidance? You have five minutes to prepare your answers starting now. Please use brief, apt quotations, with precise reference to the text."

The remainder of the session went smoothly, with the girls concentrating on making the decision as to whether or not to run round people or crash through them. They also looked at, if half stopped and it were possible, releasing quick, clean ball[23] out to support runners. By the end of the session, Caz had the feeling that the message was finally getting through: spaces not faces - running into people gets you nowhere unless they're tiny and you're huge, running into the space either side of people either gets you past them or allows you to pass on quickly if stopped. Well pleased with his efforts for the evening and the girls' progress, Caz was thinking of winding the session up early when Sib asked if they could do their traditional end of session game, that in truth, they had been offering to show him for weeks now.

"Sure, no problem," was the response. They had five minutes spare, the girls had worked hard and seemed to be taking the new lessons on board, so why not?

Eager to demonstrate their traditional warm-down game after weeks of promising, the girls split themselves into two excited teams, each team at respective ends of a grid 50 metres in length and 20 metres wide. At each end of the grid, a small tackle bag lay innocently awaiting its fate.

"What are the rules?" Caz asked.

"You'll see!"

The grid was not particularly big, so the girls were bunched into packed formations, both attackers and defenders. Sib started with the ball in the middle of the pitch and ran straight at Fi. Fi readied herself for the bosh and with the expert precision of the well-trained tackle assassin, cut her in half. Before hitting the ground, Sib threw the ball into the air and it landed behind the support who were running after her. Mands, on Fi's side, dived to the floor to recover the ball and was jumped on by three of the other girls. The ensuing mad scramble on the deck resulted in Mands elbowing someone in the chest, a bit of hair pulling, some rolling around on the ground and a retrieving of the ball on the Sib side.

If there were a pile-up of any sort on the pitch, you can bet anything you so desired that once all the bodies were cleared, the last one to emerge, with ball in hand and a sick, very-badly concealed masochistic ear to ear grin, would be Siobhan Owen. She had this knack of being in exactly the right place to either kill opposition ball, amassing many referee warnings but never a yellow card, or retrieve your own ball. The theory had been expounded that she just read the game so well so could anticipate where the ball would be. Truth was though, she just loved being at the bottom of a ruck or the middle of a maul: right in the thick of the action and pain.

Katie picked up the freed ball and whipped a pass out to Stell who bent low, pressed the ball tight to her chest with both arms, and proceeded to run straight at Mila.

Some of the boys only 30 metres away must have, at some point in their lives, probably during GCSE Physics, been asked the question: "What happens when an irresistible force meets an immovable object?"

The loud, sickening thud of muscle, flesh and bone crashing into muscle, flesh and bone that stopped them in mid-exercise and forced them to look over to the girls' training area could have provided a pretty good empirical, even though far more graphic than any science lab would allow, answer. The actual moment of impact passed, all their curious eyes encountered was, a ladies' rugby team captain lying on the floor dazed and clutching a hurting shoulder and a rather large Tongan lady gingerly picking herself up from the grass. They also saw Fi, who had swooped onto the loose ball, sprinting towards the far tackle bag.

"Crash baggy!" she shouted as she smashed the ball onto the winded tackle bag to score.

The post-battlefield scene of the prone, bruising, panting, bodies of young ladies strewn all over the grid was an intriguing sight. On virtually every face Caz saw a curious half-smile, in partial anticipation of his expected approval for their warm-down. Unfortunately, there seemed to be no way of stopping the feeling of horror that came over Caz from making its way to his face, despite his best efforts to feign approval of this, well, unrestricted violence which clearly wasn't bothered about even pretending to be rugby-related.

"Er, that's certainly interesting," his mouth said, whilst his face screamed something altogether different.

A weary little bearded man in Caz' head, with half moon glasses and shirt rolled up at the sleeves, got down from his little stool and shuffled towards the filing cabinet marked "Hammersmith and Fulham Ladies' Rugby Team Coaching Progress", thumbed through the files until he arrived at the one marked "Spaces Not Faces: how to avoid the tackler and not shovel on shit[24]," extracted the file and carefully tore it into tiny pieces, before throwing them into the air and shuffling resignedly back to his stool.

Chapter 18: Siobhan Owen

Siobhan left the 'Sheaf a disturbed woman. The irritating thing was that she didn't quite know why. She had had a couple of drinks in the bar after rugby training, plus something to eat as she wasn't going to make herself anything when she got home – home being a shared house 10 minutes walk away - but for some strange reason, she didn't feel like hanging round the club for too long.

She ran through in her head what had happened that evening and tried to find out why she was feeling a bit low. OK, there had been the usual nonsense with Larry: it was quite normal now to have to try to locate her kit before training, but as Larry's imagination was not his greatest quality, he had a limited number of good hiding places left.

She remembered the other kit-hiding instances involving all the studs of her boots being removed, the shorts being cut into ribbons and the famous occasion last summer when her whole kit had been placed on the barbeque at her parents' house, just after the spare ribs. It took ages to get that sticky goo out, but that was her favourite training top (an old tour one from Uni, "Sirens to Amsterdam!": her first experience of playing rugby while stoned...) and she would be damned if she'd throw it away just because of Larry's disapproval. The worst thing though at the barbeque was that she had to try to explain to Mum what the burning items actually were.

"No Mum, of course it's not rugby kit! You know I told you I wouldn't play any more, good God no! Larry and I were just having a laugh with some old rags..."

No, the problem this evening was something Caz had said.

Siobhan was the elder of two sisters. Her brother Evan had died when he was 4 – Siobhan doesn't exactly know what of – but throughout her life, she always felt that there was a gloom over her family, almost as if someone wasn't there who should have been.

Dad had always been absolutely brilliant: always around to give hugs and praise and generally to be Mr Can-Do. There was even that time he bought an old Rolls Royce Silver Shadow and, with Sib's help, had stripped it to nothing and restored it to probably a much better condition than it had ever been in. He'd learnt to fly light aircraft in his spare time, managed a farm, teaching Sib to milk cows, goats and pigs(!) virtually before she knew the proper words for the animals. When most children were learning how to ride bikes, Dad had taught her to ride motorbikes and before she was 14, Sib, straining to reach the footpedals, could drive a car on the private road leading to the barns at the bottom of field 3.

Being a true Welshman though, Dad's real passion was rugby. Many times before she actually knew what was happening on the pitch, she would be a regular little assistant at Cardiff Arms Park, where she would be wrapped up in woollens and jackets and hat, Dad's large presence next to her, singing, laughing, rapturously applauding and, once or twice, openly weeping along with the assembled red and white masses on the terraces. She never really watched the game as firstly, she couldn't see much and secondly, she was only interested in watching her father. The noise of the crowd and her Dad's reactions were enough anyway to tell her how Wales were doing and after a game in which the home side were victorious and played well, the warmth and glow of contentment that so rarely pierced her father's overall sadness was recompense enough for having to brave the cold and endure the tiredness in her legs. Going to sleep in her father's arms on the long train journey home and waking up miraculously in her own bed on the Sunday morning was all the magic a little girl could ever want.

Siobhan wasn't her Dad's favourite daughter – he would never show preference between her and Caitlin – but Caitlin just didn't seem to be interested in doing fun things like camping and white-water rafting, preferring to hang around Mum for as long as Sib could remember, sewing, baking cakes and being generally pathetic. Sib threw herself into all the "fun" things and every new achievement was met with enthusiastic praise from her father. The harder and tougher the sport, the more her Dad seemed to be pleased. It was a bit confusing that he seemed to be just as enthusiastic about Caite's sewing and singing, but it didn't really matter because for her, that sort of stuff was just way down the priority list.

It was no surprise that Caitlin was already married to Peter, a nice, English Accountant from a good family, had one sprog down and was expecting her second in moments' time. Mum, of Irish Catholic descent, obviously thought Caitlin was normal and that Siobhan would hopefully find herself a similarly nice boy and settle down. Mum was of course oblivious to the fact that Peter was as drippy as melted lard and that, when Caitlin had had a few drinks and the guard slipped, she confessed to Sib that she hadn't had an orgasm in two years! She'd virtually given up on having the sort of sex life that the girly magazines always talked about and was virtually scratching off the wallpaper now that she couldn't even have a drink to calm her nerves. And they'd only been married three years....

No, settling down with a nice boy, even though her nephew (plus hopefully a niece!) would be great fun, was clearly not something Sib had in mind, "Not now, not ever, no way." Consequently, the types of boys she went for were very much the opposite of her brother-in-law.....

In total, there were six previous Plus Ones (if she didn't include teenage hayshed fumblings). The first, Martin, did not occur until she'd gone off to University. It was Freshers' Week and basically, this guy looked like a young, fit, demi-God. Sib and her new-found friends of all of one week had spotted him at the Freshers' Ball and had made bets as to who would pull him first. Sib lost out to Rachel on that occasion, but got her own back two weeks later when a distraught Martin came knocking on her halls of residence door at stupid o'clock, apparently after having been chucked by Rache. The alleged "chucking" was simply a ploy to get Sib into bed, as Martin, on encouragement from his mates, was embarking on a "circle of friends" exercise[25].

The sex, that evening, was spectacular!

Probably as a result of the personal confidence he felt with his own body (a consequence of which was the numerous opportunities it offered him with a plethora of appreciative female bodies), Martin felt no need to rush either his or Siobhan's pleasures that evening. She would come to hate the constant inquisition of well-meaning future boyfriends, forever and annoyingly asking, "Do you like that, am I hurting you, should I go faster or slower, are you sure you like it?"; Martin seemed to instinctively *know* what she wanted. Every tiny movement of her body, every moan of pleasure or flinch of discomfort, Martin could, like a maestro playing a fine but unique instrument, interpret and adapt his touch - of lips, fingers, tongue, cock - to do less of what wasn't working and, by turning up the temperature degree by wonderfully lascivious degree, more – much, much more, – of what was! A lingering suspicion that her lover was more performing than fully participating did occur to Siobhan, but this was more than assuaged by the fact that even by the end of that first session, their bodies were so much more in tune than they were at the start of it, some THREE HOURS earlier...

When Sib found out about the deception, her head insisted she cease her treacherous fornications but her body screeched "Fuck it, give me MORE!"

So, Siobhan continued seeing Martin, albeit on the sly. He was big and strong and manly and he seemed to have a love for life and such an unrestrained lust for her (ok, for some of her friends too, but that didn't matter as she wasn't going to *marry* him) that she felt this warmth and glow of contentment emanate from him whenever they were together. Waking up in his arms on a Sunday morning was just bliss...

Martin also played rugby. Watching the boys crash into each other on the pitch, the hardness and physicality of the contact, the huge hairy thighs and tight shorts as well as the well stacked chests, all became a "must do" Wednesday and Saturday afternoon event.

Once the relationship with that particular rugby boy ended, the relationship with rugby boys in general took off.

When the option to play rugby herself opened up, Sib saw the opportunity to combine the physical contact she loved with the possibility to mingle with the boys.

Unfortunately, each new Martin was steadily worse (from her mother's perspective, if she'd known about them), culminating in Larry. If it were possible to paint a picture of the exact opposite of her nice-but-boring Accountant brother-in-law, Larry would be it. Tall, slim, cute, *dead* fit, funny, quirky, Australian, he was in London to enjoy himself and was the most unconventional person she had ever met. He seemed to be permanently fascinated by everything he encountered and approached life with the enthusiasm of a little boy, which she loved. He was also the most infuriating person she'd ever met as, being a natural no. 7, he never listened to anyone or anything. There were no rules that could not be broken, no conventions that could not be completely ignored, in fact, there was nothing that anyone said or did that mattered at all unless it fitted in with his opinion. The good thing though was his opinion would change every 5 minutes; all she had to do was use the right, subtle, gentle-persuasive methods and she would be be able to mould his opinion into exactly what she wanted it to be and thus achieve compliance.

Larry didn't hit her, as did nos. 2 and 4[26], nor did she have to pay half the costs towards repairing his car as she had with no.3[27], but his type of aggression was slow, meticulous, accumulative. He constantly, in his infuriatingly candid way, undermined her playing, her femininity, her sexuality, her reasons for playing as to him, it just didn't make any sense.

She'd tried to hit him once, but he just held her wrists and laughed, before tossing her on the sofa and switching on the telly to watch the Aussie Rules. The humiliation of the failed physical assault encouraged her to revert to using only words to wound (at which she was surprisingly good!) but she was determined to prove to him, to herself, to all those past boyfriends and to her exclusively male (apart from the secretaries) colleagues at the Property Management company that she could be as good as them, that she could give and take a hit, that she could be sandwiched in a scrum, be at the bottom of a ruck or in the middle of a maul and that she, basically, was as much a man as any of them.

She'd worked so hard, so fucking hard - to gain their trust, their respect - every single bloody day and even though she knew they'd always regard her as different, somehow *less* than they were, at least now they'd never dare express it to her face without the very justified expectation of a kick to their more tender parts.

"Rugby is a game of contact avoidance...."

After playing for a full 5 seasons now, this new Coach was telling her that the smashing into people, the running through people, the seeking out of people to hurt, was not rugby at all and was simply wrong, wrong, WRONG!

For as long she could remember, Sib had been an expert at fortifying the dam just behind her eyes, where amassed tears sometimes strained to break free. Now, in the dark evening, trudging home on her own, a sole escapee streaked down one cheek.

Chapter 19: Larry Mitchelle

Nobody plays rugby in Southern Australia – it's far too soft a game. Real men - the ones who wrestle crocodiles while downing a 6-pack of Fosters before breakfast - play Aussie Rules. You have to be fit, fast, strong and skilful, as well as having a propensity for dishing out, as well as receiving, not inconsiderable amounts of physical pain.

The game originated from the Irish convicts who were brought over to Australia at the end of the 18th century and started out as derivations on Gaelic Football, with a few especially Aussie twists, some say to increase the level of violence, in order to appeal to the Aussie public.

Of all the hardest, meanest, most merciless of teams in Southern Australia, the Brisbane Bruisers were by far the most successful. And of all the players who had ever graced the field of play at the Bruiser Bowl, Padraig Mitchelle was, without a doubt, the most psychopathic. And the crowd loved him!

The gratuitous tackles off the ball, the arguing with the referee, the throwing of the ice bucket over the Assistant Referee, the fighting with his own teammates when he didn't feel they were pulling their weight: all this was standard Paddy Mitchelle behaviour, so much so that "throwing a Paddy" or "doing a Mitchelle" became common parlance for over-enthusiastic participation of the extremely violent nature. The numerous red and yellow cards that Paddy acquired over the course of his career were all forgiven by the fervent home fans though as he always seemed to be acting like a lunatic "for the benefit of the team." He was also capable of combining raw aggression with sublime skill and poise, which enabled him, despite numerous injuries, to carry on playing well past the normal players' sell by date of 35.

He also was a hard drinking, hard gambling, family man who doted on his three sons. Paddy made sure that after a good night's post match drinking, he would always return home, irrespective of what time of morning, or even the morning after, to give them and his long-suffering wife Dot, an overly-affectionate, slobbery, beered-up, man-hug and kiss. The boys thought he was wonderful.

When Dot made an attempt to escape from the role of: dutiful homemaker, touchline supporter, tea, home-made cakes, beer and snacks server, general bandage-up lady, hospital bed vigil specialist, weekend, training nights and tour-time single woman and ego massager when things on the pitch didn't go so well, she was hauled back to the rambling house that Paddy had built, not so much by any of the self-recriminatory tears that Paddy shed, nor by threats of violence (rarely ever carried out), nor even by the accusations of abandoning their children. No, what really made Dot reconsider and renew her domestic career was the fact that she just did not have anywhere else to go. Nor, after 20 years of domesticity, any idea of what else she could do. Of course, Paddy did not hesitate to let the boys and all who would listen know which one of them was in the wrong.

Micky, Sean and Larry could not wait to play rugby themselves and started, along with their mates, playing for the Bruisers Tots at the age of 4, then on to the Worms (7 – 9), the Headbangers (10 – 13) and then Colts from 14. In Paddy's last game as a player for the Bruisers', he set a club record: the Mitchelle's were the first to field three members of the same family on the pitch at the same time. Mickey couldn't play as he was still injured (knee), but Paddy, Sean and Larry were all on the pitch for the last 20 minutes of what was in effect Paddy's testimonial game against Hawkes Bay Steamers. Even though Larry and Sean were both technically under age to be playing with the seniors, in true Mitchelle tradition Paddy thought it would be a fitting way to end his 18 years as a Bruiser. It was in that game that Sean broke his ankle so badly, he would never play competitive sport again.

The glory days over, Paddy and Dot settled into a functional understanding: each would perform their duties around the house, but in effect, they lived separate lives. Dot resigned herself to dead-eyed domesticity and Paddy, in more or less constant pain (knees, back, shoulder) spent his time reminiscing about the old days, surrounded by all the "Mad Paddy Mitchelle – Bruiser for life" memorabilia, permanently beered-up in his off-the-beaten-track pub paid for by two decades of physical sacrifice.

Breaking with family tradition of being born, loving and dying in or around Brisbane, Larry came to London at the age of 25 to see a bit of the world. Obviously, he would eventually go back home to settle down and have kids, but he felt uneasy about his girlfriend at the time Debbie (or Dibs, as she liked to be called) and her mates already talking about babies, planning weddings and researching suitable plots of land outside of Brisbane on which they'd build their dream house. At Brisbane airport, the last words his mother heartbreakingly whispered to him, (deliberately in earshot of Dibs only inches away,who was crying desperately even though they had planned for her to join him in a few months) were: "Don't marry someone like me, son."

He loved his parents to death and Dibs, from an unstable home, was all too keen to become them, but there just had to be more to life than *this*?

The "more than this" took the form of Siobhan Owen. When Larry met her at one of the Hammers Rugby do's[28] it was love, or total awe, at first sight. Tall, raven-dark straight hair with eyes to match, very, very cute, she was alive and bristled with energy. She drank, she laughed, she swore, she had that BBC accent that he found so sexy, as well as that fair skin and posh way about her that so many of the English (er, "I mean Welsh," he corrected himself) girls had; he'd never met anyone like her and knew that he never would again. He decided there and then that this was the woman he was going to marry.

OK, she played rugby, but it wasn't proper rugby and he could deal with it....

But, by six months into the relationship, he realised he couldn't. The thought of her at the bottom of a ruck or getting crashed into by some 20 stone lesbian made him feel sick. The bruises, the aching limbs, the "don't touch me I'm sore's", the training (OK, he did training as well – actually, he did all the other stuff too - but it was *different*!), the desire to hang around with her teammates rather than spend time with him; it was just too much for him. He ran his fingers over the scar on his cheek ("Game against Redbridge Old Boys two years previous, killing the ball and got a boot to the face," he smiled at the memory). Then there were the stud marks on his lower back ("Bexley Knights back home in Oz, killing the ball again. Hey, someone's got to!" he chuckled to himself. He'd got a pre-retaliatory punch in without the ref noticing though, so all's fair in love and war). He thought the cheek scar was "rather dashing" actually.

"But what about that on a woman?" Could he really live with a wife who had some horrible facial deformity as a result of a boot to the head, or whose nose was warped and pointing *upwards* after being punched in the face by a 20 stone lesbian? He had no idea why he was *so* obsessed with 20 stone lesbians either as he'd never met one, but there was something about rugby girls that just seemed "wrong".

And what about his mates back home? He could already hear the "pussy whipped" jibes and endless pink umbrellas in his pints for the rest of his life....

It was only after Warren, his best mate from home's visit (and general glowing approval, if it weren't for that one little thing...) that he hit upon a subtle plan: "Sib would be great, if it weren't for the rugby so, STOP HER PLAYING RUGBY. Brilliant!" What was the name of that play again "I love you, you're perfect, NOW CHANGE!"?

All he had to do now was find out how....

Chapter 20: Summer Training 2

The girls were tired and bored. They had practised trying to run around a defender, going to ground, rucking over to clear out any straggling defenders and recycling the ball until they were blue in the face. "Yeah, yeah, we get it now, can we do something else please?"

Gwen decided to voice the collective disquiet.

"Caz, I'm bored. How many more times are we going to have to do this?"

"Do you reckon you know this now then?" he replied, smiling one of his ultra-smug smiles.

"Something was definitely up. We know that face, he's planning something," they collectively thought.

"Er, yeah," came the now slightly unsure response.

"Good," he said, turning suddenly and heading towards lamp post two and a half where the boys were training, a little too jauntily for anyone's liking. "Stell, form a team," he yelled behind him, "go and get a drink and I'll be back in two minutes!"

Caz returned seconds later with Ben and a few of the rugby boys who had finished their training early.

"Right," Caz said. "Boys against girls. Full tackling, girls to start from the centre. Ball please?"

The girls looked up, all traces of tiredness disappearing instantaneously as the realisation of what was going to happen suddenly hit them.

"Full contact against the boys?!! Fucking hell!"

If they didn't concentrate and do this properly, they could get mullered. Obviously, Caz didn't tell them that he had briefed the boys earlier to tone down their tackling so as not to hurt anyone but to nevertheless stop the girls, but that slight omission should only serve to heighten the ladies' concentration. Collectively, without exchanging a word, the Hammers Ladies came to a decision: they had trained hard all summer, now was the chance to show the boys what they could do. It was also a chance to settle one or two old scores... This could be fun!

Caz threw the ball to Stell who ran straight into the midst of the slightly bemused rugby boys. The idea of playing against girls, the first time that any of them had ever done so, seemed initially like a laugh when Caz first approached them when they had arrived at training earlier that evening, but now that Stell was running straight at them, head down, ball tucked under her arm, to-hell-and-beyond expression on her face, they were having definite second thoughts.

Just how exactly were you supposed to tackle a girl? You can't try to wipe them out, 'cos then you'd look ungentlemanly, but then you couldn't allow them to run right through you either as you'd look like a sap. A grab-type tackle was the agreed solution but then, where would you grab? Under normal circumstances, getting physically to grips with one of the ladies' team would be fun, but if your hands accidentally strayed while trying to tackle someone without hurting them, you'd look like a perv'.

All such tortured deliberations were swiftly put to a hasty conclusion by the crash of the full force of Stell against ill-prepared rugby boy. The first defender was knocked to the side and Stell managed to gain a few yards before being hauled to the ground by the second tackler. The breach in the defences had already been made though and on hitting the dry summer earth, she turned her body to lay the ball towards her players. The sudden burst from Stell had not only caught the boys off guard but also her teammates as well, who were just too slow getting to her. One of the boys bent over her to pick up the ball in classic "ruck poacher" mode. As he reached, arms outstretched, head low and eyes focussed on the oval object partially-shielded by Stell's body, curled protectively around it in foetal position, he heard a crack, felt a sharp pain on the top of his head and woke up at the 'Sheaf, an ice-pack and strapping attached to his swollen forehead.

After Mand's clearing of the ruck and with Fi following close behind, clean ball was presented for Katie to pass on to the backs. Before she could get to it though, Larry came charging in from the side of the ruck to dive on the ball.

"Offside Sir!" called a few ladies' voices.

"Ball was out, play on," Caz replied, waving both arms forward.

"Not fucking having this!" Sib thought to herself, charging forward. Larry was almost on his feet and just about to break into his stride when Sib ripped into him from his left and, not prepared for such a hard contact, he spilled the ball forward. Gwen dived to the floor to secure the ball, ignoring the burn of dry grass against her knees and the pain from the thud of her shoulder against the deck. Swivelling on contact with the ground, so that her body formed an arc on the floor, her back towards the boys, she extended her arms, ball in hand, to present it for her teammates.

This time, Katie's movement to the ball was swift. She fizzed a long pass out to the Fly-Half Sophie who, seeing Ben, the first in a defensive line of boys, arms outstretched in preparation for the tackle, advancing towards her at speed in order to close her down before she could get the pass away, flipped out a short, lightning-quick ball to Lara. Lara threw on a seemingly far too hard pass to Ruth standing a few metres to her right and three or four metres behind. Ruth was already running to get level with Lara though and, as worked on in training, shouted out, "Ruth's ball" as she overran the pass, the ball whizzing behind her. The advancing defensive line of boys stopped in their tracks, Gus and Jack slamming on the brakes just before they crashed into the ladies' numbers 12 and 13. As ungentlemanly as it probably would have seemed and despite Caz' advice, Gus having lined Ruth up in anticipation of her receiving the pass, was ready to hit her as hard as he could. "No one turns me down," as she had three months previous, "when all I wanted was a snog and a bit of a feel." Ok he had been on the beers that night and probably wasn't the most desirable he'd ever been, but it wasn't as if she'd never been friendly with any of the rugby boys before...

The thought "Ooh, I like this," simultaneously went through the heads of Mads and Gwen.

Leafy, the intended recipient of Lara's pass was standing out wide, just slightly to the right of Ricky, the rugby boy defending in front of her. He wasn't expecting the ball to come straight to her though and so was a bit slow closing her down. This was a fatal mistake. Leafy's initial burst of acceleration made the 10 or so metres in between them disappear in moments and as Ricky shifted his weight to his right leg to give him the momentum to push off to the left to put in the tackle, Leafy was already past him. There were only about 30 metres to the tryline and Leafy's long, elegant strides ate them up in moments. Ricky readjusted his footing, swivelled round and gave chase: the foot race was on!

The boys on the other pitch, trailing in from their training session couldn't help but stop to watch as Leafy glided towards the line at cracking speed, with Ricky's short, powerful strides eating up the distance between them. A last gasp dive by Ricky two yards out and Leafy was brought to ground, crashing to the grass agonisingly short of the tryline.

But it wasn't over. As she fell forward, she managed to squeeze the ball out from under her armpit where it had been comfortably nuzzling and held it in both hands. At the same time she twisted to her left so that her right side came down hard on the dry ground. On impact with the floor, she flipped the ball into the air, slightly behind her and to her left, hoping that someone had been able to keep up with her and could catch the incredibly risky "pop pass" before the ball hit the deck....

Out of seemingly nowhere, a diving Fi, who had been sprinting to keep up with Leafy for support, caught the ball inches above the ground and fell forward through sheer momentum. She landed over the improvised tryline, almost ending up in the perimeter fencing, to touch down for a score: Hammers Ladies 1, Men 0!

It was like winning the world cup: that Johnny Wilkinson drop goal against the Aussies all over again! The girls raced to Fi and hugged her, even Stell forgetting personal enmities for a few seconds, joined in the collective hugging and cheering. It didn't matter that from the restart, the bigger, stronger and more experienced boys' team immediately ran down the other end and scored, nor that the ladies did not come anywhere near the boys' tryline for the remainder of the session. It didn't even matter that they *knew* that none of the boys, including a reluctant but nevertheless eventually complicit Gus, were tackling anywhere near as hard as they normally did. The most important thing was that the girls had shown to the boys on the sideline, the boys who had (initially) condescended to play against them and most importantly to themselves that they could do this: they were, actually, rugby players.

The ladies came off the pitch exhausted, hurting, but radiating happiness and something that had until now eluded them and to which they had never really previously given a second thought: pride.

Chapter 20: The Northerton Vipers

It is possible - and this is taken on the very best of authority - to subscribe to every society, club, protest movement, association, union and interest group, at Freshers' Fayre. The road to Hell is said to be paved with good intentions; whoever thought of the phrase had forgotten about the leaflets.

Stell, aged 18, had been at Northerton Uni' for a full three days now and after being: driven up to Birmingham with Mrs T and Huggy, being moved in, meeting her new flat mates in her new Uni' Digs, going out and getting drunk, eating chips, kebabs and getting drunk again, almost couldn't wait for lectures to start the next week.

Saying goodbye to Dermot, her boyfriend from home, was an absolute ordeal, all those tears, the "I love you 'til death's", the "I'll write to you every day's" were so, well, sweet, but in a sickly sort of way. They were also *so* inappropriate from a man...

Stell was actually relieved when her Mum's old, over-laden Range Rover finally pulled out of the Fulham street to make the couple of hours trip to Brum, Dermot's final "I'll wait for you!!!!" still ringing in her ears, more like a threat than a promise of undying love, and she was fully aware that her earnest vow to "Come back every weekend" was one that was never likely to be kept.

Here she now was, the first Saturday of her new life, at her first ever Northerton University's Freshers' Fayre. The fayre, usually held in the first week of the new academic year, was almost a glimpse into the future of the vicious market-share wars in which many of the students in the hall would be engaging, in only a few short years' time, for those lucky enough to find employment. All the university clubs and societies depended in the main on grants from the Students' Union for their very survival. These grants were allocated roughly according to the size of the membership for each club, so it was imperative to get as many students to sign up to the respective causes when they were new to the university: bushy-tailed, bright eyed, idealistic, completely naive, fresh meat. In a similar "cradle to the grave" mentality of the large banks, many of whom had impressive stands in the Great Hall themselves, the clubs and societies knew that once a new member joined, if there were no compelling enough reasons to cancel membership, the member would stay a member until graduation. No tactic was thus too low nor ploy too devious to be used against the FNGs[29].

Stell was tired, a bit bewildered by the mass of information and fed up with being canvassed. Her arms were filled to the brim with pamphlets, posters, leaflets and membership info on the Free Palestine Movement, the Zionist Independent Israel Organisation, the Save the Whale (Giant Iguana/ Panda/ Komodo Dragon: delete as appropriate) Campaign, plus a whole range of other groups whose meetings she had every intention of attending religiously, but sort of already knew she wouldn't. Her new-found friends (Ems, Alex, Jenny: all First Years and sharing her Freshers' flat on campus), had been wandering around the fayre for about an hour now and whilst pausing for breath in the centre of the hall, as if from out of nowhere, a rugby ball flew right over most of their heads and smashed the unlucky, taller Jenny full in the face.

"Whoops, sorry!" came the sheepish but not-even-slightly-apologetic voice of a rather cute young man, not very tall, reddish, compulsory floppy hair, well-scrubbed and bristling posh-boy confidence. "Is she alright?"

"I'm fine, I'm fine," protested Jen, whilst trying to struggle to her feet, Ems and Alex rushing quickly to help their stricken flatmate. Jen had clocked on immediately that this boy was a bit of a hottie, even though a good deal shorter than her, so, despite the blood oozing out of her nose, didn't want to seem like a wuss. One of the Fayre Supervisors, bespectacled and earnest, probably a Final Year Law Student, suddenly appeared, keen to press charges against the offending rugby boy.

"You chaps have been warned countless times, no throwing that stupid thing about inside!" He turned his attention to Jenny. "Would you like to make a statement? I could get these overgrown schoolboys dealt with once and for all."

"Ooh, he was cute too," Jen thought, but in a nice-for-my-little-sister-but-not-me nerdy sort of way. After a quick mental toss-up between which boy she'd like to see more of, she made a decision:

"No, honestly, I'm fine. It was probably my fault anyway....."

The rest of the conversation and her new flatmates drifted out of Stell's consciousness as she looked in the direction from which the ball seemed to have come: the Northerton Cobras Rugby Club stand. Apart from Red Rob (the ball-flinger and probably Jen's Uni' Boyfriend no. 1), there were two other rugby boys at the stand: a big, handsome, man-bull chap looking a bit worried (Russ, 1st team Captain: blonde, floppy hair as well, though balding slightly) and a much shorter, dark-haired chap with glasses, but as round as a ball, a cauliflower ear, no neck and a huge red, mischievous face. Stell found herself gliding towards them. "I didn't know they played rugby at Northerton," she thought.

"I didn't know they played rugby at Northerton," Stell was about to say to Man-Bull but, before the words could emerge, she was interrupted by the rasping, hostile voice of Round-Ball-Boy.

"Er, no, Girly," he condescended, hauling her out of her reverie, "Vipers stand's over there!" He pointed to a group of girls at a stand 10 metres away, under a black, white and red banner entitled Northerton Uni Vipers Ladies' Rugby Club, squeezed in between the Dungeons and Dragons Dreamworld Soc. and the Lesbian and Gay Soc. stands.

"Ladies Rugby? Proper rugby. Full contact rugby? Here? In Northerton?"

Stell used to love playing tag rugby, but when she was little, she hadn't realised that she was only supposed to love it *so* much, within acceptable limits, as a fun past-time for little boys and girls.

When tag stopped and full-contact began though, Jake and Huggy continued to play and learned to tackle and scrum and line-out, in order to become men and the future officer class of the country, while she was supposed to become a young lady and do lady-like things. However, these girls...

Stell could feel her throat tightening; she could barely breathe as a lump rose. Her fingers seemed to lose feeling and her arms grew weak. Unnoticed by her, the Free Palestine Movement and the Zionist Independent Israel Organisation leaflets wafted from the top of the leaflet mountain, to nestle peacefully side by side on the floor. The whole room seemed to disappear, apart from the stand in front of her and something behind and to the side of her eyes seemed to be about to burst. She walked very, very slowly, so as not to trip, towards the three girls gently tossing a rugby ball among them and engaging in some sort of banter that she couldn't hear. As she approached, the banter tailed off and they looked at her. Her heart felt as if it would explode from her chest.

"Alright," she said, as casually as she could manage.

"Here, catch!" said the short, stocky, brown-spikey-haired girl. "Played before?"

The armful of pamphlets followed its fallen comrades to join the leaflet carpet growing steadily over the fast-disappearing parquet flooring as Stell caught the ball instinctively and looked down at it. It was almost a full 10 years since she'd touched one of these things. Ok, it was a lot smaller at the time, but she hadn't had a rugby ball in her hands since *that* day...

"Er, can we have it back now please?" This was from the skinny girl with the Vipers' bobble hat, long, dyed-reddish ringletted hair and glasses. Stell handed it back to her; she didn't know what to say.

"I played a bit, but only tag. You know, when I was little. Stopped when I was about 9," she mumbled.

"Me too!" said the huge blonde girl, a large, friendly smile cracking open her rugged face. "Everything was great until I got banned when I was 11."

"You did actually break someone's arm, if you remember?" chimed in Short-Spikey Girl.

"Well, he shouldn't have tried to tackle me then!" Huge Blond Girl protested. Then, by way of explanation added, "The boys, see, were only playing 'cos they had to, whereas I just loved smashing into them. They banned me 'cos I was the only girl and said it had something to do with the RFU laws or whatever. They were just scared." She looked down towards her trainers, the sense of betrayal from eight years before still stinging. Bobble-Hat coughed. Brightening, Huge Blonde Girl added, "I'm Beth, by the way."

The girls all introduced themselves amidst much mickey-taking, rude nicknames and bawdy stories about the origins of the nicknames. The actual explanation behind why the Short-Spikey Girl (Deidra) was called Tampax was lost on Stell, even after the second explanation, but it really didn't matter.

There was a warmth and welcoming feeling about these girls, as if they were the same as her, had similar experiences and similar ideals. It felt as if she'd known them forever.

"You look like a 2nd row to me," Beth continued.

"My Dad used to play secon....," Stell began. Her voice trailed off and she fell silent. The Vipers, sensing something was wrong, looked at each other awkwardly.

Idit, (Bobble Hat), dived in with a, "First training session next Wednesday afternoon, announcements will be on the notice-board. Trials for the team take place the week after, but tonight, we have a special training programme!"

"What's that?" Stell asked, cheering up.

"Aaah, you'll see, but it does involve plenty of exercise of your right arm. And your mouth!"

Stell looked perplexed.

"No, not for THAT!" Idit replied, sensing that Stell may have been thinking along the lines of some form of perverse, sexual initiation.

"For *drinking,* you Muppet!" finished Beth, punching her on the arm in a good-naturedly sort of way.

Chapter 21: Reflections

It has been said that nobody ever persuades anyone to do anything. Real decisions are made at night, in the dark, on your own.

Later that evening, in bed in her uni' digs - a slight, almost imperceptible distance already seeming to grow between her and Ems, Alex and the newly loved-up, Jenny, possibly as a result of her choice of acquantances for the evening - and with an extremely fuzzy head after far too many Snakebites and Black, Stell thought long and hard.

She hadn't exactly been told as much, but it was made *very* clear that if you wanted to get on in life, as a woman, there were certain things you had to do (be pretty, be smart, be *thin*, get a good husband, get a nice house, have kids, send them to good schools, go on nice holidays etc. etc. etc). Playing rugby was definitely *not* one of them. You would end up broken and ugly, you'd lose teeth, have the wrong sorts of ears, no neck, maybe even be crippled or possibly even DIE as women's bodies aren't meant to take those sorts of impacts and collisions. At the very least, you'd lose all femininity and probably end up gay.

Tampax had spelled it out to her, in a drunken and amusing diatribe, earlier on that evening:

"Yusees, it's loik this," in her velvety Northern Ireland accent. "They hates us, they fockin' do!" she explained, waving an unsteady arm in the general direction of everyone else in the "Sack of Potatoes" public house. Warming to her theme, the alcohol flowing freely through her body, Tampax continued,

"Despite getting the vote and being able to wurk and be independent and all that other shite, if you don't have a man, the WHOLE WORL' considers us as sad, lonely old focks. With cats! So, we have to get a man, even though they're useless gobshites."

"Here here!" Beth ("Ox": as in, "always very horny...") had enthusiastically chimed in, waving her Snakey and Black in the air,

"I could definitely EAT Russ though, gobshite or not!" interjected Idit (or "Otter": "slippery when wet").

"I'd drink to that!" Stell found herself saying and most of the girls raised their glasses in a toast to the Men's 1st 15 Captain.

"From what I hear Otts, you virtually did!" said one of the other Vipers, who had joined the initial group for the evening's "training". "He's still got the bite marks!"

Tampax, unamused, pressed on:

"In order to get a man, we have to paint and pluck and fockin' WAX ourselves to look like bleedin' Barbie, just so we don't end up on the shelf. EVERY culture in the history of this planet, and God knows where else, has some way of treating women loik shite. Either with back-breaking corsets, or binding your feet or wearing chastity belts or burkhas or hijabs or not being allowed to wear trousers nor teach nor be a priest or having to throw yourself on some fockin' funeral pyre just so you can become a child-bearing, home-making, 2nd class citizen, nurse-maid to an overgrown, ego-filled WANKER." Heads nodded in agreement.

Tampax was liking this now, "I mean, if MARTIANS came to Earth, fockin' little green men with GREAT big antennae sticking out of their heads, you could bet your bottom euro that their women would be walking two steps behoind!"

"You'd look good in one of those burkhas Tamps!" said Ox, trying to wrest the mantle of Team Joker from the new contender. "Here," she continued, "has anyone seen one of the Middle Eastern Playboy magazines?"

"No," was the general murmured response, anticipating another priceless - well according to Ox at least - Ox joke.

"Yeah, in a move to liberalise, there's now a Playgirl of the Month spread. Only condition is, they all have to wear burkhas!"

"I don't get it," said a confused Otter. "I mean..."

One of the other girls had taken up on Tampax' theme and carried on:

"Yeah, my Mum, for example. She wanted to be an artist and fell in love with some French bloke who wanted to take her back to Paris. Obviously, my Grandad said no (after all, he was French) and she basically had to "be a good girl and set the right example"."

"Ooh, you could be half French!" another Viper jumped in. "Then we'd really have reason to hate you!" The first girl punched her on the arm but continued,

"At the end of a life-time of conforming to the family's and the whole town's ideal of "what was best for her"," she ended up with a nice house in bloody Bogworth, a nice set of divorced friends, me and my brother and a shit husband who left her for a younger version cos he didn't want to shag her anymore as her body'd been ruined by childbirth. I mean, tits don't last forever," she exclaimed, grabbing her quite large breasts with both hands and thrusting them upwards and outwards to prove her point. Not for the first time...

The general theme of "men are shit" and "we are all slaves to society's expectations of us" continued for a little while longer, until the girls eventually sidled off, in ones and twos, to meet their various boyfriends and girlfriends or just to go back to their student flats.

Now, in bed (on her own), Stell (christened Yoda: as in Stella = Stellar = Star Wars = Yoda. Simple!) thought about some of the less extreme parts of the well-lubricated conversation and tried to build some logic into it.

True: proper women aren't supposed to play rugby. Proper women married proper men who played rugby.

True: not adhering to society's expectations of you will not end well and you will be ostracised.

True: if ostracised, you end up as a lonely old spinster, polite society will shun you and small children will throw things at you on the street as you will smell of cat pee. Cats are obviously obligatory.

True: she'd never actually played "full contact" rugby before and didn't have a clue what she'd be doing. She would probably get smashed to a pulp in minutes (even though she was big enough to do quite a bit of smashing herself) and end up deformed (like that short, obnoxious ape at Fresher's Fayre. He was cute though: for an arrogant prick).

Also true: if you only ever do what people expect of you, you'd end up a miserable, sad, old lady, like her Mum. Which was worse, Cat Lady or Sad Lady? Phew, what a choice!

However....

Here was a group of girls who had had all this bullshit shoved down their throats. They had had (probably) brothers and fathers in the game, being lauded and celebrated and feted as if they'd just won the bloody world cup, but when they said, "I want some of that," they were told: "No, ladies do NOT play rugby."

Well, these girls were saying a great, big, "Fuck you world! This is me, this is what I want to do, deal with it!"

Wow. Fucking wow.

The beginnings of a hang-over were already setting in and the throbbing in her head was making further rational political and social circumspection far too difficult. Sleep was calling her name and even the trek to the kitchen for the regulation large glass of water as hangover repellent just seemed too much of an effort.

"I juss wanna play. See whaddiss like. Thass all....."

Chapter 22: Warfare

Why on earth would anyone ever want to go to Rivenstoke? Just inside the commuter belt for London but just far enough away to make it impossible to enjoy regular London social life, the town was dead, dead, dead. One of Rivenstoke's claims to fame was that it was the first town to be twinned with a sister European town which wanted to undergo the equivalent of a Siamese twin divorce.

The new rugby season was one week away and, in preparation for the league fixtures that would last from September until April, Caz had thought it would be a good idea for the Hammers' Ladies to play a warm-up friendly against a team who should be about the same level as them. No London teams were available for the hastily arranged fixture, so a trip up the M1 to Rivenstoke, one of the relatively unknown and hostile tribes which inhabited the area north of Watford, was organised.

The Rivenstoke Rugby Football Club was based in a green area right in between the Golf Club and one of the more notorious council estates. Its players were thus a strange mixture of people from Rivenstoke's two diverse and rival communities: the "Stokies" and the "Daflls".

The "Stokies" were the locals who had never been more than a few miles from their place of birth. If you were a Rivenstoke native and showed enough potential to go into higher education, once you'd been to Uni' outside of the catchment area, you'd gravitate towards the bright lights of London and normally never come back. As many of those who might have thus created their own businesses in Rivenstoke never returned, very little local industry existed. What did exist though amongst those who never left, and in abundance, was high unemployment leading to high crime, high levels of teenage drinking leading to high teenage pregnancy and subsequently lots of inexpensive and not overly-pretty council accommodation in which to house them all. Rivenstoke thus had more than its fair share of 70's Council-style blocks[30], full to the brim of Stokies born and bred and fiercely proud.

Another effect of the local brain drain was that housing, certainly for the larger properties in the leafier, more affluent parts of the town, which presumably would have been inhabited by returning university graduates with good jobs and higher salaries, was relatively cheap compared to London. This attracted many young commuter families, with no historic links to the town. Initially regarded with suspicion (and just a tinge of jealousy) by the locals, on average, a new arrival would have to live in Rivenstoke for at least 5 years before a local would even acknowledge their existence with a "How does?"[31]

However, they had made Rivenstoke their home and were determined to bring up their families there. In the face of local hostility, the new arrivals formed their own little groups, only socialising with others like themselves and considering the "locals" as being less worldly-wise and generally poorer.

The Stokies referred to the new arrivals as "DAFLLS"[32]. They did however contribute to local businesses, so they couldn't hate them too much, nor too openly[33].

One of the few things that brought the rival communities together though, (the Stokies a lot more than the Daflls) apart from the odd unpleasant incidents in the town centre on a Friday and Saturday night, was, in true drawbridge tradition, their hatred of outsiders. In the words of one particularly socially astute American rap group: "Where they're from's what they got and they don't own squat (apart from the Daflls), disrespect where they're from and you might get shot."[34]

All in all, a wonderful place for the London-based, culturally diverse, mostly University graduates of the Hammersmith and Fulham Ladies Rugby Club to come to play...

The Rivenstoke Ladies team were big. If anyone seriously ever wanted an answer to the age old question: "Who ate all the pies?" they would have to look no farther than the Rivenstoke Ladies XV forwards. Mostly of Stokie descent, the forwards had been brought up on a diet of football and fast food: the more of the one they did, the less of the other they could do. In the end, the fast food had prevailed. However, it has been noted by some important sociologists that the less fit and healthy lifestyle a person leads, the more sports clothing they tend to wear. Lack of availability of appropriately-sized alternative clothing may have something to do with it, but there is a complicated explanation somewhere that the main reason for this phenomenon was a compensation for the feelings of guilt that their lack of fitness gave rise to coupled with a genuine desire to be considered sporty. Now, where could they find an environment where they could eat, drink and smoke as much as they liked, whilst enjoying the company of their friends and *still* be considered athletes?

Having seen the crash bash wallop of male rugby on television and being big enough to really smash someone they came up against - legally and without an appearance before the local magistrate – rugby seemed like a license to print money and was embraced enthusiastically by some of the larger, perma-sportswear-attired local residents. The Rivenstoke Ladies, or Stokie Bears, thus had a large, solid forward unit capable of holding their own against anyone.

The backs were more evenly split between Dafll and Stokie and even though generally smaller, shared the same propensity for size. During matches, the normal Stokie game plan would be to kick the ball as close to the opposition tryline as possible (as it was unlikely that the forwards could run the length of the pitch) and then let the forwards take it from there.

A loud and boisterous crowd of some 50 people were in attendance when the Hammers' cars started arriving in ones and twos in the car park of the recently-Council refurbished Rivenstoke Athletics Ground.

"My God they're HUGE!" gasped Gwen on getting out of the car and seeing the already-changed and warming up Bears.

"Doesn't matter," said Stell. "We've been training hard all summer and we can do this." It sounded convincing, but even she wasn't so sure.

After a brief warm-up session and the customary, "Hammers, Hammers, Hammers!" rallying cry, the referee raised his arm to signal to the two teams that the game was ready to commence. Nobody noticed a small band of beer-tankard clutching, far-too-sunnily-dressed-for-this-time-of-year Rhodies slip into the ground near the corner flag, initially fairly quiet but becoming louder the more they advanced up the side of the pitch towards the halfway line, ignoring the touch judge's (a 16-year-old daughter of one of the Bears) pleas to move back. The more the beer flowed, the more vocal they became, cheering on the travelling Hammers' Ladies. Mrs T and Fred, who had as usual made the long journey to accompany Stell and serve in her familiar role of Sole Supporter, was glad of the fellow support, even though establishing, at least initially, enough of a distance for anyone watching to know she wasn't part of their group. She made a mental note that during the game, she could always ask them what was actually going on on the pitch.

Just before the starting whistle sounded, the group of Rhodies parted slightly and Fi could just make out the still-blonde hair and red face of her father.

The Bears kicked off. The September Sunday afternoon was bright and warm, with barely a breeze in the air, so it must have been the rustiness from the long drive, rather than the wind, that caused Fi to fumble the Stokie no.10's kick.

"Knock on, scrum, black ball."

"Forget that ladies," rasped Stell, through clenched teeth, trying hard not to look in Fi's direction so as not to display her obvious anger at the "school boy" error. Focussing on the next phase of play, she hissed, "We know that they're good in the scrum, so we need to get low and give a huge first shove. Are we gonna do this?!!"

"YES!" came the committed reply from 13 other Hammers. Fi looked to her boots, the shame of her knock on in front of her father strangling her voice.

"Crouch, touch, pause...," a few moments' hesitation, "ENGAGE!" shouted the referee.

The two multi-headed, multi-armed monsters, Stokie black (and pink!) and Hammers red, crashed together in a loud, dull thud. From the very first scrum, each pack of forwards would be able to "suss out" the other. How will the other beast be: strong, low, aggressive, or buckle and squeal like a wounded animal? This is the jump into the unknown, the leap into the dark, an almost kamikaze throwing of yourself into possibly a world of pain or of total dominance the forwards had grown to both fear and relish. Mel stared straight into the eyes of the woman at the centre of the black beast, trying to bore into her mind and soul for any signs of weakness so as to establish superiority. The centre of the beast stared back: dead eyed, malevolent, ready for what was about to come. Her heart was pounding in her chest and a fresh burst of sweat sprang out of every pore. From this first engagement, she'd know how to adapt, how her Hammers colleagues closely packed behind and all around her, would need to reposition themselves in order to improve, to protect her and her front row colleagues and ultimately, to dominate.

Mads, Mel and Gwen could smell the sweat from the warm-up, once cooled in the wait before the kick off but now starting to flow again. The familiar smell of their own team was overwhelmed by the acrid, sulphurous stench of the opposition. Mel could feel herself wanting to gag. Her impulse was to pull Mads (still too high) and Gwen even closer to her, for comfort and strength, but the alien heads in between them squeezed into her ears to make her head buzz. This queasiness wasn't helped by the fact that the Black Beast had definitely been chewing garlic, and maybe onion as well, in order to make the closed air in those few centimetres of front row, even more vile.

"Just get it in, just get it in," she prayed.

The Bears' Scrum Half fed the ball into the middle of the scrum, slightly towards her own front row, which was missed by the referee who was too busy making sure the no. 8s were still bound to the back of the scrum. From these very first seconds, this very first hit, the psychological battle and struggle for supremacy in the scrums, for the rest of the game, would be won. Or lost.

"Aaaarrrggghhh!" Mel shouted, popping her head out of the middle of the Hammers' front row. The whole Hammers' front row stood up as well, followed by their larger opponents.

"Penalty to Black, standing up in the scrum!"

"But she kicked me!!!" protested the Hammers' no.2, tears of pain and injustice welling in her eyes.

"Penalty to Black, if you argue, I'll give them another 10 yards and you a yellow card."

The Hammers shuffled back the 10 yards so the Bears' no.10 could kick for touch towards the Hammers' tryline.

"What happened?" asked a now thoroughly pissed-off Stell. "Two stupid mistakes within the first few seconds, what was the point of all that training and lugging our arses all this way?" she thought.

"When we went down for the scrum, the other Hooker eh, she was suspended in the air between her Props, swung her legs up and kicked me, two-footed in the chest. It really hurt-eh!" Stell sniggered with disbelief. In all her years of playing, she'd NEVER heard of anything like it.

"It's true!" protested Mads, the Prop. "I saw her swing both legs up and couldn't believe it, the evil cow."

All three turned to stare at the Bears' no.2, a short, pretty woman of about 30, a lot slimmer than her team-mates, with her blonde-streaked hair tied in a pony tail, her face the very picture of innocence itself. Noticing that she had been singled out, she gave the sweetest of cherubic smiles.

The resulting line-out from the kick to touch was easily won by the home team, who quickly organised themselves into a maul, with the ball at the back of their formation.

There are many ways to launch an attack in rugby. One way is to run round the opposition, being faster and fitter. Another way is to use the quickness of feet and brain to outsmart the other team, feigning to go one way but going the other. It is also possible to move the ball quickly to where the other team are not, to chip the ball over the top of them to run onto it, indeed to do many, many things to outwit your opponent so you have more men in attack than they have in defence.

The Stokie Bears' chosen method of attack, being big and possibly not as mobile as most teams, was to walk, very, *very* slowly but enormously powerfully, like a troop of very large Sherman tanks packed in close formation, right through the middle of the opposition, crushing all in their path. They had thus perfected the maul.[35]

What's really, really good about this attacking formation is that you do not have to be fast or skilful or particularly clever to do this (even though a good deal of organisation is required to get the shape right). All you need is size and the Stokie Bears definitely had this advantage by virtually two to one. Make that two and a half to one.

Picture: Polish Cavalry attacking German Panzer tanks with sabres at the beginning of the Second World War? Now replace those sabres with sticks of jelly (frozen) and double the tanks' armour? There, that's about right...

The retreating Hammers pulled, pushed, slapped, tickled and even tried to jump on top of this moving combination of muscle, fat and steely determination, which was slowly grinding forward like an unstoppable behemoth. There was simply nothing the red defence could do.

The cry from the crowd of, "Stokies, Stokies, Stokies!" drowned out the now much quieter Rhodie contingent as the Bears crunched over the line for their first of many tries.

"That's not fair, they're much bigger than our girls. They can't do that! Can they?" Mrs T asked the nearest Rhodie. He shrugged and stared into his beer, the golden surface of which was now suddenly very interesting compared to having to face the agitated Theakston gaze.

The hurt of conceding so early on for the Hammers and the taunts of the home crowd were more than eclipsed by the physical pain of being trampled.

"Captain, what do we do?" the Hammers' forwards were asking in desperation, as they gathered under the posts for the conversion attempt (missed). Stell looked over at Caz on the sideline. They'd only just about managed to get through the basics of rugby during the few short weeks of training that they'd had over the summer: defensive tactics hadn't even entered into it yet. Also, Caz hadn't realised that other ladies' teams would be SO HUGE, so had completely forgotten to even mention "Defence Against the Dark Arts".[36]

"Whoops...," he mouthed to Stell. He then said something else but, ears bound by protective tape, Stell couldn't hear.

"Fat lot of good he is, the git," she muttered to herself. "Ohhh-kay, this is gonna be tricky..."

Chapter 23: Aftermath: Rivenstoke Bears 20, Hammersmith and Fulham Ladies 5

Apart from the initial fumbled catch, Fi had not touched the ball once during the whole game.

To make matters worse, not only had she spent most of the time crashing into herds of Tellytubbies, who basically wouldn't have moved if she'd used water cannon, she'd also been trampled so many times, she felt like the coyote in the Road Runner cartoons, after he'd been flattened by his own tarmac press during one of his latest failed attempts to secure some poultry-to-go.

It's really not easy to play rugby when you don't have the ball and the Stokie Bears had virtually adopted the damn thing, sticking it up their jumpers and trundling forward, like the water buffalo they so clearly were, pushing the Hammers back on every single maul. Even when, after half time, Caz tried to teach them how to stop the maul ("Don't let it start!" "Duh," she thought at the time, "is this what we're paying him for? Well, he's worth every penny of it!"[37]) and the Stokies started to tire, it was still like trying to push a wall.

"A huge, chubby wall with big fat fingers, fat bellies, fat tits and fat hair," she concluded. "OK, maybe not fat hair, but it might as well have been!"

She had got lost trying to find the toilets, probably taking a wrong turning in the myriad of corridors that these council-built, multi-purpose sporting facilities seemed to be so fond of and now found herself standing outside the loos, probably as far as humanly possible to be - and still be in the same building - from the bar in which the post-match awards and celebrations were taking place between the "trying really hard not to gloat" Stokies and the bruised, smarting Hammers.

When she had come off the pitch at the end of the game, staring with incredible concentration at her boots to avoid any criticism in the eyes of the supporters, she could feel her father's disapproving gaze boring into the top of her head. After she'd showered and changed, even though some of the Rhodies were still hanging about, singing songs from home and swapping stories of how much better they were when they were playing, James Stanley was nowhere to be seen.

What had made things even worse for her though was that right at the very end of the game, when the Hammers finally had won a scrum 5 metres out from the Stokie line in a rare moment of attacking play, Stell had picked the ball up from a ruck, hit the Bears' defence on the right, then rolled left to score a try to record the Hammers' only points of the game.

"It was so unfair!" she protested silently. She leaned back against the wall and closed her eyes. She'd try to find her way back to the bar in just a few moments, now she just needed time away from everyone. She hated feeling like this, feelings that she had vowed she would never have to experience again: ashamed, powerless, alone.

Fi's eyes suddenly snapped open. She could hear footsteps in the corridor, coming towards her. These sorts of multi-sports places were normally empty on a Sunday late afternoon. The only thing that ever took place there at that time was the ladies' rugby, so anyone in the building would only be there for that. "So what would they be doing way out here?" she thought, "miles from the bar. Unless..."

The footsteps rounded the corner so their owner could be seen. It was the Stokies' Hooker, the no.2. As the game had progressed, the evil little imp had had many more tricks up her sleeve than just the two-footed chest kick. Mel had complained of being punched, her ear being chewed, as well as kisses being blown once Mel was really riled, which made the other front-rowers, Stokies and Hammers alike, struggle to contain their laughter at the sheer cheek.

The Stokie looked different in clothes: long, wet, blonde-streaked, slightly wavy hair, pretty face, pink lip-stick, laughter (or was it age?) lines at the corners of her eyes, combat pants, a "Stokie Bears do it in the woods" t-shirt (tight-fitting revealing medium-sized, push-up bra assisted breasts), she was unrecognisable from the hate-filled midget of only half an hour ago.

The Hooker was breathing heavily, as if she were struggling with a huge decision she was about to make. Mind apparently made up, she stared Fi straight in the eye, from the distance of about 20 metres, then turned to look directly ahead, ignoring Fi, as she walked, in a not-particularly-well-executed nonchalant way, right past her but as closely as possible so Fi could smell her shampoo and perfume. She turned her head with her lips slightly parted, challengingly, to again look Fi in the eye, before disappearing through the toilet door on Fi's right.

Fi gasped, her heart definitely started beating faster as she tried to rationalise the feelings that gripped her body.

She had never really had much time for boyfriends as they tended to be so cloying. Looking the way she did, she found she was considered more as a trophy, something to be acquired, rather than actually played with and pleasured. She was so often approached by the drunk ones, fortified by gallons of Dutch Courage[38], either on a dare from their equally drunk mates or batting seriously above their average and, even if the guy were cute and she took pity, at the business end of the deal, the "Oh my God Screaming Orgasm" end, she really hadn't got much out of the transaction at all.

The few times she had been with men, or rather boys, it had virtually always led to lying in "the damp patch" in an alien bed (never her own, in order to facilitate escape if need be), staring at the ceiling while actually relieved that the snoring, selfish bore lying next to her had finished his few seconds of humping away and was leaving her a little bruised but in relative peace. The tension in her chest that he might wake up for a repeat session would not subside until she saw the first rays of morning seeping through the curtains or blinds, signalling that the hour was decent enough for public transport to be available for her to sneak away. Then there would be the attempts to contact her again, which had led to so many changes of mobile phone that she could now open a shop selling all her accumulated chargers and protective covers and phone accessories for phones that had to be abandoned for fear of being traced. There was just no point in giving up her independence and being in a relationship for "*that*".

She'd tried the "Friends with Benefits" route of having just casual affairs, but it ended up getting complicated (she'd had to avoid going to Wayne's class for weeks, just until his ardour had cooled and he'd moved on to another regular attendee). She was really annoyed with herself for having to miss those classes.

So, eventually, through enforced practice, she had become rather good at pleasuring herself ("If a job's gotta be done....") and had a small selection of "toys" that she could manage quite expertly. "Give me "Friends with Batteries" any time!" she'd thought to herself.

It's true that sometimes she wished she could share what she could do to herself, and probably to someone else, with an actual *human being* she cared about, but so far, she'd been unfortunately disappointed.

Making a decision, Fi drew a sharp breath and pushed open the toilet door.

The Stokie was standing in the middle of the room, waiting, almost panting with the expectation.

"I thought you weren't...." she began, but Fi, walking rapidly, put her finger to the Stokie's lips to quieten her. No words.

Fi kissed her forehead, then lightly on the lips, then on the tip of her nose, returning to her lips with a fuller kiss. The Stokie smelled newly-scrubbed, but with a thin veneer of fresh perspiraton after the hot shower. Shorter than Fi, she had to raise herself to her toes in order to kiss Fi properly. Fi bent down to meet her lips fully, but drew away slightly, as if to tease, before renewing the kiss, this time deeper. As the two bodies pressed together and lips and tongues delved deeper into mouths, hands and crotches and bums were stroked, squeezed, kneaded, Fi thought, "Strange, no stubble. Lips feel softer, smell and perfume less harsh, body more yielding, muscles nowhere near as defined. Bum a bit squidgy."

Fi could feel the Stokie's heart pounding with excitement. The Stokie no. 2 had had two children, the first when she was far too young, but had kicked out her last partner, the father of her youngest, after years of being a neglected and cheated-on housewife. Having found a good job in Rivenstoke Council, she was in the process of rebuilding her life and had taken up rugby, along with some of the girls from work, for "a bit of a laugh" and to have a ready-made group of friends and social network post the friends she'd shared with her husband. Not just to impress them, but also to reinforce her image of being "the take-no-nonsense-hard one", the "rock" on whom others, her two children included, could rely, she was particularly vicious on the pitch. A downside of her carefully cultivated persona though was that no-one ever considered that *she* may need affection. She hadn't been touched, apart from the contact on the rugby pitch, in years and had effectively removed herself from the dating game and all hope of ever being sexually turned-on again. Then, this afternoon, she'd seen this blonde, golden, BEAUTIFUL goddess, hurling herself around the pitch and tackling everything that moved. The Stokie hadn't known what to do or how to react, but even before the end of the game, had felt aroused.

This Amazonian was everything any woman would want to be: strong, confident and absolutely drop-dead GORGEOUS. Women like her adorned the front covers of virtually every magazine and advertising hoarding, as the ad agencies all *know* that this is the type of woman that every woman would want to be and every man would want to shag. The Stokie felt both. There was also this feeling of sadness that she had detected emanating from the Hammers' no.7, so when she saw her sloping off out of the bar, something in her just compelled her to follow.

And now, this.

The Stokie felt the hardening of Fi's nipples under her Hammer's polo top and feverishly searched to grip the bottom of it, so as to lift it over needing-to-be-licked breasts. Her mouth felt wet with anticipation.

"Uh uh," Fi said suddenly, wagging a reproachful finger while pulling away, a wicked smile on her face. Then she left.

Chapter 24: Defence Against the Dark Arts

The training session after the defeat at Rivenstoke was attended by just over half the team. Bruised bodies simply could not be motivated to submit themselves to an hour and a half of more punishment, so text messages and emails detailing: the "sudden" extra work load given by various employers, the "surprise" company late-night audits and "unexpected" clients coming in from out of town flew through cyber-space for a good part of the Thursday afternoon. Those who were in attendance though were in no mood to be patronised for their defeat and were itching to show their defiance to anyone who crossed their path. Caz had better watch out.

"Ladies," Caz began, surveying the sparse numbers huddled around the 2nd lamp post in the fading early September light, "thanks for turning up." He was greeted by a chorus of groans.

"Sunday was hard, but I know how we can stop them."

"Yeah," said Stell, "Your words of wisdom when we needed you most were, "Don't let the maul start. Fat lot of good that was." The other girls nodded in agreement.

"Ah, rebellion," Caz thought. "Only one way to deal with it, make an example of the ringleader. Simples."

The Coach ushered the mutinous ladies over to a small grid that he had laid out with cones, about 5 meters wide by 10 metres long.

"OK Stell, I'll be the defender and I want you to start at the line of cones and walk towards the far end of the grid to score a try. If you get half-stopped, I want you to turn and look for support from three other forwards by forming a maul. Then I want you to steam-roller me beyond the try-line. He was going to add, "as you were steam-rollered on Sunday!" but, a quick glance at the still-smarting faces of the downhearted players made him think better of it.

Stell caught a ball tossed to her by Mads, stooped slightly with her right shoulder forward, the ball protected close to her chest by her right forearm, the left arm bent around slightly to offer protection from behind. She wanted to charge at Caz to knock the smugness out of him but, partly out of curiosity, decided instead to go along with his little scheme to see if it actually could be of any benefit. Before she had gone two metres, Caz slammed into her right thigh with his right shoulder, arms outstretched, harder than she'd ever been tackled before, completely knocking her off her feet and onto the still-dry earth. The girls gasped.

"Whatthefuckwasthat!" Stell wanted to scream, but all that came out was a strangled and winded, "Caz!!!!" The other players rushed to her aid, fearing that their captain had been seriously injured by this madman. "What is going on between them two?" was the question everyone thought but no-one put into words yet; they were just too shocked.

The impact from the tackle had knocked Stell back almost 2 metres. Caz had wrapped his arms around her thighs and brought them together so she couldn't stand, then as she flopped forward over his shoulders and back, she had forgotten about any attempt to retain possession of the ball and it spilled forward. The Coach had twisted his body in mid-air so that his lead shoulder, instead of following through to crash into her hip when they hit the ground, rolled harmlessly around her body, leaving them both lying on the floor on their backs. Stell, partially in shock at the unexpected brutality of the tackle, felt the adrenalin coursing through her body. She realised and was grateful that Caz had pulled out from actually trying to hurt her, but still felt inside the acute animal awareness of near-danger: and it felt good! Despite herself, she felt alive, excited and thrilled, her body still tingling from the impact.

When she and Caz had first met at a training session about two seasons before, when he was still playing, she immediately disliked him. He had this air about him of, now what's the best way to describe it? There that's it: Chicken Eater!

As a little girl, Stell had loved those wordless cartoons when all thoughts appeared as bubbles over the animated character's head. So, when Sylvester the Cat sees Tweety Bird the Budgerigar for the first time, his evil, carnivorous urgings are portrayed by a thought bubble containing a beautifully plump, freshly roasted, browned to perfection, grade A chicken. With trimmings! That was how Caz had looked at her: self-confidence, almost swaggering in his *certain* knowledge that, if he wanted to, he could feast on this helpless, tasty morsel and have her on her back without a moment's hesitation.

Obviously, he had been awfully polite and had made some sort of silly joke about them both having attended Northerton, but it was also clear that he felt attracted to her and made no attempt to hide it. However, and this was the really infuriating thing, he was using that tried-and-tested tactic of, "Look how wonderful I am, I am good looking and fit and a good laugh and suave and sophisticated and I am sexually attracted to you, but I am not going to do a single thing about it. Your move, Hun."

Stell absolutely *hated* when boys did that. "I mean," she thought, "what do you do?"

It was a bit like the old psychometric test in which you are told to not think about an elephant. The very first thing you think about is, surprisingly enough, an elephant.

"So," she and her friends, mostly the Vipers at Uni', had often debated, "there's this really nice, fit guy, who fulfils all the right physical criteria and has this confidence that exudes naughtiness and thus the suggestion of a pretty naughty sex life. You know he would quite like to include you in his obvious array of devilish tricks but he doesn't ever even mention it. What do you then think about EVERY TIME YOU SEE HIM (and actually quite often when you don't)? Aaarrrggghhh: it was so unfair!

"The very *last* thing in the world you should ever do though, irrespective as to how drunk you are or desperate for sex you are as you've not had it in AGES or turned on you are is to think of him when masturbating – oh NO, I've just done it! If you do this, then ALL IS LOST (especially if it's a good one)!"

"Alright Otter, that's probably a bit too much information!" the girls would usually chime in, even though they wanted to hear more.

"Every time you see him from then on, you can't help but get turned on. I mean, seriously, it gets embarrassing." The assorted friends, those who would admit to having these crushes, would nod sagely.

What would happen next though was even more embarrassing. At some stage, the girl in question just wouldn't be able to hold back anymore ("Why won't he *DO* something?!!!") and would throw herself at the object of her affection in such a way as to make it absolutely clear of her attentions and now intentions. The said bloke, feigning being taken totally unawares, would usually resort to one of three standard options:

1) Declare that he too felt the same way and they would swear undying love and live happily ever after

2) Pretend surprise and "blow her out" quite publically, painfully embarrassingly and in full view of his mates

3) Willingly have sex with her, dragging the affair on for as long as he could get away with, before she eventually found out that either he had a girlfriend (in Caz' case a wife and two children) or that she was not the only unsuspecting young lady to fall for his ploy. The gentleman concerned indeed had a stable of fillies among which he divided his time and this so-called Mr Wonderful, who gave the impression he was such a nice guy to the general public, was, once you actually got to know him, a dirty bastard, game-playing fraud.

In Stell's and most of the Vipers' experience, 1) never happened, 2) happened in say 20% of the time and 3) was a pretty much dead cert. "They always let you down. Always," she thought.

Stell had had one and a half no.1)s: Her first real boyfriend Greg ("poor guy, he really didn't deserve what happened to him. At least now he was married to a nice, boring girl from back home and lived in a crumbly house a few miles outside of Milesborough, which was all he ever wanted, to be fair"). Then the "half" who was a very short, but initially exotic-seeming foreign student from God knows where, who was convinced she'd make an excellent 1st wife. She'd spent the first two years at Uni', until he graduated and went back home, desperately avoiding the Former Soviet Republics Soc...

She'd had one or two no.2)s, which were all painfully embarrassing. Thank God for the invention of the "Pissed Text Message" at 1 o'clock in the morning, so now said embarrassment was at least no longer face-to-face. The Hammers were now all ardent practisers of "Safe Texts", whereby if any one of them reached for a telephone while pissed and after 12 am, the others would confiscate said item until it could be ascertained that the often *very* graphic text was not being sent to an inappropriate man they'd desperately like to shag. Well, only under the proper circumstances...

All Stell and various friends since Uni' had wanted was a bloke who, if he wanted you, would bloody well come out and say it. If he wanted to promise undying love and eternal marriage: fine. If he just wanted a shag: again, absolutely fine (as long as he approached it in the right way). What she didn't want was the deceit. She had had enough of the no.3)s and could now spot them a mile off. Mr I'm-So-Suave Edwards was so obvious, it wouldn't even be fun unmasking him for the fraud he was. "Especially as I'm convinced he still likes me," she thought. "Easy-peasy."

"As you can see," came Caz' voice, interrupting her memories, "the maul is officially stopped."

"OK," said Gwen, after helping a still slightly-dazed Stell to her feet, "we hit them hard, low and early. But what happens if we don't get them down and they form up. What do we do then?"

"Yuh," said Siobhan, "also, when it looked like we'd stopped Rivenstoke, they rolled around so we were now at the side of them and they just kept on going forward. How do we stop that?"

"OK, let's do this again, this time though Gwen, you lead." Seeing the slight hesitation as Gwen clearly had no desire to be smash-tackled, Caz added, "Sib, you go as first defender."

Siobhan went to line up next to Caz, 3 metres away from the diamond formation of Gwen, with ball in hand in the A position, Mads and Mand in B and C, with Fi in D position. Caz whispered a few words to Sib, who, after understanding, beamed a huge, manic smile, revealing her red and blue gumshield. The other girls knew this as the "Sib Psycho Face" and were duly concerned.

Gwen approached the one-man-one-woman defence cautiously, ball tucked under her left arm, leading with her right shoulder, bracing herself for the huge, thigh-level hit she was expecting from her team-mate. Instead, Siobhan hit her at chest height, shoulder first, wrapping her arms around her and trying to rip the ball from her left arm. Gwen instinctively wrapped her right arm around the ball to protect it and then turned so her back faced the direction in which she wanted to go. Mands and Mads leapt forward to protect the ball from

Sib's grasping hands as they tried to remove her body from blocking the ball's clear route back to Fi. Fi attached herself to the back of the intruded phalanx and tried to rip the ball from Sib, all four attackers temporarily forgetting about driving forward as the Rivenstoke tank formation had. At this point Caz attached himself to the front of the distorted diamond and the attackers braced themselves for the counter-push. Instead though, Caz concentrated on trying to turn the diamond, rotating it 90 degrees clockwise so position B was at the front of the diamond, position A was on the right and C at the back. Sib continued to cling onto the ball. Caz started to count, slowly and loudly: "One, two...."

The bewildered attackers, realising that if the maul stayed still for 5 seconds, the ball would be "turned over" to the other side, tried to wheel the maul by turning it 90 degrees anti-clockwise. Caz shifted his position so he too was pushing anti-clockwise, adding to the ladies' momentum.

"Three, four...," he continued.

The pace of the wheel was now too great and everyone fell to the floor in a heap. At the bottom of the pile, a muddied and red face, set to split in two with a lipstick-in-the-ears smile, belonged to Sib, still clutching onto the cherished rugby ball. "Five," Caz concluded.

A large, fluorescently-lit light bulb emerged from the tops of the heads of the watching Hammers, to linger for a few moments before evaporating into the evening sky while the players participating in the exercise got themselves back to their feet. No-one needed to say another word. The road to Damascus had been discovered, Voldemort's powers could now be opposed and bested, all that now remained was to spread the word to the unsuspecting opponents next Sunday. Masingford Ladies beware!

"Stell," Gwen whispered as they trooped over to the next exercise grid, "I think Coach fancies you. Oooooooooo!!!"

Chapter 25: Masingford Away

What on earth was going on with this weather? Bright, bright mid-September sun had followed the Hammersmith and Fulham Ladies car convoy along the A4 to Masingford, getting brighter with each mile farther from London. England in the autumn can do this sort of thing to you: pretend it was the 1st of August and bring the whole population out in shorts, rolled-up sleeves and smiles. It felt like naughtily stealing a few extra days of summer, even though everyone was supposed to be back at school or work, but most were possibly just relieved that the cold and the rain of the long winter months had been held at bay for just a little while longer.

During the drive, the Hammers couldn't contain their excitement. This was their first league game of the season and, even though they'd had a run out last week, this was so much more important. Gwen was babbling away about absolutely anything, mostly though about the previous evening's post boys' matches entertainment in the 'Sheaf and which one of the players had been the chosen subject of her attentions. Stell, Hannah and Huggy, who had not gone back to University yet for his final year, were squeezed in the back of Mrs T's Volvo, with Fred staring out the open window happily barking at everything that moved which, on a motorway, is pretty much everything. Mads sat up front next to Mrs T, having won the earlier spoof competition in order to ride shotgun.

Mel hadn't even pretended to try to justify her claim to ride shotgun in Caz' convertible, which was too posh by half and, as soon as he had taken the roof down, which should reasonably have been for the last time for the year due to the expected normal autumn weather[39], had jumped into the front seat, a triumphant and unapologetic smile on her face. Leafy and Sib had to squeeze into the back by sliding the driver's seat forward as Mel refused to budge in case her coveted position was usurped.

The recent maul practice, plus a new tactic of using rucks to get the ball away quickly from the usually much larger opposition forwards, had filled the Hammers with a confidence they hadn't experienced since the club first started and they were smashing everyone a few leagues lower down.

The Masingford Ground was large and impressive. Masingford was a club with a history at least twice as long as the Hammers' and owned their own stadium, where they had converted the roof of the pitch-side bar to a terrace, with Council-approved appropriate railings, from where, on warmer days, the game could be seen at first-floor, grandstand level. The far side of the pitch boasted a new and expensive electronic scoreboard which proudly and intimidatingly vaunted Masingford, in huge dark purple and green letters, with a much smaller and rather pathetic "Visitors" sign next to it. Unusually for many clubs, Masingford's ladies' team was allowed to play on the full first team pitch and the men's 1st team's light training session held on the Sunday morning meant that quite a few of the male players, as well as their respective other halves, would hang around after training to watch the ladies' team perform.

Caz loved away games. When he was still playing at a decent level, he and his team mates had felt like an invading army of elite professionals who, even though greatly outnumbered by the hordes of the rabble army they were about to face, were decamping right into the very heart of enemy territory, colours flying high[40], to defeat them not only on the battlefield, but to take their pride, their honour and, more often than not, their women, many of whom were keen to "score a Troub". However, the word "professional" was never to be used...[41]

Stepping into an away ground, bedecked in Troubs ties and "no.1s" (navy blazer, white or light blue shirt, beige slacks, shoes black or brown, sock colour optional...), Caz and his teammates could feel the mixture of hostility and strange fascination towards them which, in every part of England[42] was expressed by polite banter of the, "Fuck off back to London you posh gits" variety. And Caz loved it!

"Challenges against all odds" and "Proving them all wrong" seemed to be his thing. Maybe it was hereditary, with both parents being immigrants who left their respective home countries when young to go to a strange "Mother Land" thousands of miles away of which they had only ever seen pictures, determined to make successes of themselves, much to the derision of those who stayed behind. This iconoclastic streak in him had made him turn down the cosy job in the City offered by Troubs ("Why, oh why oh why did I do that?" he had often asked himself, *mostly* only jokingly), had made him set up his own investment company, had made him leave Old Rubberduckians and go to Troubs in the first place. Now, it had made him take on this newest project: to get the Hammersmith and Fulham Ladies' team (Rugby Union) to win the league.

Yep, now that he actually had put it into words, this was what he wanted to do.

As the Hammers headed towards the changing rooms, Stell and Gwen sharing the weight of the team kit (only shirts, everyone had to buy their own shorts and socks), Stell couldn't help flipping a comment at Caz, "Aren't you coming into the changing rooms for our team talk?"

"Maybe if you win, you might just get lucky!" he countered, drawing himself back from his reminiscences. She obviously hadn't forgiven him for the tackle on Thursday night...

There was a crowd of about 150 (a record for a Hammers ladies' game!), all good-humouredly bantering away in the Indian Summer sun. The now familiar Rhodie contingent were there too, some of whom lived in the area, having settled around Masingford directly from Zimbabwe, instead of moving to London as many of the younger expats did. As per normal, James Stanley was in the centre, laughing and swapping stories, having, through much practice, been able to completely conceal the nervousness he felt for his daughter.

The Hammers' no.10 Sophie, recently moved to that position by Caz from no.12, kicked off deep to the Masingford Dragons, who were of a similar size to the Stokie Bears of the previous week, with presumably the same tactical plan. The ball was fielded by a purple and green clad Dragon front row forward who, caught slightly out of sorts with the ball on her own in open space, scuttled up the field as fast as she could towards the sanctuary of her "pack". Before she could reach the safe haven of her fellow forwards, a huge and lightning fast hit smashed into her thighs and she came crashing to the ground. She turned to the side to lay the ball back, so her other forwards could gather it, but as she was behind them, they were just too slow to react. Fi jumped up quickly from the tackle and was just beaten to the now free ball by the recovering Masingford forwards, the first of whom picked it up, stuck it up her jumper (proverbially) and turned so her back was towards the Hammersmith line. Fi hit her at thigh level, with less force than the previous tackle but so as to halt any forward movement. The large Dragon had no intention of advancing though without the reserves in support. Sib, following instructions and just before the other Dragons could swarm around the ball-carrier to start the slow, ponderous march forward towards the Hammers' trenches, slipped in between her and the nearest support player, wrapping her up at chest height and laying hands on the ball. Sib and Fi felt as if they were on an enemy tank as it began the advance.

A collective red wall of Stell, Mands and Hannah smashed into the advancing formation, causing it to pause if not stop. Realising that the ball was stuck with the front player and not at the back of the maul, the Dragons tried to shuffle it backwards. Sib gripped firm: there was no way she was going to let the ball go. The pile of bodies inched closer towards the Hammers tryline, even though still some 50 metres out. Hammers attached themselves to the back of the formation in order to quell the advance and Stell's commands could be heard above the panting and straining, "Hammers, shift left!" The whole formation wheeled clockwise and the advance stopped.

The Dragons could feel that the shape of their human tortoise was being distorted so that the ball would be exposed on their left. Players on the right side of the maul broke off so they could join the exposed left flank, in order to steady it and regain the diamond shape. They instinctively pushed with their right shoulders and Stell, seeing the opportunity, called out again:

"Hammers, right shoulders!"

The collection of flesh and determination now wheeled to the right so swiftly that all nearly collapsed, which was what the Hammers had intended. The home forwards were big enough and strong enough to stop the wheel though, but did so at the cost of losing forward momentum. Having rotated 180 degrees, Masingford's heavy mechanised troops now found themselves closest to the Hammer's tryline, but with their backs to it. They tried to break off from the maul and head towards the line, sensing that they only had a few moments before the Hammers' forwards realised that they were on the wrong side and detached themselves to reform the defensive wall in between the Dragons and their own trenches. However, the immovable, highly irritating Sib just wouldn't let go of the ball, nor of the initial ball-carrier, no matter how much they tugged and pulled at her.

"The maul's static, Sir!" Caz shouted, encouraging the referee to blow the whistle and give possession to the red defenders.

"If I want your opinion I'll ask for it," came the stern rebuke from the ref. Still, he had to concede that, if the maul didn't move for 5 seconds, he would have to blow for a scrum with the defending side to put the ball in.

"I wouldn't dream of telling you what to do, Sir," was Caz' totally unconvincingly contrite reply. Then he started counting, loudly and ponderously, "One, two....."

"Will you shut him up?!" could be heard from the Masingford forwards. They tried again to push forward, but their tank had run out of steam and the tracks were, if not falling off, then looking decidedly unsteady with one or two bolts working loose.

"I'm warning you...," continued the ref. Caz shut up, but the point had been made.

After another 10 seconds of going nowhere, the referee had to blow the whistle. "Maul not going anywhere, scrum down red ball." The Hammers collectively leapt into the air cheering: "Harry Potter 1, Voldemort 0!" they thought - their first ever maul stop - even Fi and Stell exchanged mouthguard shielded smiles. They felt invincible.

The referee, a very large fellow in terms of height and girth (possibly sharing the same pie supplier as the Rivenstoke Ladies...) felt cheated. He used to play rugby in the big leagues (coincidentally having been a ball-boy and boot cleaner at the time Caz used to play there), but being his size and weight, his knees, hips and ankles just couldn't take the strain after a while and forced his premature retirement. He still wanted to be part of the general rugby atmosphere in Masingford though so had taken up refereeing and was now one of the registered refs, and occasional 4th team coach, at the club. No-one could ever accuse him of favouring the home team (no, they couldn't. Really!) but he wasn't going to be dictated to by these posh London gits, especially by a Coach who clearly was far too big for his boots. "Enough of the lip," he said directly to Carlton, as the ladies readied themselves for the Hammers' scrum.

"Sir, I thought your last decision was exceptionally good," Caz smiled, with all genuine warmth and penitence seeping out of every word. "Significantly better than your previous decision..."

The ball was put into the scrum by Katie and, although being shoved backwards, the Hammers managed to heel the ball for her to gather from in between Sib's feet. She spun a pass out to Sophie who fed her Inside Centre, Lara at no.12. Lara steamed up the middle of the park straight towards her opposing number but, just before the expected impact, she shifted her weight so as to target the defender's left shoulder. The Masingford no.12 bent low to catch Lara around the top of the thighs, both arms encircling her to bring her down. Before she fell though, Lara twisted her body so as to pass the ball behind her and to her left, directly into the path of an on-rushing Fi who, in expectation had detached herself from the scrum and was hurtling towards her tackled teammate in support, as all good no.7s should. She took the ball in her stride and with consummate ease, which tends to "come naturally" when your lifestyle revolves around the gym, punishing fitness runs and constant diets, raced right through the Masingford defensive line and under the posts to score the Hammers' first try of the new league campaign. The cheers of the travelling Rhodies were music to her ears as she allowed herself an internal smile.

"Beautiful rugby ladies, beautiful!" Caz shouted in encouragement, directly in front of the home crowd, more for their benefit than for his players on the pitch. If any of the home supporters wanted to throw something at him, they managed to conceal their feelings through polite applause.

Don't Let Them See You Cry

The opposition Coach, who himself had had to endure battles with his own club in order to give support to and have the ladies' team taken seriously, quipped to Caz, "Bloody hell, they pass the ball even better than our men's first team." He deliberately made a show of looking behind him where he knew that, only a short distance away, the home team's men's 1st 15 captain was nursing a "hair of the dog" beer.

"Attempt at bonding," Caz thought. "Olive branch time."

"You see all that passing/ catching/ running stuff their doing?" he said, waving an arm towards his players, retreating to their own territory as Sophie readied herself to take the kick between the posts for the extra 2 points. He paused for effect. The opposition Coach and home team supporters in earshot went quiet in anticipation of the possibly smart-arsed boast they fully expected. Caz continued," I don't know where they get it from 'cos I never taught them that!"

The Masingford supporters laughed, relieved. This Hammers' Coach obviously knew the unwritten rules against gloating in Rugby Union. Even though he represented the opposition and enemy for the day, he was still "one of us": a respecter of the etiquette of the game. The impending defeat would thus be made a little less bitter by the fact that they could all have a good-natured laugh and, in true rugby tradition, act as if the match itself were all about the sportsmanship and fair-play. The result was nothing more than an unimportant detail.

The pattern of the first few minutes was repeated throughout the match: the Masingford forward drives being thwarted by the increasingly confident Hammers' maul-spoiling tactics. The Hammers could pass the ball to the backs from the resulting scrums and being faster and fitter, the backs could simply run round the desperate lunges of the Masingford Dragons. If any of the fast girls were half-stopped, the ubiquitous Fi would always be found in attendance, running at pace and ready to take the ball in her stride in an unstoppable race towards the line. The Dragons looked forlorn as they trooped towards their Coach for probably a half-time rocket.

The start of the second half always brings a fresh commitment out of even the most defeated sides. There must be something in the half time oranges, or possibly in the rousing speech administered by the losing Coach which makes his tired, bruised, beaten team swell their chests with pride, forget about the score-line and prepare to once more fling themselves at the hated invaders. Bravado, passion and above all pride in the jersey of no-matter how small a club instils in players the inexplicable second-wind where, against all reason, they truly believe they can defy the odds and win.

This feeling normally lasts about 5 minutes. 10 minutes tops.

At one point during a Hammers' attack, the ball had worked its way out to Leafy. Masingford, were now wary of the speed the Hammers had out wide and were lurking way offside in order to tackle her at the moment the pass was received. Leafy indeed caught the ball with her opposing winger on her, who, rather than trying to bring her to ground, had realised that a dead Leafy was a lot less of a danger to them than a living one. She thus tried to hold her up, along with one of her centres, so the Dragons' back row could come along and try to break her. Leafy struggled to free herself and get to ground, but now she had three Dragons on her, keeping her on her feet and preparing the "target" nicely for their heavy reinforcements, who would try to end her participation in that particular afternoon's events. "Where the hell is my support?" she panicked.

Like a 1960s Western, the cavalry, in the shape of Fiona Stanley, came hurtling into the group of four players. Her first charge blew two Dragons completely away, knocking them both to the floor with her shoulder at waist-height. Attaching herself to the remaining limpet, Fi ripped her arms from Leafy and wrestled her to ground. With an astonished but very grateful nod of the head, Leafy was now free to sprint to the line. Fi wanted to tip her stetson in recognition of the thanks, but realised she wasn't wearing one. She allowed herself a small smile while the song, "Last night a back row saved my life," sprang to mind. Both sides were in awe: Fi on her game was the best ladies no.7 they'd ever seen.

At the restart (kick missed) the next few mauls were again dominated by the Hammers' defence which continued the Dragons' forwards' lesson in disorientation by not only rotating them like a top but by pushing and pulling them sideways (accompanied by shouts of, "To me!" from Caz on the sidelines, further upsetting the home team). The Dragons knew they were staring at an opening day defeat and the physical and emotional effort of their second wind had drained all of the fight out of them. Well, nearly all.

"Referee!!!" Caz shouted in protest as a straight right hook landed on Gwen's, cheek. "Even you can't have missed that?! That's got to be a red card, Sir?"

One of the less pleasant consequences of this second-wind "we will snatch victory from the jaws of defeat" stance, which has unfortunately been witnessed in far too many wars throughout history, is the terrible dilemma that then seems to naturally follow: what does a defeated army do, in the time before final surrender, which still has:

i) men (or ladies)-in-arms

ii) is pumped up with unrealistic propaganda

iii) is willing to fight "to the death"

iv) knows that it's lost and that all hostilities will soon end against the hated foe?

Caz knew from painful experience that it's in this period of time, in between the "we will turn it around" irrational optimism phase and the "heads down looking forward to a pint and a pie in the bar afterwards" phase that the atrocities start. You can call it "Bushwhacking" (American Civil War), "Werewolf Resistance" (World War II), or "guerrilla scorched earth tactics" (pick a war, any war), but the end result is always the same: unrestrained violence by defeated devotees. If he didn't step in now, his team would get pummelled right in front of the myopic ref.

"Come on Sir, we can't play against 16!"

The referee snapped. He was being forced into making a stand there and then: either he sent off the Masingford forward, who almost everyone at the ground, plus one or two lurking around the car park checking unlocked car doors, would have seen deliver the rather good punch to Gwen, who was still lying on the floor, an ice-pack being applied to her swelling cheek and eye by the Masingford Physio; or he could plead ignorance and thus send off the Hammers' Coach for far too robust and unfair criticism. The decision was easy.

"I've absolutely had enough of you, RED card!" he screamed, fumbling in his top pocket to produce and brandish the card, arm stretched high above his head, in the Hammers' Coach's direction.

"So you DO know where your cards are then?" Caz added, as he turned from the pitch. The eyes of the crowd followed him as he made his way into the club house, some sympathising as they knew that if the referee didn't start reining in the violence, someone could get seriously hurt. Most though were just glad to see the back of him.

Stell took charge on the pitch, ordering Gwen off to seek further attention and calling on Caroline, a new but inexperienced arrival to the team that season, to replace her in the front row. The first scrum was easily won by the Masingford forwards who, in the words of Wellington at Waterloo, "came at the Hammers in the same old way and were dealt with in the same old way." The attacking maul wasn't moving anywhere, but the amount of time the Dragons were allowed to keep possession was definitely much more than the allowed 5 seconds.

A booming voice could be heard from on high, as if from the Heavens themselves due to the additional acoustic assistance that the 1st floor grandstand terrace had to offer, significantly louder and more sarcastic than at any stage during the match so far, "One, two, three...."

Everyone looked up to see Caz, glass of dry white wine in hand, shouting from a comfortable chair on the terrace, "... four, five. Turnover ball, scrum down, red put in!!!"

Chapter 26: He's Our Coach, Hands Off!

Back at the 'Sheaf after the drive from Masingford, the remaining Hammers sat around the group of mismatched tables they had huddled together, in full reminiscing mode. In celebration of their victory, the drinking games were about to commence, followed by an outing into one of Fulham's many bar-cum-clubs that had good music, food and an atmosphere on a Sunday evening.

After post-match pints at the Masingford clubhouse, followed by the essential Away Team Meal, the Hammers had been as polite as possible during the speeches, Stell particularly self-deprecating in the acknowledgement of the great forward drives (always stopped) by the Masingford forwards, the heavy tackling (non-existent) of the Masingford backs and the quite justifiable sending off of the Hammers' Coach by the referee. To this last one there was a unanimous cheer by Hammer and Dragon alike and Caz raised his glass of white wine in acknowledgement. Smile fixed on lips, the Hammers' Coach couldn't help thinking, "I expected this from the Oppo, but do my team really *hate* me? Especially after all I've tried to do?" The first few lines of the old Human League song, "You were working as a waitress in a cocktail bar, when I met you" entered his head, but he kicked them out quickly to return to being deferential.

Fi had been named Man of the Match (again) but this time, even Stell felt she had deserved it. Leafy smiled her thanks in Fi's direction as she made her way up to the Awards' Table, grateful for her rescue, but Fi was too caught up in the general adulation to notice. Her superior fitness enabled her to be everywhere on the pitch, scoring four tries, saving one life and being majorly instrumental in halting the Dragons' mauls. Stell made a mental note to go to the gym more often.

Out of pure joy and unusually, without a care for the home team's feelings, the Hammers had had numerous pictures taken of themselves hugging and climbing on top of the enormous Masingford electronic scoreboard which showed Masingford Dragons 0, Visitors 36, before it was quickly changed back to "0:0" by the stadium staff in preparation for the match in a week's time. The Rhodies had carried Fi from the field at head height and for once, Stell had seen the witch beaming away with pride. Although ecstatic about the victory and enormously pleased with Fi's and the team's performance, there was something about Fi she just didn't like. She was sure it wasn't on purpose, but Fi always managed to give the impression that you weren't quite good enough for her, as if she were looking down on you all the time. No-one had put it into words yet, but Fi inspired one of two feelings in you: either you were "a lazy, fat, tub of lard who couldn't possibly get your life in order as you can't even look after your own body", or, people just totally adored her and wanted to be her love-child. She was always so hard on herself with regards to everything that she made you feel, "I don't know, yes, that's it, less."

"Come on Captain, it's your turn!" It was the Social Secretary Gwen (who else?), sporting a purple-glowering black eye, her voice dragging Stell back to the present. "You love the Hammers because..."

"I love the Hammers 'cos we're fucking AWESOME!!!" she shouted. All followed her in the self-congratulatory cheers. They were good, they knew it and they were gonna celebrate.

"I know one, I know one," the Captain was in the mood now. "We hate Caz because: he gets sent off from the sideline!" Again, more enthusiastic cheers and slightly drunken laughter. This one was so good it had to be acknowledged. A chorus began:

"She's the Captain of our ship (of our ship),

She's the Captain of our ship (of our ship),

'Cos our ship's a tanker, and she's a fucking wanker,

She's the Captain of our ship (of our ship)!"

The previous theme was seized on by all. "We hate Caz because he drinks white wine!" That was Sib.

"We hate Caz because he always makes me cry," (Gwen). Caz had been telling her at an earlier training session that she was great and didn't do herself enough justice on or off the pitch (knowing about her legendary reputation with the men's teams). In training, she always wanted to argue, even if she didn't know what she was arguing about. There was something in his voice, almost like he actually *cared*, that just got to her and she had started to blub. As soon as the words came out, tears began to well in her eyes again.

After a few more rounds of, "We hate Caz because..." (they had thought about doing a round of "We love Caz because...," but this was their chance to get him back for being so smug and they were certainly going to take it!) and a few more drinking games, all designed to make the remaining ladies and Caz drink as much and as quickly as possible, they trooped off to the nearest of the bars on Fulham Broadway, much to the relief of the 'Sheaf's other early Sunday evening patrons.

The second bar that they went to had, due to the high rents in Fulham, undergone many transformations, but had now survived for a few years as Varaderro's. It styled itself on a Mexican hacienda and played a large variety of mostly Latin American music, with Tex-Mex cuisine and copious amounts of tequila-based cocktails to match. The very good job opportunities in this affluent area of London meant that there was always a diverse crowd of people from all over the world, ready to let their hair down from Wednesday until Sunday nights, after a hard week at work, and thus there was always a Bouncer-controlled queue, patiently waiting to enter.

Caz nodded to one of the Bouncers on entrance as they bypassed the small, Sunday night queue, who smiled and nodded back. They vaguely knew each other from the local gym, but mostly, one guy with 8 women was great for the male-female ratio and would decrease the likelihood of any trouble. In his long experience, the Bouncer knew that the principal reason for fights in any of the establishments at which he'd worked was men not being able to talk to, dance with and hopefully take home, women. The less successful they were at initiating conversation, the more they drank to give them courage, the more they drank, the less successful they were. The moment would come when all hope of having an intelligent conversation had long since passed, at which point they would either have enough courage to try to accost one of the "Oh My God She's So Beautiful's", with completely expected results, or start a fight. "If there were at least 7 rather drunk women free, then that's 7 less blokes ready to have a go," he thought. "Tonight was going to be an easy one."

Caz got 9 tequila slammers from the bar and worked his way back to where the Hammers had decamped. Fi had already sloped off ("Probably to the gym," Stell thought), but the remaining ladies were in great spirits, celebrating every action on the pitch earlier that day with increasing exaggeration and poetic licence. Caz sat back and, partly due to the excessive amounts of alcohol they'd made him drink, allowed himself a warm and fuzzy smile. It was great for the girls to finally have something to be pleased about and he could definitely sense, that's if his senses were all there (which they clearly weren't) that a bond was growing between these young ladies which would forge them into a proper team. They had shared the mud and the blood and the sweat and were now celebrating their joint, although for now only modest, success. Even though he'd been partly responsible, he wasn't actually on the pitch with them and so, wasn't really part of it. "It felt more like *their* victory, than *our* victory..."

Then he saw her.

Tall, slim, long, ringletted, white blonde hair, very full lips, long eyelashes, startlingly large, blue eyes, long legs, exceptionally figure-hugging dress barely concealing an hourglass figure and, for her size, unfeasibly large breasts. Caz could feel himself gravitating out of his seat and straight towards her, standing in the middle of the dance floor, an entourage of males and females milling around her. The girls' conversation dropped off as they saw their Coach drift away.

"Hi, I'm Carlton," he said. "Best chat up lines are to just be nice," he thought. "If she likes you, she'll respond, if not, no matter what you say, you ain't got a chance."

"Ciao!" she shouted, "I'm Sylvia!"

"Yes!!!" he said to himself, "she likes me!"

Feeling eight pairs of eyes boring into her, Sylvia swivelled on the spot to turn directly towards the Hammers' ladies. "Are they a-with you?" said the Vision of Loveliness, one eyebrow raised in a mixture of incomprehension and curiosity, with a touch of admiration thrown in. "Who is this guy, with all these women after him?" passed through her head.

"Yes, but it's not like that, I'm a Coach, they're my team," Caz found himself apologising.

"Ah, capito! What sport, you look like a rugby player to me, si?"

"No way!" Caz thought. "Not only was this woman GORGEOUS, but she knew about rugby as well!"

He was in love. He can't remember how the conversation progressed from then on, but they went to get drinks, then on to a booth. To talk. From across the floor, the girls could see them getting closer and their faces were almost touching.

"That's disgusting!" said Gwen. "What on earth is wrong with him, don't his eyes *work*?"

Stell said nothing as she looked away. Her cheeks were burning red and she didn't know why. No, that's not true – she *did* know why - she just didn't want to admit it to anyone.

"I cannot believe it – Caz likes SKANKS! Our Coach is a Skank Man!!!" scoffed Sib, eyes transfixed on the love scene in front of them.

"Skank" was an expression used amongst the Hammers ladies to describe a woman of not particularly high repute. It was taken from the American Gangsta Rap terminology and was derived from the expression "Skanky Ho"." Due to the alcohol, and possibly as a result of feeling a bit left out, Caz had managed to find the thickest pair of beer goggles any man has ever worn in the history of bad choices.

Further to the Bouncer's philosophies on "Why Men Fight In Clubs", there is a stage when drunk men see the world differently (as in, through the bottom end of a raised beer glass). It is often then a good idea to start a fight in a taxi rank late at night ("leave it Darren, it's not worth it!"), or to have that late night kebab that *will* come back to manifest itself the next day in a number of ways, none of which will be pleasant. It is also possible, again with the help of beer goggles, to believe that a member of the opposite sex is stunningly attractive, when indeed the truth may be somewhat different.

Unbeknownst to Caz, but, despite their consumption of alcohol, completely blindingly obviously to the Hammers' ladies ("Why do beer goggles have the opposite effect on drunk women, especially when it comes to *other* women?" Caz would wonder later, after the hangover would subside sometime over the next few days), the Beautiful Sylvia was, indeed, a fake. Quite literally.

The first thing that was wrong were the breasts. Far too large for her size, far too prominent, far too, well, *plastic*. Or silicone. Or saline. Whatever they were though, they had nothing to do with any real woman at all (unless, of course, the plastic surgeon had been female). The lips: pure botox; skin on the cheekbones: pulled so tight you could bounce a penny off it (the girls were even looking for signs of a belly-button on her forehead, so much, to them, obvious face-lifting had been going on); hair: weave (you could see the roots at 20 paces, even in the half-light of the club); eyelashes: obviously false ("we'll give her that one as we all do it. Sometimes"); probably liposuction EVERYWHERE ("Guesswork, they concluded, "but hey, why not?") and lastly eye colour: contacts (unless she actually *is* a cat) and eye size so huge that her permanently startled expression could only have been achieved if the dial on the blepharoplasty machine had been whacked up to "Saucers" level. "The only thing this woman had going for her," Leafy, the trainee Nurse added, "was she must be loaded as all that surgery must have cost a fortune!"

After very little deliberation, the Snakey and Black (chased with Tequila Slammers) plan to "Save the Coach" was hatched.

First it was Gwen. "Coach," she said, sidling up to the two lovebirds, "are you going to take me home tonight?"

Sylvia looked from her black-eyed face to Caz, her eyebrow raised inquisitively.

"Not with a face like that Hun," he responded quickly.

Gwen was joined at the side of the booth by Sib, "We're weeks into the season now and you've only slept with numbers 1 to

3. I'm no.8 so can you skip over a few and let me have my turn now!"

"Siobhan, it will *never* be your turn. I told you that last week," he added for good measure. When the third Hammer was halfway across the floor Sylvia, who had realised that there was a definite "cock blocking" exercise being executed and was not too displeased (as it probably meant that the young ladies had good reason to not want to let their stud go into another stable for the evening) suddenly jumped up. "I a-love this song, let's dance!" she blurted out, grabbing the slightly unsteady Caz out of the booth and over to the dance floor.

Mads, who had thrown a quick glance at Stell staring uncomfortably at the floor, decided to take matters into her own hands. She grabbed the nearest camera phone she could find and, while Gwen and Sib were making silly faces behind Caz and Sylvia, took a picture of them, while yelling a very loud, "Smile, you're on Candid Camera!" as the flash went. Sylvia suddenly exploded.

"Give me da camera, give me da camera!" she shouted, desperately lunging at Madeleine.

Mads, surprised by the outburst and explosion of anger, managed to jump backwards, knocking into a couple who were dancing in the middle of the floor. As she tried to stop herself from falling, the Italian jumped at her, in an attempt to claw the camera out of her hands, but was caught, in mid-air, by the alert Bouncer, who was trying hard not to laugh.

"Give a me, give a me!" Sylvia continued to shout, flailing with hands and feet as she hung suspended by the Bouncer. A small crowd of revellers formed around the little scene, initially in shock but, realising it was just a non-serious spat as opposed to a full-on fight, were finding the evening's entertainment quite a diversion. Then the lights went on. When Sylvia was set down to earth, Caz was able to get a good look at his newfound love.

One cure for the state brought on by the wearing of beer goggles is *really good lighting*.

"OK," said Caz, instantly sober and trying very badly not to look at the newly-revealed Sylvia with more fascination than horror, "Mads, if you took some pictures, could you delete them? Please," he added, imploring the Hammer to not prolong the embarrassment.

"I don't know," she replied. "There's a lot of pictures on here and it may take a while to find them. I took loads, you know when the camera does that "photo burst" thing so you can select the best one. It's really very clever." She was definitely enjoying this now.

"I kill you, you beeeetch!" hissed the fuming Frankensteina. The Bouncer was having a great time and, in mid-chuckle, managed to say, "Ladies, if you don't sort this out soon, I'll have to ask you to do so outside." Followed by more laughter.

"Mads," Carlton implored. He tried to look at her meaningfully, in order to avoid looking anywhere else.

"Oh, ok then," came her over-exaggerated reply and with a dramatic shrug of the shoulders and theatrical sigh, she scrolled to the one picture on the phone of the lovely Sylvia and pressed delete.

"Huh!" Sylvia grunted, indignant, but satisfied. The lights went back off and the party-goers went back to partying. Sylvia, heading towards the door, turned to face Caz.

"You call me, ok?" she whispered, making the sign with little finger to mouth and raised thumb to her ear. At least *that* belonged to her.

"Er, yeah. Sure" he replied, very, very unconvincingly, whilst the Hammers' ladies high-fived in the background, unanimously agreeing to call their Coach Skank-Man from then on.

Returning to his place amongst them, the subject of conversation changing from the feats of the day to the defeat of the patchwork quilt Italian, Caz' addled head was struggling to work out what exactly had just happened. All day so far, and for most of the summer training, the girls had acted as if *he* were the enemy, the evil torturer who just wanted to lord it over them, showing how clever and important he was. Then, this evening, when he almost got close to having to saw his arm off the next morning (so as not to have to wake the lovely Sylvia, once he had seen her sober and in the bright light of day), they had risked getting thrown out of one of their favourite haunts in Fulham by jumping in to defend his drunken honour.

"Why would they care what I got up to and with whom?" he wondered. "All I do is shout at them two and a half times a week." And then he fell asleep.

Chapter 27: Roger Theakston Post Divorce

Elsewhere that evening, in a luxury flat on the 7th floor of a high-rise apartment complex above the Barbican in the City, Roger Theakston's fingers did not tremble. There was also no tightening in his chest and he did not hold his breath through anxiety. All such feelings had been mastered long ago and he was extremely cool and clinical as his index finger glided expertly over the touchpad mouse of one of the two laptops he had open on his office desk. Both displayed a dizzying array of figures that he needed to memorise for the next morning's early meeting. In the task bar of his internet browser, he began typing the letters "www.rf" and immediately, the link to the "Fixtures and Results" page appeared. He quickly found the further link "RFUW Leagues" but, before he could click on the even further link to the Rugby Football Union Women's South East West League 2" results, he paused.

Since the divorce, all contact with the kids had been strained to say the least. His ex-wife Anna hadn't taken him to the cleaners as expected, almost preferring to leave the marriage with the children and what she'd come into it with, which was just her make-up shop and the clothes in her many, many bags. However, "friends" of friends got involved, claiming that she "had a right" to the family home and at least half of everything he'd built up and so, taking the practical option, he had prepared for a legal war. Even though he could gain access to really expensive City Law firms run by *his* friends, who had been willing to help out at "mates' rates", he was told by his father, in no uncertain terms, that he should "be a man and pay up". He'd had to borrow a pile from J, which had taken him a good few bonuses to pay back and Anna was subsequently left with a generous monthly allowance and a good deal of capital, that she invested in property in an up-and-coming area of London called Fulham. He could retain the family home in Milesborough, which would eventually go to Jake anyway, but he hardly spent any time there, preferring his flat in the City as it was so much easier for work, but also to avoid the local gossips as the scandal had been, for Milesborough's standards, huge. He also had access to the three children one weekend in three.

He still spoke to Jake, although the relationship, initially very uncomfortable, would never be what it had been. For Jake, when he was little, his father had been the font of all knowledge, the Great Man on whom he tried to construct his whole system of values ("What would Dad do?" he could almost see Jake asking himself whenever faced with a new problem or unfamiliar situation). All that had gone now. It had helped that Jake was technically-minded and so Roger was able to pull a few behind the scenes strings to facilitate his entry into one of the Asset Management firms to which he'd applied after University for a position as an Analyst. They now had common ground and could hold a conversation on the phone or on Skype. To rebuild the trust though, well, it would take him his whole lifetime, but it was something he *had* to do.

With Huggy, things had been a lot easier: Huggy simply refused to talk to him. In fact, Huggy refused to acknowledge that he had a father at all. Right from the very first awkward "weekend parent" custody meetings, Huggy would scream and cry and refuse to leave Anna's house, then, when he was eventually dragged out, be a snotty, red-faced, miserable little monster for a full 51 hours (from 5 pm on a Friday until 8pm on a Sunday evening). Yes, Roger *was* counting. Even though it hurt, Roger was more comfortable with clarity: "He hates me, move on." This is what he'd always told himself and there were times, especially in the early years, when he came close to believing it. It was a relief when he and Anna both decided that Huggy shouldn't come along on the "Nightmare to Milesborough" weekends anymore.

Stell though was the difficult one. She refused to touch him and treated him like he physically *did* have leprosy. These were the bad days. Other times, she could get quite enthusiastic about telling him all the things she'd done, almost forgetting that she was supposed to be angry with him, but then when she remembered, she'd clam up and revert to one word answers. As soon as they got back to Milesborough though, in front of Grandma and Grandpa, she'd again become the Stell she'd always been: happy, full of light, the entertainer to all comers. Roger took these opportunities to try to spend time with Jake alone, maybe horse-riding, shooting or just rambling in the open countryside.

When the children had gotten to the rebellious teenage years, they hadn't wanted to go up to Milesborough anymore and preferred to meet in Fulham, their adopted home. Jake would discuss banking with his father, at various restaurants or cafes at the cinema complexes where he'd take them after the films they'd always go to see, but the main topic of conversation the 15 year-old Stell could manage was, "Have you got any money?"

The only time Roger could get anything out of her at all, apart from the need to be remunerated for her time with him, was if she perceived there was any criticism of their mother in anything he said. She would leap into attack mode and defend to the hilt anything Mrs T did, had done or may do at some point in the future, normally ending up with an incredibly acidic, "It's all *your* fault anyway." She didn't need to state the reasons why. Roger almost couldn't wait until she was old enough to go to University and thus liberate him from the Jeckyll and Hyde performances of one weekend in every three.

Between those weekends though, and for a few short years after the divorce, Roger was free to relive his bachelorhood. Problem was, he realised very soon afterwards, that being a man-about-town in your forties is really not all it's cracked up to be. You drink too much, eat meals on the hop, your friends are either tucked up at home with their families or you drag them out to the displeasure of their other halves and become labelled, by women you've know for 15 years, as "a bad penny who'll get their respective partners into trouble." He often found himself in places with people much younger than him, which were really intended for singles who were either: "Second Time Arounder's" (too much baggage – how many times had he had to pretend to be interested in all the evil things a fellow 40-something's Ex had gotten up to?); "Desperate Late 30's" (as per description, mostly career women who had realised, a bit too late, that the biological clock was ticking and if they didn't get a man soon, motherhood would pass them by and ubiquitous cats would be waiting) and Gold-diggers (young, attractive, looking for Sugar Daddies or at least a leg up the corporate ladder. Very tempting, but they were young enough to be his daughter! In fact, he even once bumped into Half-Pint's daughter Janine in a City drinking establishment whilst she was out celebrating with colleagues from work. He was sure she'd actually come onto him as well! "Oh God, I need to change my life RIGHT NOW!" was his conclusion. Before taking her back to his flat..)

What really made him give up the single life and indeed, bore heavily on his conscience like exam revision you know you should do but can't quite start yet, was his father. Even though J had never said it, reflected in his father's eyes, Roger saw himself as a failure. He had so wanted to be like his father, to *be* his father even: the patriarch of a strong dynasty of "good blokes", but instead had wrecked not only his life but that of his heirs as well. Running around after young fillies would eventually lead to the sort of indiscretions whereby he'd wake up one morning and find himself married to 19-year-old Svetlana from the Ukraine, his inheritance and the bank accounts already in joint names and 23 "seeck relatives needing oprayshn" camping on the doorstep looking for "a little financial hjelp." Ouch. Also, getting married again to anyone wanting children and producing more offspring would only complicate succession. What he needed was a good, stable, attractive but above all *nice* woman, of about the same age, whom he could be with and with whom he could share a "normal" life.

So Roger had gone online (why not? "it's quick, effective and fun!" as the advertising says...) and found himself a nice, early 40s arts teacher. She'd been divorced and had two small children: all three just needed to be looked after and loved. His family didn't need him anymore, so why not? The relationship was easy: she was grateful to have a man in her life who was charming, attractive, rich, easy going and good in bed (actually GREAT in bed: all that experience had produced definite advantages!); he was happy to be a normal family man again, even though with somebody else's family.

When J was on his death bed, Roger was able to look him in the eye and say, internally at least, "Look Dad, I've made amends." His father never responded and died moments later.

Now that the stepchildren had grown up and left the house they'd shared in a comfortable part of London (one to Arts College, the other to live with a boyfriend somewhere on the south coast), the relationship had crumbled. They were just from completely different worlds and with nothing in common anymore, they just went their separate ways. He had no contact with the stepchildren as the bond of blood never existed. Maybe at some stage, after they'd "found" themselves, they may re-establish a relationship, but they had stopped calling him Dad well before they reached their teens and, if they ever had to speak to him, always referred to him as "Rodge" (which he loathed).

Roger Theakston clicked the final link: "Masingford Ladies 0: Hammersmith and Fulham Ladies: 36."

"Yes!!!!"

Chapter 28: Court Martial

The Hammersmith and Fulham Rugby Club monthly committee meeting was due to start at 7.30 pm prompt. The Alikadoos (elder, no longer playing, usually founder members of the club) had been arriving since 7.00 pm, in order to get their drinks in and reserve the best places at the meeting table, which was to be held in the upstairs room of Hannover Rooms Private Members Club on Parsons Green.

Siobhan, being the Women's Liaison Officer on the Committee and Stell, the Ladies' Team Captain, were waiting downstairs in the lounge bar, Stell armed with a pint of lager and Sib a sensible orange juice and lemonade. They had both had contrasting weeks so far.

Stell had got into work at BetNow! on the Monday morning walking on air. The bruising in her shoulder, the sore ears and slight ache in the knees were completely insignificant to the elation she felt due to the previous day's victory and she couldn't wait to tell everyone in the office of *her* team's performance. However, who could she tell? Apart from Ancient Stanley in the mail room, who'd played rugby 150 years ago when he was at school, no-one was in the slightest bit interested. Even though they knew she played (a couple of work mates had accompanied her to the 'Sheaf the previous season to watch one of the 6 Nations internationals), it was extremely unlikely that anyone would ever enquire how she'd got on. She'd have to give them a little encouragement.

"What did you do over the weekend?" she called over the desk to Geordana, a fellow Account Manager who sat directly in front of her in the shared group of eight tables. "Obviously, she'll have to ask me in return," she schemed.

Geordana launched into an explanation of her Friday night's drinking, her Saturday shopping, her Saturday night's clubbing, but before she could get on to the all-important "what I did on Sunday" part, Trish, the Team Leader, descended onto the pod of tables and whisked Geordana away for some meeting or another. Trish shot a: "Are you just going to gossip all day or are you actually going to get some work done?" look at Stell, who immediately found some "very important papers" to stare at on her desk.

"Rats," she thought.

When Stell had first joined the online gambling company as an administrator a couple of years before, she knew absolutely zero about the industry. Trish had shown her around the company and the people, taking her under her wing and treating her more as a friend than a subordinate. Stell thus quickly felt "in": a part of the company and "one of the crowd". She had held Trish in a kind of awe as a super-efficient saleswoman and the two had got on so well that Stell had even invited her to watch rugby at the 'Sheaf, with a couple of other colleagues. It was only after Stell had been at BetNow! for a while and had transferred to sales that she'd noticed that all of Trish' accounts, for which she was now responsible, were managed shockingly poorly. The vast majority of the customers, totally fed up with Trish' aggressive sales pestering and total disregard for ever delivering on any of the many promises she had made in order to secure the sale, now simply refused to even answer Stell's phone calls. Over the last year, Stell had set about trying to pacify the more irate ones and then repair the broken bridges with many of the recipients of BetNow!'s services. Through sheer force of character and bloody hard work, she had even managed to generate some new business with previous dormant accounts and her sales figures, initially really poor, were turning around. Expecting some form of praise or recognition from her mentor, Stell was surprised how, little by little, Trish' friendship seemed to be withdrawn, receding now to almost open hostility. Stell was now definitely "out" and Trish had her new office pets to go to lunch with.

After an hour of calling prospective new customers, (all of whom would simply die to advertise BetNow! on their respective websites...) Stell, feeling that the coast was clear, with exaggerated limp ("Why doesn't anyone ask me *why* I'm limping?!") made the short trip to the mailroom. A young temp smiled at her.

"Where's Stan?" she asked nonchalantly, leaning forward to peer through the hutch opening into the mailroom to see if Stan were hiding behind one of the packing crates or under the pile of empty, flat-packed cardboard boxes.

"No, Stanley off on holidays. He back Wednesday," came the reply in a thick Indian accent.

"Double rats!"

Everybody had seemed busy doing something all morning ("Why are they all *working*?! Somebody ask me about the rugby. Pllllleeeaasseee!!!") and Stell was convinced that they had some sort of game going on, a conspiracy of silence probably concocted by Bob, another Account Manager and fierce rival, (as well as being a fellow "out" as his sales figures were way in excess of both Trish' and Stell's, "But only for now," Stell had plotted), to torture her by not asking her how the team had fared on the Sunday. They *knew* she had played. "Just bloody well get on and ASK me!" If Monday went past and it got to Tuesday, no-one would ask about the previous weekend as they would all be looking forward to the next. However, to just blurt out, "I played rugby yesterday and we won" would seem so out of place, as well as give the impression of boasting. "There's nothing for it," she thought. "I just have to wait for someone to ask. Fucking rats are really annoying me now!"

It wasn't until late afternoon, eating sandwiches at their desks, that Bob, with his "I sound like I'm just about to tell a joke" Australian accent asked, "So, what did you get up to over the weekend?"

"Thank bloody Christ!"

Sib's week had been different. Her equivalent of Old Stanley was a young, fit Kiwi who sat right next to her at Bramwell and Westminsters Property Services. Knowing that she played rugby, virtually the first question he asked her every Monday morning was, "How did you get on yesterday?" They would then spend a good half hour going through every detail of the game. Monday mornings were slow times in property management: all the burst water pipes; tenants locking themselves out; complaints about noisy neighbour parties over the weekend etc. could all wait until after the first cup of coffee. Maybe even the second...

Sib suspected that Devon's reasons for his keen interest in her were not completely platonic but it didn't really matter: all that effort she put in on the training pitch every week in order to be able to play needed to be recognised and appreciated by *someone*. She couldn't call home to tell Dad as she "wasn't supposed to be playing any more" and trying to say anything to Larry, especially if his team had done badly, was almost like rubbing salt into whatever wounds he'd picked up on the pitch the day before. Last night, he was also probably angry because he had run out of hiding places for her kit and the strain of finding new ones was just too much for him.

Her half hour of "basking in the warm glow of appreciation" over, as well as perhaps a more intimate than absolutely necessary appreciative examination of the bruises on her lower back, she could now turn her attention to Mrs Podrowski's blocked drains.

Caz arrived with only seconds to spare at the Hannover Rooms, as per usual, and rushed upstairs to squeeze into whatever seat was left unoccupied. There were 10 in the room including himself: the three representatives of the Ladies' team, the President, Chairman, Social Secretary, two Founding Members, the Club Captain and the Treasurer, all of whom were either existing or former players and all on friendly terms.

"Sorry I'm late," Caz apologised as he took out a sheet of A4 and pen. He looked around at the faces which, in contrast to the normal variety of expressions (some pleased to have finished work for the day and happy to spend time with mates discussing the sport they loved, some nervous at having to speak in public), were uniform in their seriousness, ("Like Hanging Judges," Caz thought) apart from the girls who seemed to be pleading forgiveness, their eyes wide in contrition.

The Chairman spoke. "Carlton Edwards, it has come to our attention that last week Sunday, at Masingford Rugby Club, you were awarded a red card for abuse of the referee. Is this correct?"

Whilst waiting for the meeting to start, Stell and Sib had been joking about the previous weekend's game and had thus mentioned the Coach's sending off. One of the committee members had overheard and, according to RFU laws, if the club did not conduct its own disciplinary hearing and mete out commensurate punishment for any offence committed by any club member - including player, coach or spectator - it could be fined.

Caz played along with the obvious wind-up. "Yes, for some strange reason, the referee objected to being called an idiot!"

Nobody smiled. Stell was frantically making cut-throat gestures, drawing her index finger across her throat and grimacing as if to say, "They aren't joking, SHUT UP or you'll make it worse."

Finally clocking on, Caz more stated than asked, "You're not joking. Are you?" as hope that this was just a gentlemanly "spiffing wheeze" disappeared downstairs for a quick pint before dinner.

Like synchronised swimmers (minus the smiles and swimming caps), everyone shook their heads at the same time.

The Chairman continued, "Mr Edwards, could you describe, in your own words, what happened? We shall then ask you to leave the room, along with the other non-executive committee members, whilst we decide on the appropriate disciplinary measures to take." Seeing Caz' worried face, he added an, "if any."

After giving his account of events from the Masingford game, the two ladies and Carlton left the room, expulsed to the corridor to await the outcome of the deliberations inside. Caz couldn't believe it: here he was, at least 30 years after he'd left school but right back outside the Headmaster's study, dutifully waiting to be punished, after he had performed one of his usual "experiments" at school.

The streaming system in schools when Caz was young had led to children being "labelled", from an early age, as Future Prime Ministers or Production Line-Destined Factory Workers and it would take a monumental effort on either the part of an ambitious and particularly determined child, an interested parent or a keen, eagle-eyed teacher to move anyone out of their designated stream. Ever.

Caz, like his father before him back in Guyana in the 40's, had been placed in the top stream since virtually birth and so believed all the privileges the world had to offer were indeed his for the taking. Like the recidivist criminal who *knows* he can beat the system as he is clearly significantly more intelligent than anyone else (but still spends half his life in jail), Caz wasn't going to let mere evidence, like virtually always being caught for whatever spiffing wheeze he'd decided on committing in class (such as using a magnifying glass to burn a hole in the back of the head of the girl in front of him) get in the way of his belief that due to his God-given abilities, he could do what he liked and escape all consequences.

Very differently to his father though, Caz would never have to: sweep floors, run errands and, in the baking heat, pick fruit on the family's citrus farm from dawn till dusk just to afford even a basic education. Nor would he have to change countries in order to give himself a chance at going on to university whilst simultaneously juggling working, raising a family, attending night school and cramming studying into every waking moment. For Caz, with all the benefits of a healthcare system, free education and free university entrance that England offered at the time, the tremendous hardships of growing up in the Caribbean would never exist, even if he were in the slightest bit interested in what went on in those distant and alien lands, which he was not.

There was thus probably no jealousy involved whatsoever when his father used whatever implement he could get his hands on (cricket bat, curtain wire, belt buckle, probably the most terrifying of them all, his bare HANDS), at whatever opportunity he could, to thrash some "common sense, as all you have is book-learning" into Caz and his 4 siblings. Caz always wondered why the corners of his father's mouth: contorted in pure rage and eyes: exploding with the flames of relish, did seem to betray just a bit too much zeal when extracting physical penitence for whatever latest misdemeanour he or his brothers and sisters had got up to. Branded into his subconscious forever, like the evil mantra of a comedy villain, was his father's favourite phrase: "Beat them in the head, it's the only way they'll understand."

What does one do when, on the one hand, you're told that Harold Wilson is just keeping your seat warm for you at no. 10 Downing Street, but apparently, according to your nearest and dearest, you have no common sense and will never be as intelligent as them? From about the age of 9, Carlton Edwards made a decision: whatever his father did or said, whatever he believed or how he acted, Caz would do the complete opposite!

He became the iconoclast of his school year, the maverick left-wing intellectual, the sportsman (Captain of everything he was eligible for, including rugby until the ref caught him using someone's head for elbow target practice), the organiser of school strikes and founder of students' rights movements. Being introduced to existentialism through his French lessons at the age of 15 really didn't help, as it was too much of an ask for anyone to have much empathy with him when he permanently sported a black beret and had the constant companion of L'Etre et le Neant by Sartre under his arm for a full 2 years!

In brief, Carlton Edwards became a right pompous pain in the arse.

None of this was done out of any care for any of the causes he stood up for, he simply wanted to do what he thought his Dad would hate. It was also so easy to argue whatever cause he'd decided to support as all you needed was a posh accent, be obviously very earnest in what you said and most importantly of all, BE GOOD LOOKING and people would buy into whatever it was you were promoting. "Maybe Downing Street would look good on my CV after all?" he began thinking...

Then, years later, Caz went to Troubadours. It is really quite difficult to be pompous when you're being run into the ground, gasping for breath. The smart-Alec superiority complex lasted the customary first five minutes of summer training and he found a new respect - not only for the other guys exhausted on the floor who probably all had similar views on their own self-importance when they had first arrived at the club, but were now desperately trying not to wretch the lining of their empty stomachs - but for himself.

Despite outwardly rejecting his father's accusations of stupidity, Caz had never realised that somewhere, deep within his very essence, part of him wasn't so sure. If he coasted along without ever putting in the effort, he would always have the ready-made excuse of "I could have achieved if I'd been bothered" to appease any failures in his life. He would also never be in the position to either confirm or refute – to himself – if he were indeed as hopeless as he'd always been told.

But Troubadours didn't work that way.

He now knew what he could endure and, eventually, triumph over. Working hard *could* produce results and from that point on and without realising it, he would throw himself totally into anything he did, no matter how seemingly trivial, to be the best Carlton Edwards he could be. There was now no need for the cockiness, born of insecurity, nor its protective outer wall which had kept everyone, even his wife Britta, at a safe emotional distance. With her being Scandinavian, a people renowned for their sang-froid, the marriage hadn't stood a chance. The distrust and envy he encountered every day from people who just *knew* he wasn't being sincere and genuine would all simply melt away. "Hey, people may even be able to just relax with me and maybe even *like* me after all these years of being the Outsider (Whoops, slip into pompous existentialism again...)" he thought.

But, it all never completely did.

He stared at his shoes, fully expecting to see the scuffed, standard brogues of his childhood rather than his modern trainers. Sib was still babbling apologies, trying to explain that they had only been joking together and hadn't expected *this*. Caz looked up and saw Stell staring at him. He tried to make some joke about hoping he wasn't going to be given "six of the best" as his trousers weren't big enough to put a book down the back, but Stell could see that, behind all the cockiness and air of infallibility that he tried so hard to give off, somewhere inside he was hurting. Just like any normal person, not the Smug Skank Man they'd grown to love to hate, Coach just wanted to do some good and be appreciated for it. Also, just like everybody, he needed someone to just be there for him when he screwed up.

While Sib continued to ramble, Stell mouthed a simple, "Sorry."

Chapter 29: B.A.G.S.

The first few weeks of the season had gone better than anyone had planned. Caz had sat out his "one match touchline ban" punishment against one of the weaker teams in the league, the committee being lenient with their sanction as the referee had not reported the incident to the RFU. They had only been defeated once: Ellingham away. The girls had travelled the 3 hours to the New Forest to play against a team who had the audacity to play like the Hammers, with fast, open rugby and not a Tellytubby in sight! They couldn't even use the excuse of the free-roaming New Forest Ponies wandering on and off the pitch during the game: Ellingham were just better at Hammers' rugby than they were, well certainly for the moment. However, the ladies now had a style of play that they were getting more and more comfortable with, with each fresh victory and were now ready to face their biggest test of the season: the hated Kingston Tusks.

Every superhero has a nemesis. Like Superman and Lex Luther, Tom and Jerry, Microsoft and Macintosh[43], the Mighty Hammers' evil adversary was the Kingston Tusks.

The Hammers ladies' team had been formed only a few years earlier by ex Tusks, in one of the many schisms with which rugby union is all too familiar and, as with many schisms, the bitterness and sense of betrayal from the old faction and the inbuilt need for self-justification of the new underdog leads to more, er, enthusiastic participation[44] from both sides when the inevitable confrontations arise. Further adding to the rivalry between the two clubs was the fact that their players formed the backbone of the Surrey County Ladies' Team (currently more Tusk than Hammer but the balance changing), as well as this being the Tusks' first visit to Fortress Hurlingham since their narrow victory at the end of the previous season (which would have doomed the Hammers to relegation if the RFU hadn't saved them by changing the league structure at the last minute). A tiny glimmer of hope lay with some of the older Hammers that, due to a change in the team's tactics (i.e. they now trained), if luck fell their way, the ref was favourable, the grass wasn't too long and with a fair wind, this was the best chance to date that they could possibly record their first ever win over the club that spawned them. Maybe.

However, as fierce as the competition would be on the pitch, many girls had friends in both camps and, once hostilities had ceased, the partying together would be hard. All week, the Social Secretaries had been planning the theme for the "special" after-match celebrations but first, there was business to contend with.

The day was bright, although chilly, so many of the weekend Dads from the children's tag rugby earlier on that day had stayed around to watch at least the first half of the ladies' game, whilst the Mums enjoyed their cherished couple of hours kiddie-free-time at home . Mrs T and Fred were well wrapped up on the sidelines, no Rhodies had braved the cold to attend, apart from James Stanley who arrived at the start of the second half, conspicuous without his usually omnipresent support. He sheepishly deferred to Mrs T, who obviously had no clue what was going on, to find out the score. The club Chairman, in his self-appointed role as prominent supporter of the ladies' team, was as usual sitting in preferred position, on the top stair at the halfway line, approximately 20 metres back from the pitch, with a customary bottle of port under his chair that he would present to the ladies' captain at the end of the game to help with the post-match celebrations, irrespective as to how the team had fared.

Today, for the first home game of the season, there was an unusually large number of Boyfriends and Girlfriends (or BAGs) along the sidelines boosting the numbers of spectators to way above normal levels. In total, probably about 100 people were in attendance, eager to cheer on their respective teams.

Generally, the BAGS could be split into three distinct types:

Bag type 1) was the "I Love You So Much and think Everything You do Is Awesome's" (ILYS or LUPs, as in Loved Up Pups).

The ILYs, predominantly men but who come in both sexes, were usually recent acquisitions (Gwen's latest one was an Army Officer she had met at a friend's wedding a couple of weeks before) and on the whole were considerably less attractive than their rugby-playing partner. They found the whole rugby experience - the drinking games, the strange, upper-class(ish) people and the whole environment – fascinating. You could always tell an ILY by the perma-loved up grin on their faces and the particularly uninformed and annoying commentary on the game as they tried just a little too hard to understand what was happening on the pitch, in order to be a perfect partner for their fabulous "catch" whom, deep down, they suspected was too good for them.

The conversation, usually after training, with regards to why any player would ever go for an ILY was a tricky one, as no-one ever wanted to admit that they were. If a player felt the ILY tag was directed at her partner, undying love was professed and lioness fangs and claws bared. No-one thus dared refer to a BAG as an ILY in front of their partner. However, you *knew* what your teammates thought of your BAG and *they* knew you knew. Worst of all though, the ILY knew *they* knew, which was the source of many a heated argument of the "Your friends don't like me" variety. Gwen's ILY, having met Stell the week before, waved at her and gave a sheepish "Remember me?" grin, whilst she was in the middle of her pre-match team talk. Stell ignored him.

BAG type 2) was the "When Are You Going to Stop This Nonsense?"-ers (or, the Haters). Haters are evenly split between both sexes and their loathing for their rugby-playing partner actually playing rugby could have sprung from a variety of feasible origins. In Larry's case, "women don't play rugby": there was no further explanation necessary. However, the women who didn't play rugby, many of whom he'd dated and to whom his mates were now getting married, were definitely not the sort of women he liked. They were a bit too "wet" for him, only wanting to settle down, get a mortgage and basically become his parents. Any attempt to vocalise and justify his particular views was shot down in flames by Siobhan's well-rehearsed, reasoned arguments well before it had even reached fighting altitude. If he had to admit it, his "Women don't play rugby" plane hadn't even made it off the ground, having been strafed in the hangar by Miss Fighter Ace Owen. She knew all the lines by heart and had had this particular conversation just too many times to regard his "plane-less pilots desperately hurtling towards the hangar doors" arguments with anything more than affectionate contempt.

Some BAGS hated their partner playing as they just wanted company to do something *normal* with over the weekend, like wandering around the shops on a relaxing Sunday afternoon together ("But do we have to wander round shops on a Saturday *and* a Sunday as well?") Life with a rugby player seemed to always be about *them*: the training two nights a week; the obsession with what you can and can't eat; the gym attendance; the early morning running; the having to behave on a Saturday night in preparation for the game on Sunday; the "I'm out getting pissed with my mates" after the game and then, to add insult to injury, the requirement to nurse the Monday morning hangover or attend to and sympathise with the effectively self-inflicted injuries.

At Troubadours, after training, everyone went their separate ways as soon as they could and wouldn't meet again until the next session. At a more grass-roots level, like at Hammersmith and Fulham, friendships were generally stronger, as players tended to spend time away from the club together as well as on the pitch. However, what Caz had noticed over the last few weeks, watching the girls train and laugh and cry together, was the closeness that was growing between these young women as, for many of them, just being on the pitch was a small achievement. Most players had some story or another of having to overcome the attitudes of others - ranging from mild disapproval to open hostility – normally of someone close to them, who just didn't want them to play. Sharing the pain, the sweat, the mud and the blood and then ultimately, the victory of all that collective effort was something that made the team more like a family than just a group of individuals playing an amateur sport and Caz witnessed that, even if a player were injured for a short period of time, until she had again taken to the pitch with her comrades in arms, she felt a little like an outsider. The reason a Hater hated was simply because they knew they would always be an outsider.

It is difficult to detect a Hater as they are normally not at the game. If, by some force of nature, they are dragged there kicking and screaming, they will be pretending not to watch. As opposed to the ILYs, who comment enthusiastically on everything that happens, even in the warm-up, Haters disparage everything, ranging from the knobbliness of the ref's knees to the ugly kit of the opposition. Haters have no friends, apart from other Haters.

3) The Psychos. This category of BAG, mostly women, just hates everyone. They may simultaneously belong to both of the above categories as, the person they love deeply and passionately and will KILL for, is doing this thing that they absolutely hate and can't wait for them to finish. Obviously, they feel their partner loves her Rugger Bugger mates more than she loves them. Their minds are constantly filled with images of the lust-crazed orgies their partner *must* be getting up to as soon as the changing room doors shut and they believe that every nod, wink or smile from or to their loved one from a fellow player, or even from anyone on the touchline who just so happens to be passing through Hurlingham Park whilst the

game is on, is a sign for a secret sex-tryst that will *definitely* take place as soon as their back is turned.

It is quite easy to spot a Psycho as they will be having an argument with their partner. If they are not having an argument with their partner, then they will be staring intently at everything around them, taking note of all the coded messages that only they can see are being passed, to use as ammunition in preparation for the next argument with their partner. They may also be spotted giving everyone around the Evil Eye: staring into their souls in an attempt to uncover the blackness of their intentions towards their loved ones, as well as to dissuade them from going *anywhere near* their girlfriend. It is best not to look in a Psycho's direction. Psychos don't last long as the rugby-playing partner eventually gets fed up with the constant accusations and will exchange them for – now here's the bit Caz didn't quite understand – another Psycho!

"Maybe Psychos were just better in bed?" he wondered...

There is also a fourth category of BAG. This is someone who just likes watching their girlfriend play rugby. Their numbers are far too small, and they are far too uninteresting, for them to merit any further mention here.

All three (plus one) categories of BAGS were eagerly waiting on the touchline, either making inane comments, disapproving ones or just staring malignantly. Oh, or being normal.

With less than 5 minutes to go before kick-off, Lara, the Hammers no.12, had a panic attack. A very pretty, incredibly intelligent young lady from a highly educated family, the expectation of generations of academia had always weighed heavily on her shoulders, a weight she had always carried well (even though she had had to work bloody hard to carry it).

So as not to disappoint her very tolerant, liberal parents, she had excelled at school and university, played excellent piano, wrote poetry in her spare time and, in a move that came as a complete surprise to no-one, had followed her parents into the teaching profession, which she could obviously do at the same time as writing her first novel. Her effortless success had come at a cost though.

Like the ducks which seem to glide seamlessly across lakes, Lara's feet were, below the surface, always pedalling away like fury. The private girls' school at which she had recently begun lecturing gave her so much work to do outside of school hours, it almost seemed as if she had been singled out specifically by the Head of Department to take on everybody else's slack[45] and Miss Baines was going to make sure this particular academic over-achiever had not a single moment's spare time to lord it over her less-gifted colleagues. With the pressure of work and thus less time for the gym and training, Lara had recently lost her place as the no.10 in the Surrey team and, over the last few weeks, had lost her place at 10 in the Hammers' squad too. She'd also just seen the prospective referee arriving a few moments before and, as Bad Luck seemed to have taken a particular interest in her that day (he and his mates following her around and throwing bits of rolled up paper at her from behind whilst pretending it wasn't him), the girl turned out to be from the same Jewish community in North London where she'd grown up. They'd exchanged polite smiles, Lara's a definite: "Bloody Hell, NOOOOO!!!!" and the ref's more of a: "Ah, I see your parents are still allowing you to play rugby, are they?" She was a ref so obviously sympathetic to the cause, but the news would filter back through the community nevertheless.

Her inhaler, energy drink, Mars bar and oranges had suddenly gone missing (Bad Luck having mischievously hidden them in a corner of her training bag in which she simply hadn't looked), her blood sugar was low and she needed to just get away from everyone and everything. Struggling to breathe and heavy, dry-for-the-moment sobs wracking her chest, Caz took her back towards the changing rooms.

The Coach rested his hands gently on Lara's shoulders as she leaned backwards onto the wall, her hands on her knees to support her weakened body. Tear-streaked face turned towards the floor, her medium-length, curly brown hair only partially hid the shame and nausea she was feeling.

"Listen, you don't have to play if you don't want to." No reaction. The sobs continued. "But you are absolutely fantastic with the ball in hand, your pass is amazing, you *can* run, I've seen you do it once or twice in training (pause for reaction) and you are by far the best tackler I've ever seen. Or felt." No, that didn't come out quite right.

"And I mean out of both men and women," he added.

At this, Lara couldn't help but let escape a tiny smile. At training during the week, when they were practising defence in the backs, Caz ran at the line so they could rearrange themselves in order to "guard" the correct bit of pitch. It wasn't supposed to be a "full contact" drill, but Lara just couldn't resist the opportunity to try to waste the Coach and had put in the hardest tackle he'd felt in years.

"Yeah, I did put you on your arse, didn't I?" she managed to say, her voice stronger now.

"Alright, don't boast, I'll get you back." Then, for encouragement, he added. "But it did bloody hurt though."

Lara raised her face to his. They were only inches apart. Her breathe was hot against his skin, his lips. They looked into each other's eyes, lips parting as hearts beat just a little faster. Regaining focus, Caz continued.

"You are not my second choice no.10, you are my first choice no.12." He pressed on: "We've only lost two games so far this year and I think you can tell me why?" Lara hadn't been at the defeats at Rivenstoke or Ellingham.

" 'Cos I wasn't there," she brightened.

"Correct. With you at 12, our whole back line comes to life. Who knows, today we may even see you run with the ball."

Lara's smile now was wider, more open. The Coach tried to not look at his watch: there were probably only a couple of minutes left until kick off. "Also, the Surrey Coach will be watching today and most of Kingston are his first choices. I reckon this may be the opportunity to demonstrate to him who he should be selecting at 12."

Lara straightened up. She wiped the snot and tears from her face with the back of her sleeve, a fresh look of intent illuminating her eyes and skin. "Yes I can. Yes I can. Yes I WILL!" the unuttered words went through her head. The hairs on the backs of her forearms and neck stood up.

"Coach," she said.

"Yes Lara?"

"Get me a Mars bar."

Imogen, who had been in the England squad only a few years before, looked at her regional club mate, twenty metres or so away over the No Man's Land between the two teams, and smiled. The Tusks normally beat the Hammers, for whom they were a definite bogey team. Being big, strong, fast (although her pace was slipping in recent years) and athletic, she was employed by the Kingston Coach as a utility player, changing position as he felt the game and the opposition demanded. Today, she was at Inside Centre - no.12 - and was facing her former Surrey Fly Half, Lara, who had been identified as the weak link. County had lost the previous game as the opposition forwards had just run over Lara like she wasn't there. When she was substituted mid-way through the game, she seemed to physically shrink and since then, at County training, Lara had become so invisible that no-one was surprised when she was dropped completely from the squad.

Imogen put her black gum-shield back into her mouth, shaking off the built-up spit from the back, and bit down hard for it to fit in snugly. The move the Tusks were going to execute was simple but effective. From the scrum, the ball was going to be passed straight to her and she would run right into and over the Hammers 12, creating a breach in the red defences that they would have to fill by abandoning other positions, leaving them unmanned and vulnerable.

"And so, the Tusks would win another battle against the Hapless Hammers."

She crouched down, right foot in front, left behind, ready for the pass which would be just a little in front of her so she could accelerate onto it for maximum effectiveness. "Here it comes...."

The sound of the slam as junction of scapula and clavicle (collar bone and shoulder blade, to you and me: both *very* hard) crunched into vastus lateralis (largest thigh muscle: soft) caused all 100 spectators to wince, grimace and suddenly jolt their heads back a couple of inches in the automatic natural reaction of trying to get themselves out of harm's way (even though already a good 30 metres from the on-pitch collision). All immediately ceased whatever conversations they were having: even the ILYs stopped talking.

From her prostrate position on the floor, lying on her back, Imogen could already feel the hematoma forming as her thigh burned. Steeling herself against the pain and successfully biting back the tears, she knew that she'd be able to last until the end of the game, but if there were bruising to the femur, she could be out for a number of weeks. "Fuck, fuck, fuck!" she thought, I'll miss out on the regionals,"[46]

Stell reached down to help her up, "You alright girl?" she asked, genuinely concerned for her fellow Captain. Lara, the tackler, got to her feet, trying hard to suppress any instinct to jump in the air and shout, "Yes!!" into the heavens. In the attic of the large family home in North London, a fictitious covered picture that was painted of Lara when she had just turned 16, a la Dorian Gray, allowed an almost imperceptible half-smile, dripping with malevolence, to curl one corner of its lips.[47]

Lara looked over at Caz. "Whoops," she mouthed, with no hint of remorse.

Caz, although surprised at the ferocity of the tackle, mouthed back, "Great hit Lar." It would be "bad form" to show too much pleasure in someone getting hurt.

Reassured that no serious injury had taken place, the crowd resumed its general banter. "What just happened?" Gwen's ILY asked Caz. Caz ignored him.

"Ball knocked forward, scrum down red ball," the Ref shouted.

The ILY was just about to ask one of the Hammers' subs what that meant, but then thought better of it.

The ball was put into the scrum by Katie and, although being shoved backwards, the Hammers managed to hook the ball back to her again, who spun a pass out left to Sophie. The ball travelled along the line to Cysk at full back (no.15), who appeared completely unexpectedly in the gap between nos. 13 and 11. The Tusks' fullback was slow to realise that her opposite number had "come into the line" and could do nothing to stop the Hammer flying through the defence to score, under the posts, to the cheers of the watching crowd.

Larry, (Hater with borderline Psycho tendencies), come to watch the Love of His Life for only the second time ever, had formed a curious union of opposites with a scary-looking Future-Ex-Girlfriend (a Pyscho, with Hater tendencies and wearing far too much mascara, probably for even greater Evil Eye effect), to not watch the game with.

"Typical eh, ran straight into the man instead of going round him and then, couldn't defend a simple split-hit out wide." He was unsure of his use of the expression, "the man".

"Uh, yeah," FEG said, not understanding a single word, nor really paying too much attention. She was too busy surveying the retreating and celebrating Hammers for any signs of unnecessary *over*-celebration.

"Great try ladies, same again!" Caz shouted from the sideline, as Sophie kicked the extra points.

The pattern of the game continued in the way it had started. Possession won by the forwards of both teams was evenly shared, but whereas the Tusks' attacks were continually repelled by Team Lara, whose tackling remained as hard, if not as ferocious, as at the very beginning, the Hammers could pass the ball along their lines to the fleet-footed trio of Leafy, Cysk and Katia, who were having a field day. If any of the fast girls got caught, Fi the Ubiquitous was on hand to gather the ball and score herself.

At 28 – 6 up, with only 2 minutes left on the clock until full time, the girls were happy but exhausted. Running and passing was much more fun than smashing into people, especially when the scoreboard seemed to agree! This was perhaps their best performance EVER and the evening's celebrations were definitely going to reflect this landmark in the ladies' team's history. However, before thoughts could turn to post-match drinking games, there was still one more matter to attend to.

The Tusks had been awarded a penalty in front of the Hammers' posts, in what would probably be the last move of the game. The match had been lost, there was no way back, all that was to play for now was pride.

Larry leaned his head towards his new-found Psycho-Hater friend. She'd turned out to be Shezza, a girlfriend of one of the visiting team and hailed from a small town not too far from Brisbane. Despite her obvious hatred for all things rugby, she was actually a decent laugh. "I bet they run it," he confided, having given up on feigning indifference and sure in the knowledge of what the Tusks' Captain's decision would be.

To "run it" would mean to go for the try, which would bring the Tusks a possible 7 points (5 for the try, 2 for the following conversion) but would involve having to face the Hammers' tackling one more time. If they went for the penalty kick though, it would bring them only 3 points but would be contact-free. The try was, even though completely pointless as far as the outcome of the game was concerned, the honourable thing to do.

Towards the end of the battle of Waterloo, A French general named Cambronne, his troops completely surrounded and running low on ammunition, when asked to surrender by the English and Prussian forces, is famously claimed to have given the one word answer: "Merde!"[48]. He would rather die in a heroic but ultimately futile final act than surrender meekly to the dominant powers. This "Mot de Cambronne" from the Tusks would be their defeated army's final act of defiance.

Imogen looked over at the posts, then looked at the tryline and the Hammers' defenders massing on it to protect their territory. Then she looked over at Lara, who stared back. The smile from the fictional painting in the attic had transferred to her lips.

"We'll go for the kick, Sir."

Those in the know on the sidelines looked at each other in stunned silence: resistance had been broken.

"What are they doing now?" Gwen's ILY asked. Everyone ignored him.

Chapter 30: The Dilemma of the Well-Meaning Precedent

If we ignore the leaflets for the moment, the road to Hell is supposed to be paved with good intentions.

Roger Theakston had not had much time to answer any of the non-urgent emails from the week just finished, so Sunday afternoon, after a swim and steam at his club, was as good a time as any. Now, back at his City flat, he had some time to clear out his inbox and had started scanning through the dozens of unreads that had evaded the spam filter. Banks in general and his firm in particular were coming under increasing completely unfair criticism from the media-inspired public for gambling and losing lots of money and never having to face the consequences, so part of his duties as a Director, in the absence of doing any real work now that he had a multitude of subordinates to order about, was to try to identify any opportunities to redeem the bank's image. He had employed Esme, a 19-year-old Temp from a nearby agency ("Too pretty by half: is this some sort of test?" he'd thought to himself), to sift through the press and forward any mentions or good publicity opportunities to him. Eager to secure a permanent job and impress, she had also agreed to cut out, scan and email to him any other bits of information from the newspapers that she believed he would find of interest.

Just above the email forwarded from the Temp entitled: "Hammersmith and Fulham Gazette, Sports Review", his touchpad mouse hesitated over one marked: "City Mentoring: helping under-privileged school children understand the Square Mile". He smiled ruefully.

When he was nearing the end of his rugby playing days[49], the desire for Roger Theakston to "put something back" into the game coincided with his reaching the higher echelons of his career at the bank. He thus found himself with more time on his hands than at any occasion during the previous decade, the most obvious use of which would have been increased participation in the family home: playing with the kids, helping wth homework, participating in the preparation of meals, possibly even doing DIY ("Thank God for Polish builders!" he thought) but a combination of Anna's clockwork domestic regimentation which suffered no interference and rendered his half-hearted attempts to "lend a hand" redundant, plus a total lack of desire on his part to actually interfere anyway meant that some other activity, to fill the gap in his life, would have to make do. Roger hadn't realised what a huge gap not playing rugby anymore would be.

His last 1st team game took place at the age of 38. If it weren't for the fact that players in his position on the pitch (2nd row) don't actually run very much, nor touch the ball (plus he was best mates with the Captain who doubled up as selector in chief), Roger should have never been allowed on the pitch, albeit for the 20 minutes he lasted. Younger, fitter rivals were queuing up to take his place and, in order to avoid the embarrassment of highlighting the obvious lack of meritocracy in team selection, he subsequently retired to the

Vets team, which played a maximum of twice per year against players as old and battered as he was.

With the reduced number of games, the need to train as hard as he had done for the last almost 30 years of his life also diminished, as was the desire to participate in the Saturday night drinking sessions with his old mates. It just didn't "feel right" - going to the club as a pure spectator and listening to the tales of honour and glory won that afternoon on the field of play; hearing about the dark deeds of the front row or commenting on the incompetence of the ref - without having been the centre of attention on the pitch himself.

Instead, his wife Anna introduced him to the joys of Saturday afternoon shopping!

"My God, where do all these people *come* from?" he thought, being dragged from one completely identical store to the next.

Then there was the ferrying around of the children between their multiplicitous activities from Friday close of school until late on Sunday afternoon.

"They go to more parties than we ever did!" he had once expressed to his wife[50].

Anna blushed internally, smiled sweetly but said nothing.

There was also no longer the excuse of being tired or bruised or hungover on the Sunday to avoid full-on family days out to visit his parents or any one of a number of places labelled "family excursion venues" all over middle England. Being a responsible Dad was hard work, especially as he would never be able to complete the myriad of tasks and "appropriate clothing and suitable present" requirements that each child-focussed activity demanded. After a few months, he and Anna were both tacitly hugely relieved when he eventually decided to seek another focus for his rugby-barren existence. She could now go back to her usual, uncompromisingly ruthless schedules and could, once again, be *actually on time* at the various events. He could go back to, well what? The gap in his life needed to be filled, but how? Another sport maybe?

Naturally, he was drawn again to the rugby club.

With two budding young players (plus Stell) and not wishing to commit to any coaching courses in order to be involved with the seniors, the most sensible thing to do was to turn his hand to coaching the Minis at Milesborough. He already knew most of the parents and very often, the children - many of whom attended Milesborough Prep and lived in the affluent "Lanes" – who would come over to his house after school for play and homework dates with his unruly trio. He thus completed a few "on site"[51] courses, filled in a few forms and emerged as the Milesborough Minis u11s Rugby Coach within the space of a few short weeks.

It was during the very first training session that it struck Roger that most, if not virtually all the Minis either attended the private schools of Milesborough Prep, or its local rival the Milesborough Rhetoric. Children from the local, non-fee paying schools never seemed to last very long and while they were at training, stumbled around shouting "Pass, pass" but hardly ever received the ball. Attending the sessions in all loud, excited keenness, eager to be involved in every phase of the action at the start of the season, by mid-first term, they had been transformed into moping, peripheral figures, getting into regular fights with their teammates or raking up daisies with their studs on the sidelines, hands deep in pockets, chins desperately trying to bore holes in their chests. He would receive the inevitable phone call from their mothers only days after saying that little Kevin would "no longer be attending and could I perhaps sell his hardly-used kit back to the club?"

After the first five occurences, Roger, forever the Defender of the Disadvantaged (inherited from his father who encouraged him to always "spare a thought for the less well-off") decided he wanted to find out why.

He couldn't believe his ears when he discovered - through his covert campaign of sounding out various Mums, former team mates and club officials - that children from the less-priveliged backgrounds were deemed "too rough for rugby."

"Eh," he'd thought at the time, "an oxymoron if ever there were one. How can you be too rough for the roughest sport on the planet?"

The club's promotional school visits were only ever targeted towards the Prep, the Rhetoric, or any of the other fee-paying schools in the area and, if by chance, a mother and her hooligan brat were to wander onto the pristine lawns of Milesborough Old Boys RFC on a Sunday morning, they were actively discouraged to not repeat their obvious error by nobody talking to them.

A more vocal campaign against the snobbery was considered, but Anna had quite rightly pointed out that former 1st team Captain or not, the club would not hesitate to make the Theakstons feel unwelcome, if they felt their cosy status quo[52] was being threatened. Posh parents didn't want their children rubbing shoulders with "The Great Unwashed" and so would take them somewhere else. Fuming, Roger had decided to do something about it.

Darren Murray, Scottish parents but brought up on a London Council Estate, had first come to the Minis rugby at the club during Roger's 2nd term as u11s Coach. He had "Front Row Forward" written all over him: of average height for his age, but wide in shoulders and chest, with strong, stocky arms and legs[53].

Roger's eldest son Jake was keen to show off his father to his new disciple and he and best friend Matt tried hard not to burst with pride when pointing out Roger's name on the Club Captain's honours board, as well as his face in various guises in generations of Milesborough Old Boys RFC team photos which adorned the clubhouse walls. Darren was clearly impressed and Roger could see the determination in his 10 year-old eyes to try to prove his worth to Jake's "celebrity" father.

On the pitch, Darren was hopeless.

He clearly didn't have a clue how to play and, with each buckled scrum or dropped ball, the derision and sarcastic comments from not only the opposition but his own team were building up in the poor boy, who was clearly out of his depth. The hostile environment and the increasing frustration in his own performance were going to inevitably lead to Darren exploding, using his fists on the nearest tormentor, as was totally expected of "that sort of boy". The club's prejudices would once again be vindicated.

The game was about to restart with a tap penalty to Darren's team and Darren, red-cheeked with burning fury in his eyes, approached the penalty taker, a gangly, skinny Tormenter in Chief (relieved and thoroughly indulging in taking as much pleasure as possible from someone else being bullied, for once).

"Uh oh, better intervene now," Roger had decided, intending to spare the poor boy from further embarrassment.

"When the whistle blows, pass me the ball," Darren had rasped. Tormenter in Chief was about to say, "What, so you can drop it again like you do with your "aitches"," but seeing the resolve in this Council boy, who admittedly could have snapped him in two, thought better of it.

"Er, OK," he answered, looking up at Roger, who was acting as Coach and referee, to make sure it *was* OK.

"Iss awright Mr T, I know whot I'm doin'," Darren assured him.

Roger looked at the boys' respective faces: a pleading "get this psycho away from me" from the one and a psychopathic determination from the other. He came to a decision: "Let's see what he does," he thought to himself and nodded his agreement.

From the restart, Darren accelerated onto the pass, which he caught for once ("He probably think's it's a dole cheque!" his teammates thought) and ran straight towards the defenders who were expecting this brainless, full-frontal assault. They crouched low readying themselves for the impact. At the last possible moment, Darren changed direction and, keeping a low centre of gravity, targeted the skinniest of the defenders, running straight through and over him. Breach made, he sped towards the tryline.

The defensive line collapsed back in on itself, with the wingers out wide racing back to intercept the slower boy before he got to the line. The first winger was closest, but, before he could put in a tackle, Darren changed his angle of run so he was virtually parallel to the try line, running straight at the winger. The winger tried to slow down to lessen the impact, but it was too late. The hunched ball of acceleration that Darren had become ricocheted off him like a buffer in a penny arcade game (a buffer that became detatched from the game and landed in a quivering heap in the mud), changing direction again to target the other winger who was approaching from the other side. This winger did have time to slow down though and not only that, managed to find a pretty hasty reverse gear as well! Darren raced after him for a few steps before once more changing direction and heading towards the tryline.

By now, the other defenders were catching up and, to cheers from his own team, who had forgotten about trying to keep pace with him to offer support, Darren was left to outrace the chasing pack. They clawed, snarled and grabbed at the human bullet, just hauling him down before the tryline in a huge pile of 10-year-old boy, agonisingly inches short. The cheers came to an abrupt end.

However, two chubby arms shot out from under the pile of players, grounding the ball on the line.

"Try scored!" Roger shouted and all of the attacking team, Matt and Jake the loudest, whooped with delight.

Roger smiled at the memory.

Roger had recognised that feeling of disorientation that Darren must have had that day, as he himself had felt when way out of his depth all those years before at Troubs and was hugely impressed by the way the 10-year-old had reacted. Roger had been taught that limited expectation leads to limited ambition which leads to limited success which goes right back to the limited expectation again in a circle of failure which, if not nipped early enough, could last for generations.

"Give me the boy until age 7 and I'll give you the man," kept on playing over and over in his mind. The sound of a phone ringing brought him back from his reverie and he lightly touched the cursor of his laptop on the "City Mentor" email. He considered opening it, but his thoughts took him back to Darren Murray.

Darren had demonstrated to everyone watching that day that he was willing to fight to prove he was just as capable as anyone else at the school, even though he'd been given a different starting point in life, rather than just wallowing in self-pity and continuing on the well-worn road to failure that probably countless generations of Murrays had trodden over the years. Well, if Darren were willing to fight, then Roger was going to increase this one 10-year-old boy's expectations.

That same day, after driving the children home as usual after training, he had taken Darren back to his house, so he could explain to Mrs Murray that her son had a special ability which he, Roger Theakston, was willing to help him develop. Naively, Roger thought he could save the world, or at least that small part of it that had impacted on his world, a piece at a time.

He had no idea what was in store for him.

Roger clicked on the "delete" tab and the "City Mentoring" email wound its way to his laptop's Recycle Bin.

The phone continued ringing.

It was probably the clients from Japan he was supposed to be "entertaining" this evening (dinner, casino, strip club: standard behaviour) so he'd have to answer it. He opened the next email, without reading whatever hopeful and unsubtle plea for a permanent job Esme had attached, right clicked the attachment entitled "H & F Gazette Hammers Photos", then opened up the "Personal" folder, the "Family" sub-folder then the "Munchkin" sub-sub-folder. A thousand saved pictures of his daughter, from her very first days as a yellow-faced newborn (she'd had jaundice at birth) to the latest ones on the rugby pitch of only the previous week, plus articles, copies of every certificate she'd ever gained (exams, swimming, baby-pilates, even the egg and spoon race!) flooded the screen.

Roger clicked on "save" and got up to answer the phone.

Chapter 31: Cowboys and Indians

During the aftermath of the Kingston victory, James Stanley was confused.

No fellow Rhodies in sight meant he had had to prepare himself with rapid-fire liquid fortification in order to face the terrifying prospect of having to converse with the lady rugby players who, to him, were the equivalent of Marty Martian and the Moomies. He loved Fi with all his heart and all his soul and would have done everything and anything for his daughter, but for the life of him, he just didn't "get" her, nor any of the other girls bawdily exchanging slaps on the back while downing pints like a bunch of cross-dressing blokes.

Much of the emotion and compassion that he may have once possessed had been forcibly expulsed from his much younger self by the war, but when this blonde-ringletted angel had been born, he had made a tear-streaked vow to do all he could to protect his little princess, to keep her safe and to bring her up as an elegant, sophisticated, paragon of feminine virtue who would never want for anything. Visions of 1950's debutantes with too much make up, extravagant hair piled for miles on top of their heads and trussed in acres of flowing, flamboyantly coloured silks and taffetas wafted around his alcohol-blurred front brain which, after eight voluminous whiskey and cokes, was in an unusually insightful, pre-melancholic, state of euphoria.

Fi had just pipped Lara to Man of the Match, the official part (speeches) of the post-match celebrations in the 'Sheaf had just ended and he had been talking to the Coach ("Strange man but he understands his rugby though") who had been full of praise for his eldest daughter. He could now wallow in his pride, without the requirement of having to put on any facade of disapproval for his normal entourage. However...

As he looked over at his daughter, trying hard not to evacuate the contents of her stomach after her regulation celebratory dirty pint, dressed in cowboy hat, denim skirt, check shirt (he was sure that had belonged to him at one point), rodeo boots and tasselled, leather waistcoat ("That was *definitely* mine!" he protested silently and through the rum-fog of his mind), he couldn't help but think how different things were - here and in California - to back home.

For years, James had thought that the best way to be a man was to go out and earn: hunting and gathering and forging one's way in the world, then to bring home the bacon for pretty wifey to make something wonderful with so they could all sit around the braai and swap stories of their respective days. The men would recount tales of feats of strength traditionally involving besting wild animals in hand-to-hand combat, but more recently the most hostile things he encountered were business partners and takeover bids. The women would talk about shopping, whilst dressed in impossible-to-do-any-housework-in ball gowns. OK, he realised that the ball gown thing was probably a bit dated, but the general idea was they had certain gender roles where the man did the stuff to impress (slaughtering the largest wildebeest, opening doors for his woman, making huge amounts of money, twisting the opposition hooker like a length of rope: you know, MAN-stuff) and the women looked pretty and looked after you. Nowadays though, women wanted to do the impressive stuff (cover every blade of grass on the pitch, score tries, run a business) and Jimmy had to admit, they could be pretty good at it. If he had to be completely truthful, Cheryl Stanley, his extremely ambitious and multi-talented 2nd wife, had been effectively running his business for years. His eyes had been truly opened by this dynamic go-getter who must have clearly marked *him* out as husband material ("Surely *he* should have been choosing *her*?" he queried) from the moment he employed her and way before his first marriage had collapsed.

His moving country, burying so much of his past and adapting to his new environment had forced him to change his age-old views on everything, and his Cherry seemed to be the embodiment of all the new realities. She differed from the women back home so dramatically that he felt they were virtually a different sex. "And this is what these "modern" women seem to be like," he continued.

And then there was Fi.

His daughters both had this extraordinary athleticism that they must have inherited from their mother's side and an un-shakeable ambition that they must have picked up from their Stepmom. There was no doubting though where Fi got her hard-headed work ethic and desire to win from. She was almost obsessive: he had often seen her working out in the gym so ferociously that she could barely stand afterwards and she would apply this resolve of winning at all costs to everything she did, be it sport or school work or just generally being fabulous.

It was only since she'd taken up playing rugby though, when Cheryl had finally managed to drag him along to a game, that he now began to see that she was basically a taller, leaner, *female* version of himself: stubborn and determined to the extreme. He'd also noticed that even though she feigned indifference most of the time, he could tell when the resistance and determination were building up in her by the curious way she bunched her lips together, almost as if she were making a deliberate effort to hold in words that she knew would betray her true feelings.

"Bloody hell," he suddenly realised, "I do that!"

Jimmy knew that, if Fi allowed any words to escape during this period, the accent would be unmistakably Rhodie.

He could tell at times (like now for example, when she would every-so-often shoot him a "My God you're so embarrassing!" look) that mostly, she just didn't want him around. Then, there were other times, when she was on the pitch, that her eyes would nervously scan the touchlines desperately seeking him out, just for reassurance that he was there. There was also the sloping-shouldered, gazing-at-the-ground look of shame all over her after the defeat at Rivenstoke. She couldn't bring herself to look him in the eye and he couldn't bear the, well, the sense of *despair*, as if *she* had disappointed *him,* seeping from every part of her body. He left the rugby club before she even came out of the showers, the thoughts, "Doesn't she know I'm here for her, to look after and protect her?!!!" easily defeating any tinge of pain he might have felt at the loss on the pitch.

Then suddenly, with an alcohol-dissipating bolt of clarity, came the sudden understanding: His eldest daughter, Fiona Stanley, this miniature *female* version of a cross between him, her Mother Penny and some strange, outer-worldly presence that he had absolutely no clue about,[54] was *never* going to be a fairy tale princess who needed to be protected!

"Most of the time she doesn't *want* me there, she doesn't *need* me there, but wants to know that *if* she needed me, I *would* be there!"[55]

Realising he was probably being profound and thus on unfamiliar territory, Jimmy Stanley tried to retreat:

""*There*" being where though?"

Through his stinging eyes, he surveyed the battered, bruised, swollen, wet-haired, laughing, drinking and occasionally singing young ladies in every corner of the pub. The smile started from the upper left side of his chest, stretched up towards his mouth and ended in the "too many Rum and Coke" tears welling in the corners of his eyes.

"Anywhere she bloody pleases!" he vowed, in answer to his own question, his gaze coming to rest on his daughter as if for the first time that evening.

Fi must have sensed she was being stared at and shot a quick glance over to her father, who immediately turned to examine the suddenly exceptionally interesting contents of his emptying glass.

"Fancy another drink Mr Stanley?" interrupted Caz, dressed like an Apache Indian, with a long, straight black wig topped off by a huge red and white feather. He was wearing a light brown tasselled suede waistcoat with matching chaps ("Very strange man," Jimmy thought).

The Hammersmith and Fulham and the Kingston Tusks Ladies' Rugby Clubs had one or two strange traditions between them, which had started since the former's inception only 3 years before. Old Tusks who had relocated east just a few miles along the Thames into London had more or less founded the Hammers Ladies' team, so the tradition of post-match fancy dress, where the home team would co-ordinate with the visitors what the outfits would be, was really a Tusks' custom passed on. The theme for today was a particular favourite of Stell's as she already had most of the gear (from a line-dancing past that she'd prefer not to talk too much about). Former outfits had included: Good and Evil Cartoon Characters, Pirates and Fairies, Star Trekkies and Clingons, so the Cowboys and Indians theme was a fairly easy one for most players to make a good stab at.

Stell, propped up by the bar, whilst ordering the next round of cheeky pints and just before the "Disney game," looked around the room to see Hammer and Antler alike, dressed in the most silly Wild West outfits she could think of. There were Big Chiefs, Cowhands, US Cavalry Officers, a few Wild West Belles, and a few semi-naked Squaws with war-painted faces hiding reddening bruises. The two teams and BAGS had shifted positions from their original respective huddles and were now all mingled together to form a huge, smiling, beered-up group of happy faces. A warm feeling of achievement swept over her: *she* had created this, all these girls out having a good time after playing hard and winning, finally beating Kingston after so many times of trying. Most of the 'Sheaf's non-rugby Sunday afternoon patrons had already either left or relocated to the other end of the bar, so those who remained were all either part of the group or were just generally sympathetic to Stell's amusingly dressed Band of Brothers. "Er, I mean Sisters," she corrected herself.

Something didn't feel right though. In the middle of the bar was Fi's Dad: very ruddy faced and clearly very drunk. Stell had only ever seen him scowl before, but now he was beaming away, whilst swaying slightly from side to side. Every once in a while, he would pretend not to look at his daughter who was heavily involved in some conversation or another with Caz, in order to disguise the obvious pride swelling his still broad chest and nowadays even broader stomach. Fi again sensed eyes boring into her and looked up momentarily to meet Stell's gaze, allowing a tiny smile to flash over her lips, before returning to conversation with the Coach with even more interest than before, virtually dripping at every word he uttered.

Something pierced the upper left part of Stell's chest like the sharpest of knives.

To her surprise and annoyance though, it wasn't at the way that Fi was exaggerating her interest in what Caz had to say – Stell knew that Fi was only capable of paying close attention to any conversation where she wasn't the subject for a maximum of 2 minutes – it was the expression on James Stanley's face. Usually so tight-lipped and grim, the man seemed to actually be enjoying himself, not exactly basking in the reflected glory emanating from his daughter, but at least taking his hat, gloves and scarf off and having a bit of a sit down. Stell felt slightly nauseous.

Her thoughts were quickly cut off by Gwen's voice, calling all to attention. "Ladies and gentlemen, for all those participating in the Disney Game, please take your seats, with alternate Hammer and Tusk."

The noise of chairs being re-arranged and tired but newly excited bodies being moved suddenly rose to drown out all other preoccupations and Stell filed her feelings for later examination.

The rules of the game were simple enough. A player would sing a line from a well-known Disney song and the person to her right would have to sing the next line, plus a new line from another song. If she were able to meet the challenge, the player who had first sung would have to finish her drink and go buy another one. If the challenger could not finish the song nor find another one, she would have to drink up and then get another drink. The game normally started off quite sensibly, with known favourites being heartily belted out by all, but as it progressed and songs became more obscure, the amounts of alcohol consumed increased dramatically as participants simply became too addled to remember any words at all.

Gwen started with, "Chim-chiminey, chim-chiminey, chim chim, cheree!"

Imogen, the Tusks' captain, nursing a large ice-pack on her thigh continued, "A sweep is as lucky as lucky can be!" The Tusks all cheered as Gwen downed her Snakey and Black and got up to go to the bar.

Imogen continued, "From the day we arrive on the planet, And blinking, step into the sun." "I know that one, I know that one!" blurted out Mads, out of turn. "But that's the first verse, surely it should be just choruses?"

There was a quick consultation between captains, after which it was decided that first verses were allowed.

"Do you know it then?" asked one of the Tusks.

"Too easy," replied Mads. "It's the Circle of Life from the Lion King. It goes: There's more to see than can ever be seen, More to do than can ever be done. Take the shame," she added, amongst Hammers' cheers. Imogen hobbled over to the bar.

"Let's get down to business," Mads continued, "To defeat the Huns," she added, gesticulating at the Kingston players. "Ooooh!!!" The Hammers added for sound effects, "Naughty."

"Did they send me daughters, when I asked for sons?" was the next Tusk reply, as she pointed at the Hammers girls. This got a collective laugh as Mads embarked on finishing her pint.

The game carried on for a few rounds, with scores between both teams fairly even. You could tell how old the players were by their choice of Disney song: older players like Caz chose songs from the Disney classics (Jungle Book, Bedknobs and Broomsticks), players with children from the newer films (Mulan, the Little Mermaid).

"Ooh, that's given me an idea," Mads suddenly exclaimed. "Let me have a go!"

As most people were too drunk to object and smiling rather inanely at each other with no further care about the rules, she pressed ahead, "De seaweed is always greener," she sung, in a very heavy, pseudo Caribbean accent, "in somebody else's lake."

A Tusk joined in, in an accent even heavier than Mads', "You dream about going up der, but dat is a BIG mistake!"

"Jus' look at the world around you, right here pon de ocean floor," came another voice. This was completely unprecedented, a third line of a song without the challenge forfeit. Whatever would happen next?

Caz continued, "Such wonderful things around you, what more is you lookin' for? Oh-oh!"

All joined in with the chorus of "Under the sea, under the sea!" to huge guffaws of laughter. Players, BAGS, anyone in that part of the pub added their voices to the now deafening and tuneless chorus, and one or two began tapping out a percussion accompaniment with spoons on tables, hands on thighs, anything that could make a noise.

When the singing eventually died down, somewhere around the middle of the second verse, James Stanley was thoroughly convinced that they were all mad. He sloped towards the exit, swaying slightly as he navigated his way around the sports bags heaped in piles on the floor and the grinning rugby players who were all congratulating themselves on a job well done. Just before he slipped out of the door, he turned back to have one last look at them all. Someone had noticed his attempted escape and started up with the opening line of a well-rehearsed song: "Bye bye Fi's Dad." The lone voice was joined by others from both teams:

"Bye bye Fi's Dad,

Bye bye Fi's Dad,

Bye bye Fi's Dad,

We're sad to see you go,

Fuck Off!!!"

Jimmy held up an imaginary glass in his right hand, acknowledging the recognition with a toast.

"Bloody crazy," he muttered to himself. But he was smiling broadly as he exited into the cold evening air.

"Ah, guys, one last thing before we go," announced Imogen. "One of our players, Jen, you all know her," some of the Hammers nodded their heads. Imogen continued, "She's not been well all season and been in and out of hospital. We're having a bit of a whip round as she can't work at the moment. You know, to help with hospital bills and all that. If you can give anything at all, it would be greatly appreciated."

The sudden seriousness of the announcement, after the previous half hour's general silliness dampened the mood only a little, and the players each went to their bags or dug around in their pockets to make a small contribution to the Kingston bobble hat as it was passed round. As the Tusks filed towards the door, dressed in the main as extras from a really bad Western, the familiar leaving song started up:

"Bye bye Tusks,

Bye bye Tusks,

Bye bye Tusks,

We're sad to see you go..."

As soon as the last Kingston player had left the bar, Stell shouted: "YESSSS!!!! First time we've ever beaten Kingston, now PAAAR-TAAAAYYYY!!!"

Chapter 32: An Inconvenient Truth

Stell did not do jealousy. Jealousy was a thing that small-minded people, who are insecure and don't know their own worth, do. In fact, jealousy was so far from her normal frame of being that it must have been the drink that had made her do it. After all, she had consumed gallons of Snakey and Black, depth-charged with Jagermeister (Jager bombs!), so she *must* have been drunk, even though she knew that she definitely wasn't. Stell tried to fall asleep in the taxi into which Caz had bundled her, but the drive home from the 'Sheaf was too short and the sleeping policemen on the way between the 'Sheaf and the Mansion far too awake at that time of night, for her to nod off for even a few minutes. Besides, her head was buzzing too much for her to even think about sleep until she sorted out exactly what she was feeling and why she had reacted *that* way.

"I mean, it's not as if punching your Coach in the face was an over-reaction," she tried to convince herself. "He is, after all, a big-headed Skank Man and probably deserved it."

There were a number of things that Caz had done over the last few months that had really got under her skin and, in order to justify the punch, Stell started going through them one by one.

Firstly, there was his god-awful arrogance. He seemed to believe he had this ability to change things into his own image and the players – *her* team - were just pawns playing out his megalomaniacal fantasies. She had played rugby for years now and knew what to do: who was he to tell her it was all wrong and they should change? Rugby was about smashing into people. She *liked* smashing into people. All this "running round people, spaces not faces" crap was just being sissy...

But, they were now winning. The girls seemed happier, they were having fewer injuries and the numbers at training were increasing all the time. Maybe he was right and *she* was wrong? "Aaarrggghhh!!!" she thought.

Another thing was that one of the universally accepted perks of the job of a male coach in a ladies' team is, first refusal of any of the goods on offer. In some rugby clubs, it was almost an initiation into the team for the Coach to "try it on" with any new players and often, selection could be based on who his "favourites" were rather than on playing ability. Stell had slept with the Northerton Coach (only the once though), but this was because she liked him, not to advance her position in the team at all. Well, "like" as in they were the last few people left at a party after a night of serious drinking and she hadn't wanted to go back to her cold, student bed on her own. As they were both rather drunk and neither of them were that keen on the other, they had decided to extol to the other rugby girls, in the highest possible terms, the magnificence of their sex that night, rather than admit to the unfulfilling and embarrassing five minutes of nervous flopping around that so many people make so much fuss about.

In fact, sex, for Stell, had always been pretty much of a non-event. She did like boys – she liked the size and strength and the smell; the natural smell of sweat and testosterone and, if she had to admit it, of sperm – so she could never convert to the Sapphic pleasures offered by some of her team mates, even though this would have been far less hassle than trying to fathom exactly what was going on in a boy's mind. Problem was, she just didn't trust men.

When she had first started to be interested in discovering how bodies liked being touched, which was a good few years after all of her friends as she'd previously found the idea of naked men "disgusting", the boys of her age didn't have a clue what they were doing. Everything seemed to be over so quickly and even though brief moments of pleasure could be had with a fellow spotty teenager who scored 10/10 for effort but less than half that for what to actually do with it, there was just *too* much emphasis on the "brief".

Sex became like an Olympic 100m dash: you had a maximum of 10 seconds in which to come first! Or not at all... Also, she found that most men were intimidated by women who were bigger than them, so due to her size (which fluctuated between 14, when anaemic and 18, when not training), the pool of prospective partners was narrowed to only the larger, more confident blokes. Of these though and in order to prove their virility, some thought they were entering into a physical challenge with a huge beast that needed to be broken (and not loved) and were convinced they were actually doing her a favour by jumping on and roger-ing away like the Duracell Bunny on acid. For a time though, Stell actually believed this to be true and was almost *grateful*, especially if she could close her eyes and through gritted teeth, bring herself to climax by imagining a gentler, more attentive lover instead of Marathon Man bashing away like he was trying to come out the other side. She would boast to teammates, who were now virtually her sole friends at Uni, about how, after various athletic encounters, she couldn't walk for days...

There was another type of guy at Uni who simply spelt trouble. Out of the Rugger Buggers (and some of the non-rugby playing blokes), there was always someone who had a special type of confidence, a naughty type of smile and something in his general demeanour that suggested that he was rather expert in what to do with a woman's body. In fact, so strong was the allure of this chap, it was impossible to NOT think of him in sexual ways (which often took place even when the latest Marathon Man was giving his current performance of the role of Piston Packing Pete). This man was EVIL personified because, as earlier described, you could not hide from him the fact that you'd made yourself orgasm by thinking of him, he already *knew* that you had made yourself orgasm by thinking about him and so, logically, if he suggested to you to drag your hot and steamy fantasies into the world of reality, you would gladly drop knickers, current boyfriend and all scruples in order to make it happen.

This type of man, even if *initially* the most morally pristine human being in civilisation, would *never* be faithful as there was just too much temptation. Every moment that he was out of your sight, you would be wondering where he was and who he was up to. Stray hairs, strange perfume, unrecognised numbers on his mobile phone, delayed arrivals of even only 20 minutes: all would indicate that he was out with someone else doing something that he wasn't supposed to and the constant suspicion would be crushing. "No wonder Mum was always so miserable," Stell thought.

Then, there was the time when you were actually *with* him. Stell *knew* women. She knew that the most important thing a man could have to make him irresistible to women was an attractive girlfriend. A woman on the hunt would stop at *absolutely nothing* in order to steal a tried-and-tested winning partner and she remembered once (when younger and less worldly wise) when she'd attended a function at her brother Jake's work. She'd gone with one of his mates, who even though a Shagger was just a good friend, but by the end of the evening she had wanted to gratuitously beat about the head and neck the very next woman who either thrust their business card, phone number or cleavage into his face or gave him one of those sad, longing, but extremely effective, flicked-hair, searing looks, completely ignoring the person beside him whom they had no reason not to suspect was his GIRLFRIEND! She could have sworn that one woman even mouthed "burning and yearning" to him when they were dancing. She tried to mouth back, "You will be when I set fire to you," but it was a bit of a mouthful for the full meaning to be conveyed across a crowded dance floor. Depressingly though, Stell also knew that her date for that evening would be, as soon as her back was turned, gathering numbers for later secret trysts, thus giving the impression to the ladies in waiting that, to him, Stell meant absolutely nothing.

She had felt invisible, humiliated and insanely jealous, even though he was only a friend (although maybe she had had the tiniest of crushes on him). Stell vowed to never again put herself in the position of going out with, or being seen with, an out and out Shagger.

A Shagger was thus great in theory (if you can stand the humiliation) but the worst person in the world to love (for more than the regulation couple of hours). Stell's father was a Shagger. So too, she was absolutely sure, was Carlton Edwards. Life, in the main, would be so much simpler if one could have sex in one's head, accompanied by all the Carlton Edwards you could think of, indulging in the wildest of sexual perversions (within reason), but not have one of them actually in your life to cause major havoc and seriously affect your mental health[56].

But there were things with Caz that didn't seem to add up. He had made an announcement at the beginning of the season that all over-fraternising with the troops was strictly off limits. Either he was playing a "hard to get" game, just to feed his ego, or he actually was really only interested in getting the team to play as well as they could.

"It's sometimes like he really cares, like he believes we've got this ability that, with a little bit of mucking around, we could develop into something special. He even really makes an effort in the fancy dress," Stell continued (which, due to his ex-costume-designer Mum, was far less of an effort than the team actually realised), "just so he can show that he buys into what we do, that he's the same as us and so we'd trust him just that little bit more. This was *soooo* annoying, the manipulative bastard..." she concluded.

Worse of all though was his overwhelming smugness. He knew what to say to people to get them really riled and wanting to smash his face in (like: calling the front row "Fat Po-po's." Every time they scrimmaged from then on, they only had to imagine his smug face in front of them and they would tear into the opposition; then he would change, being all compassionate and caring, telling Lar' how indispensable she was to the team).

"Or licking Fi's skinny arse whenever she won a Man of the Match award," she thought.

The last image of the two of them in the bar, Fi dangerously close to Caz' face, pretending to listen to what he was saying but still managing to find the time to smirk at Stell, made the nausea rise again.

Then there was the image of Fi's father, Jimmy, standing in the middle of the bar, rocking from side to side with that dumb, adoring grin on his face.

Stell had felt herself float over to where Caz and Fi were standing, approaching the coach from behind. The expression on Fi's face shifted to one of incomprehension as Stell clenched her fist behind her back and brought it crashing into Carlton Edwards' right cheek. Fi looked shocked, then tried to bury a burgeoning smile.

"What the hell did you do that for?!" Caz had shouted. The remaining girls in the bar stopped what they were doing and stared. Sib and Mands, fearing that Caz was going to hit back, rushed over to stand between them. Stell didn't know what to say or where to look, anger, frustration and jealousy coursing through her veins like blood.

"Oh-kaaaay," Caz had said slowly and deliberately. "If you're going to hit me, at least do it properly. You hit like a girl." Nobody expected this reaction and, ignoring the obvious paradox, stood silent.

"Right," he continued. "Stell, I want you to hit me as hard as possible but this time do it properly." Stell, Fi, Sib and Mads looked at each other nonplussed, then into Caz' face. He wasn't joking.

"Then, it's my turn," he had continued, in the same eerily cold voice. The face was composed but his black eyes burned with barely controlled fury.

Fear struck in Stell's heart. She also, for a very brief moment, had felt incredibly turned on. The fear wrestled the feelings of sexual excitement to the ground.

"I've just had too much to drink, I think I'm going to be sick," she had said, pretending to stumble.

Gwen and Mands both said in unison, "I'll help you to the loo," more to get out of the way and lead Stell out of potential harm. You could almost hear Stell's and Caz' hearts beating violently, Stell's in terror and excitement, Caz' in anger.

When Stell returned from the loo (not having been sick), Caz had already hailed a taxi from the rank outside and, supporting Stell on one side, Gwen on the other, opened the door and helped her in. He gave the driver a fiver, told him the address and said, expertly disguising what was going on in his head, "Just take her home, please."

"I don't need him anyway. I don't need any of them." Stell thought to herself as the taxi drew up outside the Mansion.

Chapter 33: The Morning After the Night Before

"Grooooooaaaaannn!!!"

Stell's head was *seriously* throbbing from the indulgences of the previous evening and the most intelligible thing she was able to utter, in fact, the *only* noise she was capable of making, was the mumbled sound which emerged from somewhere in between the stomach and throat, bypassing the mouth but miraculously working its way up to the brain (whilst bashing off brain cells like sweets from a piñata), before double-backing and emerging between almost closed lips.

"Sunday nights drinking when you've got work in the morning is a *very* bad idea," she thought to herself, while leaning over the sink in the Betnow! bathroom, splashing cold water on her face as if it made any difference. She'd travelled to work on the tube without make-up (fellow passengers paid even closer attention than normal to their morning newspapers to avoid staring too intently at the white-faced zombie, obviously travelling home from a very late night blood-fest), not that she wore very much anyway, and had slipped into the bathroom to try to create a face that didn't look too bad on the phone. The realisation and shame of what a total tit she'd made of herself the previous evening was standing in the bathroom just behind her, either laying a very heavy Hand of Doom on her shoulder whilst shaking his head in sorrow, or simply just poking her in the temple. Really, *really* hard.

Plan of action for the day was to get in early (achieved), avoid everyone (so far so good), say nothing and crawl back to bed as soon as possible. Maybe, by Thursday's training, all would be forgotten.

The bathroom door opened and Geordana came in, bright and breezy after another fabulous weekend. Upon seeing Stell, who turned to look up from the sink, she staggered backwards into the door.

"Bloody hell, what happened to YOU?!" she managed to gasp.

"Bad pint last night," Stell lied.

"More like loads of good pints, if you ask me!" Geordana laughed. "C'mon, let's get you looking respectable," she added, while reaching into her bag for her travel make-up kit. Stell let her colleague dry her face with a soft towel, then, taking her chin in one hand, stare at her closely, in order to assess the extent of the salvage operation required.

"I take it you must have won yesterday then?" she asked, while applying foundation under the red-blotched eyes. "That's three in a row now, if I'm not mistaken."

"Grooooaaaaaannnnn....." came the reply, from even further down in the depths of Stell's stomach. Realisation and Shame's face lit up as he pressed both Stell's shoulders down as heavily as he could. For him, this was going to be a fun day!

By the time Stell had made it to her desk, Bob, a couple of Betnow! customers on the phone, even Trish had asked her how the Hammers had got on the day before. Throughout the course of the morning, Ancient Stanley from the Mail Room had come to her desk so many times, with a big, enthusiastic "Tell Me All!" puppy dog smile on his face, that she knew she would *have* to talk to him at some point, but she really didn't have the stomach to go into great detail on the team's, and her, performances ("Oh gawd....") of the previous day. She had thus pretended to be deep in conversation on the phone whenever she heard the creak of the mail trolley's wheels. The poor man had looked crestfallen when he saw her occupied and, suspecting foul play after the eighth time, had tried to sneak up on her minus the trolley. Geordana though, serving as early warning system, was able to alert Stell to look busy via the tried and tested office communication method of hurled scrunched-up bit of paper. Stell felt pangs of guilt for the treatment of Ancient Stanley shoot through her, but she was *convinced* that someone was responsible for all this sudden Hammers' rugby interest. She swivelled round in her chair to catch Realisation and Shame sniggering. He shrugged his shoulders and gave a picture of innocence, "What, me?" face in response.

"Rats," she thought. "Oh Gods of Rugby, please make this day end!" she silently prayed, whilst, partly in fear of what she'd find, opening up her email inbox for the first time that day, even though it was nearly lunchtime. And there it was.

"Inbox. Arranged by: Date. Today. Sender: Carlton Edwards. Subject: We need to talk."

"Oh fucking THANK YOU, Gods!" the sarcasm dripping from every word. "Now I'm for it."

A good day's work completed in less than half a morning, Realisation and Shame sauntered off, whistling nonchalantly to himself in satisfaction.

Caz' email was brief. No recriminations, no finger pointing, just a simple: "We need to discuss the team and what's happening between us. Lunch today?"

Stell's heart beat faster. "What was he asking? Does he want to discuss "us" as in personal stuff, or is it about the team? Is he going to say something like, "I hate you, you stupid fat cow and never want to see you again," or will it be more of a "I've been in love with you from the first moment I laid eyes on you, let's get married and have babies"?"

Then, the realisation hit her. "He's going to resign! He's going to say something like, "There's obviously weird stuff of a personal nature going on between us and so I can no longer coach you nor the team. Seyonara Fatso"!"

"More time, more time. I need to figure out how I'm going to play this." With trembling fingers, Stell typed, "Busy today, how about tomorrow, 12.30? You can pick where."

She closed her laptop, asked Geordana for a cigarette, ("But you don't sm...," her colleague began, but then realising that Stell was shaking, rummaged in her bag to produce fag and lighter, handing them over with concern etched on her face), then headed towards the smoking balcony.

Chapter 34: Lunar Reflections

The moon can be a real bastard at times.

Just when you really need to catch up on a missed night's sleep from the previous evening, alcohol-induced coma not really qualifying as an entry into the Land of Nod, the moon decided to be full and high and *smirking* as it threw its cold light through every window, every gap and every corner of every household where the occupants were wrestling with whatever problems lay unresolved in their consciousness after another busy London day. "Why do dogs, wolves and werewolves howl at a full moon?" Stell thought to herself. "Because it won't just shut the fuck up and leave them alone!"

Stell covered her head with her pillow, pressing the sides of it into her ears to blot out the inaudible moonlight from seeping into her brain and disturbing even further the myriad of thoughts swirling round her head. She had shut her window - which was normally kept slightly ajar, even on these cold nights, for a gust of "Good clean London air," as Mrs T always maintained, only half-jokingly - and had rolled down the blinds, drawn the curtains, hidden under the duvet and now, last resort, was using the pillow to block the lunar gravitational tugging on her subconscious. She would have had a good howl at the moon too, if it would help, but she thought that the neighbours of south Fulham probably wouldn't have appreciated it.

She needed to prepare a defence for her behaviour the previous evening - even she was surprised she'd just got up and whacked the Coach upside his head – but there was "stuff" bubbling up under the surface, issues that she couldn't quite put her finger on (apart from the Green Eyed Envy Monster, obviously) which just seemed to come to a head, right there, right then.

And, she actually did have concerns with regards to the way the team was going...

The Hammers, to her, had always been *her* team. When she'd played rugby at Uni, it was more for a laugh than anything else. She was with a bunch of mates and they were doing something that they enjoyed together, but it was more for the camaraderie and the licence that being a rugby player allowed you, rather than actually taking the thing too seriously. She remembered her first "training" session at Uni being about how much you could drink (and how sick you could get), rather than doing any running around with the ball. The actual playing of rugby wasn't really that important, as it normally always culminated in her being bruised, hurting or not able to walk for a week. "No, not *that* "not being able to walk"," she quickly corrected herself, "the *other* kind." She did quite like the smashing into people bit though! In order to really put a good "hit" in, all she had to do was imagine a member of the opposition as being a useless ex-boyfriend, her latest rival in love or one of her pervy lecturers and no further motivation was necessary!

Losing games was not really important either as it was the being together – and being seen as being "different" from the other girls on campus – that had given her the buzz.

Moving on to the Hammers, where she was now the captain, she had the opportunity to mould the team into what she wanted and what other commitments on her time would allow it to be. They were a "social" club who didn't want to be muscle-bound, fitness-focussed freaks (even though having one of them on their side really did help). She wanted to create the same camaraderie she had enjoyed at Northerton so results were of no consequence if you knew that, irrespective, you were going to have a good night out with the girls, most of whom had either come to London for a job after university or who hailed from abroad. What many of them had in common was that they knew next to no-one in London outside the club and for them, the Hammers *was* their social life. In fact, arriving at a game on a Sunday *still* drunk, without having slept and in whatever kit you could cobble together (which hadn't seen the inside of a washing machine since before the previous week's training), was indeed legendary behaviour and a testimony to the great night out you must have had with the men's team on the Saturday. "It also meant you had a ready-made excuse for losing...," Stell now thought to herself.

With the window closed, her bedroom was unusually hot and the duvet, giving a good impersonation of a heavy, suffocating tent, caused Stell to feel even more restless than ever. She gave the duvet a few solid kicks, in order to get some air under it and as it collapsed on top of her, her mind turned towards why she had enlisted the services of one Carlton Edwards in the first place.

A consequence of the Hammers being a "social" rugby team was that they had come perilously close to relegation the previous season. If that had happened, they would have definitely lost most of their better players[57]. Without these, there would simply not be enough people left and the Hammersmith and Fulham Ladies' Rugby Club would probably have had to fold. Stell and one or two of the core team members had realised that the status quo would lead to extinction and that going forward was the only option. Hence, Caz.

It had been quite subtle at first, but now she and one or two of the stalwarts had become increasingly aware that he was trying to change them ("Which was sort of the point," she had to admit, "but it still didn't mean she had to like it!")

Firstly, he had insisted that he didn't believe in fitness, which was great. He had then got them to work so hard on the training pitch, with the ball in hand at every possible moment that they completely forgot that they didn't like running around! Each training session was different from the last and, if they were not fully concentrating - which it's really difficult to do when you're dog tired and had last night's cheeky pint and curry swishing around in your belly - they could be completely lost and look like idiots. So, Stell and the others had secretly started going to the gym and watching what they ate.

Caz had gotten them to organise themselves into the little groups that they would be in on the pitch (i.e. numbers 1 – 3 and 6 – 8 would always be working together), so they could plan attacks to defeat the other groups. When this all joined together to form a team, they would frequently take on and sometimes even beat the startled, press-ganged men's team players that Caz would cobble together to act as opposition.

At the thought of their last Thursday night victory over a few members of the Fourths, she couldn't help herself from smiling.

Numbers were significantly up for training as well, since now that they weren't smashing into people so much on the pitch, she nor any of the other Hammers had the excuse of being injured to avoid attendance. There was even now - which was a first for the Hammers Ladies' team - competition for places! A consequence of this was that if anyone even thought about turning up drunk or ill-prepared for the game on the Sunday, they knew there were at least one or two other girls waiting in the wings to take their place. "That's what I don't like about the way the team is changing!" she suddenly realised, "it's all getting just a bit too serious."

What she did like though were the results. To finally beat teams like Kingston and Masingford would have been a dream-come-true only a season before. Now, it just didn't seem enough. The Hammers were moving up the league table, everyone was interested in hearing how they had got on on the Sunday (she made a mental note to buy something nice for Ancient Stanley's birthday to make up for avoiding him the day before) and even some of the players from the previously disparaging men's teams started coming along to watch the girls play. She felt, rather uncomfortably, like a *sportswoman*. Someone had shown her she could do this thing, that it wasn't just a stupid pastime that she should drop at the age of 8 and that she could be good at it, and bloody good at that.

"After all, we *did* bring him in to make the team better and so we can't have any complaints that that's what he's doing," she concluded. Smiling internally at the thought of the Masingford scoreboard, she kicked off the duvet and walked over to open the window. "Moon, you lose," she thought and went back to bed. "I was just drunk last night. I'll apologise to him at lunch tomorrow, especially if he's paying!" Stell tried to convince herself, "And that will be that."

Something still wasn't right though, but by now, sleep-deprivation was taking over. Before her eyes closed, the image of Fi's Dad, as proud as punch, drinking in the atmosphere (as well as all the spirits in the bar) of the band of players and supporters *she* had created made her feel slightly queasy. The last waking thought to leave her head, as her mind floated along on the lunar tide into the arms of Morpheus, was the image of Fi's triumphant, sneering face.

Chapter 35: Something to Prove Too

Exactly one mile north of the Mansion, in a large, almost deserted house, the single occupant was also not having the easiest of times getting to sleep.

The evening of the punch to the side of the face and bundling Stell into the taxi, Carlton Edwards had walked home absolutely livid. He had poured himself a large whisky and had gone into the living room, turned on the TV and, as he did whenever he was really angry and had to calm down before he did himself a mischief, turned on the Xbox (FIFA football: Liverpool v Chelsea[58], Skill setting: World Class). He took great pleasure in thrashing Stell's team 7 – 0.

This evening, in anticipation of the peace summit the next morning, he just couldn't sleep. As he booted up the Xbox again (Liverpool v Chelsea rematch, Champions Cup Final, this time Skill Setting: Legendary for extra "Gamer History" points) he couldn't help but protest: "Why on earth do I always get myself into these stupid situations?"

Deep down, he already knew the answer.

When he worked in the City in investment sales, his job had been to get potential investors so enthused by whatever investment product his bank was trying to sell that they would merrily sign their nest eggs away without looking at the small print, which was written in such a complicated way, they wouldn't have understood it even if they had. The rich, old punters, many of whom were self-made men, would base their decision on whether or not to invest purely on trust. "If you looked them in the eye and they could shake you firmly by the hand, you could trust 'em" was a mantra that he was amazed to find that people still used, even when talking about squillions of pounds.

Obtaining that trust was initially enormously difficult, as all the sales people Caz had ever spoken to had told him that it was a question of coming up with the "killer line", the "objection handling", "getting the positioning right" and a whole load of other completely over-the-top, "huge smile and firm handshake" claptrap.

Over time, he had eliminated all superflous advice on sales (from those trying to *sell you* books on how to "do" sales) and had arrived at what he believed to be the very *essence* of how to get anyone to do anything he wanted: "There are only *two* things the prospective victim/punter/sales prospect cares about:

1) Does the seller know what he's doing?

2) Does he have my best interests at heart?"

The first one was easy. A little bit of studying (including experience in the field) was essential to knowing the subject, but far more important was looking the part. He'd never considered himself attractive[59], but as he was never really short of female attention, he assumed he probably wasn't a Worzel Gummidge[60] lookalike. Dressing well, having the right accoutrements[61] for the job, being relaxed, easy-going and confident enough to not need to exert undue pressure: all "Standard Operating Procedure" to help make the prospect feel in the hands of someone who'd done "this" before.

The second bit was slightly more tricky. What he had to do in order to fast-forward the gaining of trust[62] was ascertain what the punter "really, really wanted", then *give them the impression* he was giving it to them.

With men, this bit was straightforward: ask them directly and they'd normally tell you. You then repeated this back and they'd be convinced you "got" them. With women, "straightforward" was perhaps not the most appropriate adjective.

It was almost a taboo to ask a woman directly what she wanted as it demonstrated that you didn't understand her and just weren't listening to the non-verbal signs she was sending.[63] Rather than appearing caring and considerate, repeatedly asking, "Tell me what you want, go on, tell me, is it ok? Really?" made you seem clueless and basically, *really* annoying.

You had to *listen* intently to all she said, didn't say, alluded to, vaguely hinted at, reacted most strongly against and then and only then, would you know what she really, really wanted. Sort of. You'd have to keep on listening to make sure there weren't any variations in priority list (as there invariably would be) but hey, no-one said it was going to be easy!

This unintended but nevertheless cynical manipulation of people's feelings, in the business world, had the inevitable side effect of spilling over into Caz' private life.

It hadn't occurred to him that possibly some of the sexual advances made by one or two clients (both male and female), over-familiarity of work colleagues who had clearly "gotten the wrong message" and general feelings of anger and betrayal when he eventually left various companies he worked for had anything to do with his sales technique. Instead, he practised with gay abandon his highly successful ploy of: listening to his interlocutor's innermost feelings; repeating them so they felt he "really understood them"; using this tactic for everything from obtaining good seats in restaurants and theatres, getting young ladies into bed or even inspiring a team to play better than they had done previously.

He had heard from the Hammers the oft repeated[64] protest "we're a social club" so much that he was *convinced* there must be some underlying, undeclared feeling shared by all. It *had* occurred to him though, during another game of Xbox, that if he could find this common "thing", he could perform a group sale on the players to maybe change the way they thought about the game and indeed, played? A bit of analysis was thus required.

For most of the players, their first male role models and initial heroes were their fathers. Being of a certain age, most of these men were "old school" (brought up to believe they should be the "strong, silent type" and as a consequence, were not particularly comfortable with expressing the obvious – well to them at least - feelings of love they had for their children). Over time - and by one of those strange quirks of fate that seem to have almost been purposefully created just to make things interesting - the daughters' realisation of flaws in their hero-fathers' character just about coincides with the awkward time at the onset of puberty, when the first pieces of the dam to their developing bodies and sexuality begin to work themselves loose. To futher add to the mix, the gathering maelstrom does not go unnoticed by Dad, in whom the need to defend and (maybe over?) protect his darling little girl[65] is only surpassed by his inability to express it without causing offence[66].

From the adoring relationship of only a few short years before, two rival camps are now created: the one of the: "I don't understand you, you're crazy, I'm trying to protect you, all I want is what's best for you (but as defined by me)!" variety, the second, more of a "Fuck you, this is me doing what I know you don't want me to do, deal with it."

Fast forward 10 years to the age of most of the Hammers and the positions between fathers and daughters had become even more entrenched; hostilities ceasing temporarily only over family gatherings at holiday or birthday times. *Or possibly over some shared activity.*

"But he won't ever even bother to come down to watch me play..."

Into this environment steps a Caz: a slightly younger, good-looking, well-spoken, *ideal* version of their fathers (with his cynical "I really care about you and am listening to your most heart-felt desires" hat on). The sudden explosion of feeling (and pain) two nights before was scarily reminiscent of many of his other endeavours, where manoeuvring his way into hearts to get what he wanted ("To win the league: hell, why not?") had, once achieved, led to people eventually realising that he actually really didn't care about them at all.[67]

"But I do care!" he protested to himself while the Liverpool left back, after robbing the gangly French Chelsea winger, crossed for a header to thunder past the keeper. 1 – 0 the 'pool!

During his playing days, he had never given much thought to the lady rugby players hanging around him and his teammates on a Saturday evening in the various club houses and converted pubs up and down the country, tending to the bruised bodies and often egos of the men after the game in the hope of being with one of them later that evening. Apart from maybe, that they reminded him of Napoleonic war camp followers: ghost-like creatures drifting from battlefield to battlefield with no purpose of their own in virtual self-imposed servitude. In fact, as most of the ladies' team hadn't even played that day, their games normally being on a Sunday, the *only* reason they were at the club that night was for the men, who would take their pick of the keenest camp followers for the purposes of that evening's entertainment. Very, very rarely would that particular liaison last beyond days (if not just the one night) and the merry-go-round of matching camp follower to bruised warrior would continue the next week.

"Funny how, at the end of season Dinner Dances, the rugby boys would virtually all turn up with some skinny, non-rugby-playing "girlfriend" and virtually all the rugby girls would turn up in a partner-less group," he had observed once or twice. However, as previously stated, he never really gave it much thought.

Now, he saw the rugby girls in a different light. He had grown up in the generation of women's lib': big improvements in women's pay, equal rights and feminism, so was just completely unaware that the accumulated effect of centuries of conditioning (which constantly re-iterated women's inferior status) could not fail to leave at least some tiny, almost infinitesimal trace, even in the most confident. There always seemed to be - either lurking in the background beneath all sorts of physical, mental or emotional layers or right out front, as in the case of the career women he'd known through banking (and universally referred to as the "Ball-breakers") - something to prove. Over the season, Caz had come to realise that what women *really* wanted was for someone they respected to help sweep away that last vestige of self-doubt (and thus need to prove themselves). To have faith in them, to believe in them so they could show their various doubters that they were actually good at this male-dominated thing[68] they had chosen to do, sometimes in the face of vociferous objection from people who were supposed to love them. Then to give them the recognition they deserved once they'd achieved it.

Recognition from the boys' teams, from employers, from their parents (mostly their fathers), from friends, BAGS, anyone close to them really.

To counteract this lack of self-belief, the rugby girls had formed themselves into a little entrenched community, the slogan of which seemed to be: "Nobody likes us, we don't care!" The "not caring" included: not taking training seriously; not looking after their bodies properly for what is a very hard and unforgiving sport; the *worst* pre-game preparation imaginable almost as a badge of pride nor caring whether they won or lost. It was his job to shake the players out of this discomfort zone by *making* them care. "About something, anything."

For him rugby was a game of passion, of total commitment, of working your body as hard as physically possible, in training as well as on the pitch, so you can be at your physical peak in order to put the very best of yourself in the line of fire for the benefit of your teammates. The game had transformed him from being the cocky, fear-of-failure-fraud[69] that he had been before Troubadors; why not his team?

You couldn't consider yourself a *proper* rugby player if your only concern was whom you were going to shag on a Saturday night. The girls themselves didn't consider themselves proper rugby players, nor did the boys they were often after. Consequentially, they then weren't treated as such.

As the greatest insult to anything is indifference (sales training platitudes, even though he hated them, were never too far from Caz' train of thought), he would shake this indifference out of them.

A *sensible* Coach would have kept a safe distance from this particular potential emotional minefield and definitely *not* fanned the flames of the confusing feelings towards their first heroes who just weren't bothered in even making an attempt to see them for whom they really were (of which they weren't too sure themselves, but were working on...). Caz' start of the season declaration of saintly chastity was a deliberate tease ("I thought it was fun!" he mused, thinking back to elephants again) and he had made a deliberate show of *not* flirting with them, just to keep them interested.

(2 – 0 to Liverpool! The talismanic midfielder and captain completed a mazy run with a sweet, curling drive into the bottom corner).

Caz had also, unwittingly, stumbled on another tactic to get his players to react. He had once accidentally referred to the front row as being gravitationally challenged. Well, actually he'd called them "Fat PoPo's." The sheer ferocity of the anger that *that* one tiny comment had generated was enough to fire the pack through the first part of the season, enabling them to make up for lack of size and perhaps technique by just wanting to SMASH (him, probably). "I wish I'd dreamed that up on purpose!"

(Oh no, Chelsea have pulled one back: 2 – 1).

So, his tactic had been to get them to either love him or hate him, leaving no room for indifference, all while giving the impression he understood them, was one of them and could "feel their pain" (sometimes literally as now he knew these young ladies better - what they did for a living, who they were seeing, what motivated them, what they drank and what effects it would have on them the day after – the more he began to wince when he saw one of "his girls" go down injured on the pitch.)

It should have clicked in his head that the fanned flames had now become roaring furnaces, uncontrollable to any normal man-child when, one by one, various players would introduce him to their parents, who had finally come to see them play after often years of disaproval. The sheepish grins of the players and mostly grudging acknowledgement from the parents that the team wasn't that bad really reminded him scarily of the awkwardness of meeting parents of former girlfriends for the first time...

He and Gwen had had a conversation, once the winning had started, about why the boys' attitude towards them seemed to be changing from one of almost contempt, to respect, then to almost envy.

"It's because they have respect for *you*," she'd let slip in an intoxicated slur. "They believe if *you* think we're worth something, then we must be. Then, when they see us play, they wish they could play like we do!"

Caz didn't answer (she was too drunk to listen anyway and would probably have burst into tears, as she had a habit of doing) but he knew that the real reason was because the team was gaining respect for themselves. "If you're willing to make an ass of yourself, there's always someone willing to ride you." That's it, I've got to stop this now or I'll be platitude-ed to death....

Red card! Liverpool goalkeeper sent off! "It wasn't even a foul ref, come on!"

And then there was Stell.

The first impression he had had of her at that training session a couple of years before was she just seemed to be an open and perhaps slightly naive, very pretty-without-realising-it young lady[70]. Initially, she appeared in awe of the male players whom she was convinced knew so much more about the game than she did. When someone mentioned that Caz used to play for Troubadours, she just gawped in wild-eyed wonder and would have fallen off her chair, if they weren't already prostrate on the floor doing the pre-warm down stretches.

It wasn't the big, wild, blondish hair, nor the scarily large blue eyes and long lashes that had first attracted him though. Beneath all this, the thing that had got to him was a fierce, lioness-like pride and desire to protect from any criticism or ill-treatment the fledgling team she was trying to build.

At that time, the ladies' team normally trained on a tiny, hilled space - which didn't even extend as far as the 1st lamp post - next to the men's training area. That evening, their training area had virtually been taken away from them, encroached upon by the men's teams so much that Stell had little choice other than to abandon it. She had thus taken her 5 disciples over to the main pitch where they had joined in a game of touch rugby with some of the men's 4th team. Stell was putting a brave face on the low turnout and the forced eviction by shouting enthusiastically but, if anyone had paid close attention to her features, they would have noticed see was seething. The tackle she put in on the 4th team hooker, even though supposedly a game of touch and to which thankfully, he was too surprised to react, let all know she was not a happy bunny. It was obvious to Caz that the ladies in her charge that evening had complete trust in her, though it was also obvious to anyone who'd ever been anywhere near a rugby pitch that devising rugby training session plans was clearly not one of her strong points.

Curiosity tweaked by this woman of contrasts, he made a vow to try to get to know Stell better, if the opportunity ever presented itself. Over the last couple of years though, the opportunity, nor really the desire for him to do anything about it, ever did.

He had once been told, before he went into banking and had to "toughen up", that he used to wear his heart on his sleeve. Well Stell, all 6'1, 180 lbs of her, had a whole suit made out of every part of her vital organs you could stitch together with a needle and thread! Completely unlike him, if she thought or felt or had the slightest inkling of anything, it showed first on her ears which could go from pale to crimson in under 3 seconds, then the freckles on her cheeks would do a lightning fast game of Join the Dots so they would match the ears, then the nostrils would flare and she'd either eff and blind like a trooper or, if she went silent, it was a clear sign to beat a hasty retreat as, at the very least, the totally unexpected, including physical violence, was an odds-on certainty to follow.

"My God," he thought, that night, "she may even sack me!"

(Goal Chelsea! The referee had awarded a penalty, coolly slotted away by the popular chubby funster midfielder! 2 – 2. Noooooo!!!!!)

But when she laughed, which did happen sometimes, the eyes would water at the outside corners and her whole face would explode with the radiance of the opening of a sunflower on fast forward. The beauteous image would only last for seconds though as a swine snort or two would quickly put an end to any floral imagery.

The night before, after the Kingston game, he had known that Stell was watching him talking to Fi and he had strung the conversation out longer than necessary, just to see how she'd react. He hadn't accounted for the fact that maybe the Pandora's Box of conflicting emotions he had deliberately opened would come back to bite him in the bum. "Or punch him in the face," he winced. He knew that he had purposely started a chain of events that could lead to, well, who knows where. "That was clever."

He had thus sent the email this morning to arrange not an armistice, but a free and frank exchange of views. One of the major drawbacks with his particular controlling behaviour attribute of "aloof" was that you never entered into personal conversations about feelings, unless absolutely imperative. And then you still tried not to.

If he were going to get the sack though (for any number of reasons: conflict of interest, personal feelings getting in the way of professionalism etc), then they might as well clear the air first. Caz had decided to tell her what he really thought of her, of Fi, of the team, irrespective of what the outcome would be.

"I'm going to be an honest man for once," he'd said to himself, and clicked on the "send" button.

That was this morning, a whole 12 hours ago. He wasn't so sure now....

(Chelsea players celebrate as with the final kick of the game (header from a corner), they win the Champions Cup final 3 - 2. "Och, they now have the bragging rights over their bitter rivals," the Scottish commentator's voice was purring. "Well done lads.")

"Great," he thought. "Even Xbox hates me." And with that, Caz switched off the console (before the loss could be recorded on his Gamer History) and went upstairs to get some sleep in preparation for the peace summit to come.

Chapter 36: Armistice

Stell had taken a half day off so she could either have a good cry, if the coach did actually resign, or get drunk in the afternoon without colleagues asking what was wrong. During the course of her restless night, the thought of an alternative scenario of undying love being declared and an afternoon of passionate tumblings in billowing white sheets had made the briefest of appearances, but had just as quickly faded into the image of her boss Trish at work, 10 ft tall and stabbing her in the back with a pitchfork while screeching, "You're below target, you're below target!"...

She was seated at a small side table by the window, in the Duke of Monmouth "gastro-pub" on Parsons Green. Only a couple of years before, it had been the home of the Hammers and you could get a pint, a pie and even a game of snooker in. The owners had then realised that, due to the general gentrification of certain parts of London, if you kicked all the rugby players out, whacked up the prices and sold attempts at Michelin-starred food and fine wines, you could make a killing off the recently graduated offspring of the Nouveau London Riche.

Looking over the park, Stell could see scores of foreign Nannies bonding on the park benches, while ignoring the attention-seeking whining of the English (and quite a large number of French, given that certain parts of south Fulham were fast resembling more another arrondissement of Paris than a quiet London suburb) toddlers in their charge.

"Where did the word "toddler" come from anyway?" she mused. "I thought either you're a baby or a kid - nothing in between. Then, you're a teenager, you go to Uni then, when you come out and before you know it, you're an old git who has to balance job, social life, money, boyfriend/husband-to-be and somehow, miraculously *know* how to do it all! It's just not fair......"

"Can I get you another drink, Madmoiselle?" came the waiter's voice, interrupting her silent protest.

Louis, originally from Paris but having been a waiter in London for so long he had to work hard to preserve his accent (just so people didn't mistake him for an Englishman), couldn't work out why this nervous looking young lady was sitting alone in a gastro-pub at lunch time, but not ordering food or drinking alcohol. She was wearing a tight grey skirt, well-cut grey jacket and low, really low black silk blouse revealing just a suspicion of lacey black bra. Louis had to make an effort to not look down her cleavage.

"Dressed for work but not quite comfortable in how she's wearing her clothes," Louis appraised silently. "The make-up too, not applied with enough subtlety, like by someone not used to doing it." She had also obviously made a special effort with her appearance today, but she was unsure of the final effect. Plus, she was definitely waiting for someone.

"Ah, office affair!" he concluded.

Sudden raised voices from outside and a quick-fire burst of panicky Tagalog made them both look out the window. "Little Jeremy or Francois must have fallen off his bike," they thought absentmindedly.

"Er, no, I'm alright thanks," Stell replied, looking down at her tonic water and lime. She needed a clear head in order to express to Caz why she wasn't happy with the way things were progressing with the team. Hopefully, talk about why she'd clobbered him two nights before would be relegated to second place. "After all, attack *is* the best form of defence," she tried to convince herself.

Another Nanny shout from outside, in a strange South African sounding twang of, "Victor, Olivier, you get yourselves down from there or you *know* what will happen to you!" The voice sounded vaguely familiar, but Stell wanted to continue her train of thought.

The main problem with Carlton Edwards, she had decided over the course of last night and this morning, was this: for reasons of his own ("Probably 'cos he was beaten as a child to be the "Best of the Best" a la Great British Empire crap," she wanted to believe), he was dragging the team to places they didn't want to go (or maybe they did, but were too frightened of failing to even attempt?)

He was seeing in them all this ability that they never knew they had and, as a result, they were – *she* was - gaining confidence in themselves. Not just in rugby but in everything else they did as well. It was like he had put his finger on an "Insecurity on-off switch" and made them want to train and play as hard as they could. Not for themselves, or for her, but for *him*. Or rather against whomever it was who said they couldn't in the first place.

He was also not too bad looking, with still a fairly fit body ("Like an aging gigolo," she thought. She tried to fight the follow on thoughts of "with probably loads of experience as well," but with very little success), so it was possible that some players could confuse the "being touched spiritually by the coach" to a "being touched physically."

"Aaaarrrggghhhh! I hope that's not me.....," Stell realised. A flush of embarrassment suddenly attacked her cheeks, as well as a slight twitch in the general vicinity of her heart. These coincided with a twinge slightly lower. Her cheeks burned crimson.

"Hi, Stell, sorry I'm a bit late," Caz apologised as he slid into the seat in front of her.

"Ah, le boss est arrivé!" Louis smiled, spying from behind the bar.

Chapter 36: Armistice 2

Stell looked down into her drink so Caz wouldn't see her blushing. He was wearing a light pink shirt, open at the neck by one more button than absolutely necessary and a pair of designer ripped jeans. Caz was tall, slim(ish) with a powerfully built chest, arms, thighs. The scars he had picked up from all those years on the rugby field were mostly hidden from view, apart from the gash above his right eye, which she actually quite liked!

As opposed to wearing his backwards facing cap, which seemed to accompany him everywhere when he was coaching, he wore his hair in a regulation short back and sides cut, with a wavy mass of tiny curls on top. Stell realised it was the first time she'd seen him not in training kit, fancy dress or black tie. He looked edible.

Caz too had hardly ever seen Stell in normal clothes. The curves that went on for days in all directions were usually invisible underneath that manky old ex-Northerton Viper rugby shirt and stupidly baggy jogging pants she was sporting that Tuesday evening when he had first met her 2 years before. In fact, he could now laugh at the fact that under all that rugby gear, he actually had thought she appeared rather flat-chested, an idea which, given her current work attire, was clearly preposterous. "Oh dear, very nice!" he thought.

After ordering drinks (another tonic and lime for Stell, a glass of white wine for himself), Caz cut straight to the chase.

"I know why you thumped me on Sunday," he ventured.

"Oh God, here it comes....," Stell braced herself.

"It's because you think I'm taking over."

"Eh?!!!" Stell thought. "He's completely missed the point!"

However, now that Caz had said it, she could imagine him wanting to be in control of team selection, as well as tactics, which traditionally, she had always been in sole charge of. This control of selection would naturally include the appointment of team captain...

In general, male coaches weren't really that bothered about the fine minutiae of how the team worked or was put together, as they were there mostly for the "fringe benefits". Up until now, she had thus wielded complete control over who played where, over who was "in" or who was "out". She hadn't realised until that very moment that her popularity within the group, the reason why all the girls had looked up to her, was not due to respect and love for their leader, but because if they didn't, they could be out on their ear, rejected by the pride and left to wander the plains on their own (or join another club). She suddenly felt very small.

Caz continued, "I think you ladies are brilliant. You guys have got so much ability; you can definitely win not only this league, but the next couple above as well. But, going forward, you'll need to get the right people in the right positions and the roles of who does what sorted out."

"He said "you" and not "we"," Stell noticed. "He *is* going to resign after all!"

"Stell, do you know what makes a team?" Caz carried on. She gave an almost imperceptible shake of the head.

"It's been proven that collective thought or will actually does have a physical effect on events, like a gravitational pull. But there has to be a focus for that collective will, a central thing or person that pulls everyone together and makes each and every player want to fully commit on the pitch and in training, so they won't let that central person down."

"It's HIM! He wants to be the main man in an all girls team!" Stell almost blurted out.

Caz continued, "As I'm not actually on the pitch with you guys, the main person can't and shouldn't be me."

"Oh," she thought. "Who then?" she had the sneaky suspicion what the answer to her unasked question was...

Caz pressed on, almost reading her thoughts. "Fi is playing as a one-woman team at the moment and simply, she's everywhere."

"Oh," again Stell thought, repressing the desire to say, "Oh Gawd, not again."

"She's definitely got the ability to play at a much higher level and, as Vice Captain, the team listen to her. She does have a habit of popping up in the backs though when she shouldn't be."

Stell tried not to choke on her tonic water. She knew that *she* was the one responsible for telling Fi to "Just go out in the backs," as she simply didn't know what else to do with her.

Correction, she *did* know what to do with her (omitting the option of slow strangulation, but only for the time being), but as Fi never listened anyway, the best way to deal with her complete disobedience was to banish her to the backs where hopefully, her insubordination would be less noticed.

"We can't have two central points in the team, Stell," Caz hesitated, "we can only have one leader on the pitch, one point of focus."

She looked up at Caz who seemed to be trying to study her face for a reaction to his opening words. ("Oooh, that smells nice!" entered her head. "Was that Issey Miyake he was wearing?")

Banishing thoughts of just ripping his clothes off there and then and to hell with rugby, she sighed resignedly. "Oh well, better to jump than be pushed."

"You want Fi as captain, don't you!?" It came out more as an accusation than a question. "It was so unfair though," she thought, "that Fi always seemed to get whatever she wanted. If only I were a few pounds lighter....."

The realisation that Caz was making a mess of what he was trying to say hit him like a brick to the back of the head. He almost turned to the side to see the God of Realisation and Shame pretending he hadn't thrown it.

"No, no, no, no, no, no!" he spluttered. "That's not what I meant at all!" How could he explain this, in words that not only Stell, but *he* could understand?

After their training session two years before, he had completely forgotten about the strains of injustice he had seen on Stell's face that day until he had watched the ladies play a season later. He could see what was going wrong with their play, could see who needed to play in which position, what they needed to do and how, like a big jigsaw puzzle that just needed a bit of rearranging, all that was required was a little tweak here and there. He could also see who the centre of the team should be, around whom everything would flow nicely, based purely on her passion, determination, her standing amongst the other players and selfless and absolutely crazy desire to be right in the thick of the action, inspiring all around her to do the same.

Once he'd been asked to coach the ladies' team and his marriage had well and truly fallen apart, any lust on his part that may have been hovering around waiting for the ideal moment to strike, was replaced almost entirely by the desire to just help. Almost.

Caz heard Stell cough, bringing him back to the present. In order to take control of where this conversation was heading, Stell thought she should say something else. Caz cut her off before she could open her mouth.

"The centre of the team is YOU, Stell," he blurted out, completely forgetting about trying to measure his words carefully so as to not reveal any signs of the pounding in his chest nor the dizziness swirling round his head. "She really did look good...."

"I need you strong and in control."

"Eh?" Stell thought.

"Your drinks sir," the waiter said, returning with Stell's soft drink and Caz' white wine. Stell grabbed the wine and took a long, deep swig.

Louis raised an eyebrow. He was about to condescend with a: "May I get you another glass sir?" but he thought twice, internally smiling to himself as he decided to go for the "longer term financial gain option" over the "instant gratification that the condescension towards the uncouth English," would grant.

From many years experience, Louis knew these types of situations and their respective stages, all too well:

"Stage 1) Boy meets girl,

2) Boy likes girl,

3) Girl likes boy,

4) Other issues involved (wives, husbands, etc) so can't get together in normal environment (office, gym, sports club),

5) Boy and girl arrange to meet outside of normal environment,

6) Boy/girl reveal how they feel about each other,

7) Boy and girl, how do the Ingleesh say, "shag the rest of the afternoon away!"[71]

It wouldn't be doing his job properly if he didn't assist them with moving on from stage 5) through to stage 7) ("After all, I am French!" he thought to himself) whereby The Duke of Monmouth would forever be "their special place" and, if he played his cards right and stayed around, he would be "their" special waiter. A lifetime of VERY LARGE TIPS would be his just reward[72].

"Or should I make that a bottle, sir?" he added with an immensely straight face, fully committing himself to not appending the French equivalent of: "Fnaar, fnaar!" even though clearly appropriate.

"Er, yes please," Caz stuttered. He was flushed as well now.

Triumphantly, the waiter oozed away. "Le début de l'affaire!" he smiled to himself. "She's his secretary or Personal Assistant, he's married of course, he's shown faith in her and she believes she can make him happier than his wife."

Louis allowed his imagination to not only race, but go for a Personal Best. "A wife who, after the birth of their, 2 or is it 3 kids, has neglected him and has let herself go," at which he pulled a distasteful face.

Coming into the final bend, just before the home straight, if his imagination kept up its incredible pace, it could get its hands on that elusive gold medal! "A fat wife who devotes all her time to the kids, lives in a tracksuit, has cut her hair short and who wears no make-up." This was starting to sound a bit too much like his messy divorce, but his imagination was on the last leg of the home straight, only centimetres left to the winner's tape.

Making a last-gasp dash for the line, the imagination continued: "She," he tilted his head slightly towards Stell, "is thinking to be the next Mrs Sportsman" (Louis was sure that Caz had probably been some sort of sportsperson but retired from it and now pushed a pen around a desk), "he is after, how you say, only the extra nookie. It will be a désastre!" he said, shaking his head.

Olympic gold!

"Oh dear," he thought, "I've been in England too long..."

He glanced again over to the uncomfortable-looking couple trying hard not to say with words what every part of their bodies was expressing.

"Plus ça change....."

Stell raised her head from out of the large wine glass to tune back in to what Caz was saying. She took another swig whilst Caz continued to babble.

"....she's much slower than the backs, so we'd prefer them to go on the runs, not her. She can get away with it against the worst teams, but against the better ones, she'll get tackled and we'll get stuffed."

"Yes!!! At last!! Not everyone thought Fi was some sort of superwoman! *This* is what she wanted to hear, music from the Gods!"

"...plus, when she plays, YOU don't. She undermines you and you sort of, shrink."

"Nope, no idea what he's on about," Stell jumped to the defensive. She'd already criticised herself enough for one day and wasn't prepared for someone else to have a go as well. However, she really didn't know what he was talking about as he had a habit of getting carried away with his own voice and getting *way* too technical! It was kind of sweet though.

The good news was that he hadn't threatened to resign yet, she was off work for an afternoon and he was getting the drinks in! "Hey, it could be much worse!" she thought.

Caz continued with some impassioned plea about "getting the back row to work as a unit etc" and Stell reclined in her chair, pretending to listen intently. The wine was starting to have an effect and Caz' words were becoming hazier and hazier. She liked how he was saying them though and started to feel warm and fuzzy, the tension from the last two days slowly lifting, like post-exam euphoria. Stell moved forward in her seat, her mouth felt moist but her lips dry. She was desperate for another glass of wine. She licked the left-hand corner of her lips and ran her finger gently round the rim of the empty glass. One shoe fell off.

Suddenly, Caz stopped rambling. He laid his hand on top of hers, which was still resting on her glass, halting the gyrations of her finger. He moved a few inches towards her and looked her right in the eye. His Issey Miyake smelt stronger to her up close.

"Eh eh," Louis thought, while half-heartedly polishing two white wine flutes, to show he was busy. "Ç'arrive: the "pounce"."

Caz paused, their faces were within inches of each other. He could smell her perfume, her lipstick, the wine on her breath, then said, "Stell, will you be my captain?" He was staring straight into her.

Stell felt as if she were going to cry. She wasn't expecting *this*. Caz was asking her, *pleading* with her, to inspire and motivate, to encourage and fight for and *lead* her team into possibly even winning the league. A slight pang of irritation flared within her that he had somehow changed things so that *he* was asking *her* for help with *his* team, but she was too elated to dwell on it for too long. To win the league would mean so much more than just getting more points than anyone else. It would mean that they were *right* and everybody else - boyfriends, Dads, the men's teams – were wrong, that they were good. They would also be able to attract new players and continue to be a club.

She wanted to say yes, but somehow, this didn't seem enough. The Issey Miyake was drawing her in and, for the first time, she saw honesty, almost vulnerability in his imploring eyes. Their lips parted at the same time, only inches apart, instinctively expecting what was to come. The whole room disappeared.

Louis, dropping all pretentions of not following every action of the infidelity about to be born in his bar, was fascinated. He had witnessed similar situations so many times before, but, maybe this was different, not just the start of "just another affair" after all. In spite of the inevitable stages 8) to 11), these two people were embarking on this road of hope that would lead them they didn't know where, desperately trying to escape whatever disappointing relationships they were in, in their quest to find the elusive happy-ending that the human condition is committed to seek, "L'inaccessible étoile"[73] of the songs. Life is giving them a second chance at happiness and, even though it may destroy them, they are willing to dive into it, head-first and uninhibited, open-hearted and empty-headed, come what may.

The romantic in him smiled as he placed the flutes on a silver tray, next to the selected chilled white wine in its cooler. He draped a fresh cloth over his forearm and set off towards their table. "After all, I am French!"

He looked over at the lovers-to-be and felt almost like an intruder in his own bar. "What are you waiting for, kiss her, nom de Dieu!" he silently proclaimed as he made his way over, very, very slowly, in order to time his arrival *just* so.

Suddenly, there was a banging on the window. Stell and Caz both jumped back to the safety of their respective chairs.

"I thought I recognised you two there! What you up to?" Fi's smiling face was pressed against the window, with her twin charges playing in the street behind her. Caz' and Stell's embarassed expressions were enough to make the smile disappear, only momentarily, to be replaced by an even bigger, fixed one.

"Ohhhhhhh-kay," Fi said, evaluating. Then, as cheerfully as she could muster, she added, "Have a good lunch!" and turned on her heels to walk off down the street.

As the sound of Fi barking "Victor, Olivier, come with me NOW!!!" faded into the distance and Stell and Caz sat in shame-faced silence for a few seconds, midway between the bar and their table, Louis the waiter, stopped in his tracks.

He puffed out his cheeks, gave a little "Brrppp" sound as he let the air escape between closed lips, shrugged his shoulders and replaced the bottle of wine back in the fridge.

Chapter 37: Vengeance of a Gym Queen

"What on earth am I letting myself in for?" Stell wondered as she stared at her reflection in the full-length mirror.

Here she was at Top Trumps' Gym in Fulham, wearing lycra leggings, an old "Northerton Vipers on Tour" rugby shirt with "Yoda: Drunk I am" written on the back, hair up, no make-up and preparing for the undoubted torture that was surely about to befall. The loo flushed as Fi emerged, figure-hugging lycra everywhere, with a "more like a bra than a top" piece of material on her torso revealing taut obviously painted-on abs and *full make up*!

There had been an embarassed silence between Fi, Caz and Stell at the Thursday night's training session following Duke of Monmouthgate. Fi hadn't been able to make the game the following Sunday due to "work commitments", but the Hammers had recorded their biggest victory of the season. The tactic of forwards trying to run into spaces and not directly into opposing players was paying off as it meant that when they did get tackled, they could go to ground and present the ball in such a way that it could then be moved by Katie pretty quickly to the fast girls out wide.

Stell was quite justifiably awarded Man-of-the-Match as she had simply been unstoppable. Revelling in her renewed authority and finally buying into Caz' philosophy of "spaces not faces", the one-woman wrecking ball had run straight at the heart of the bigger Hartsey forwards, but instead of crashing into them, had re-found her side-step of almost 20 years ago and made them have to try to move to tackle her which, if you are 5' nothing and 115 kilos, is a very big ask. Sometimes, it would take up to three defenders to slow her down and then, once the ball was released, gaps in the opposition defence were everywhere. By midway through the second half, Stell was absolutely exhausted and received a standing ovation from Mrs T and the 10 travelling Hammers supporters, as well as from the grudging home support, on her eventual substitution. Even Fred did a little "Hail the Conquering Hero" somersault!

Inevitably though, the question of fitness had again come up, with Caz, in her absence (and partly in contrition), praising Fi's ability to cover every blade of grass ("giving 110% for the full 70 minutes and feeling over the moon and not sick as a parrot"), in a well-known parody of various football commentators.

However, these commentaries were only well-known to the British-born Hammers and so when Fi was informed of the Coach's compliments and believing he was being sincere, she had emailed all the players so enthusiastically about her fitness regime at the gym, where she had a part time job as a fitness instructor, that Caz didn't have the heart to point out the joke.

All had thus agreed to submit to a fitness session at Top Trumps, under Fi's able tutelage, that they could then use as the basis for their own individual training programmes. Needless to say, in the week that had elapsed since that particular resolution, appropriate excuses for non-attendance were found by all, except Stell who, as the Captain, couldn't really back out of it. All the other experimental victims having deserted (probably due to cut backs in the science budget), Stell felt like the last remaining monkey in the laboratory cage, being led out onto the operating slab by the Evil Scientist. "Rats" was no-where near strong enough to express the taut feeling in her stomach. "Lab Rats," she thought. "There, that's better."

Her stomach was just about to get a whole lot tauter.

Having spent some time looking for gainful employment after leaving Uni', Stell could recount all the programmes on the various TV channels, from the morning chat shows, through the ultra tacky ads to the "understated in the UK but massive spin-off version in the States" early evening game shows. Fi looked like one of those women in the latest "multi-abdominal crunch" contraption adverts[74] that were featured on every channel, at about "morning biccy and cuppa time"[75], just when you were feeling a bit full and guilty for eating between breakfast and lunch.

Stell had initially found such ladies like permanently grinning, big-haired, wiry-bodied, insincere, "bouncing about like the Duracell Bunny" ALIENS. After months of unemployment, self-esteem being ground down by constant job rejections from those companies which bothered to respond, she found herself grabbing at the perfectly normal tiny trouser roll of flesh above her jogging pants and actually contemplating a small investment in *Absoblitzer*, so she could be more like the women on screen who so obviously had these perfect lives as a result of their perfect bodies. The BetNow! job, when it eventually came, had saved not only her brain from turning to mush but also her emaciated bank account from an investment into a soon-to-be-discarded pile of plastic, springs and rubber bands that, unsurprisingly, would not deliver the life-style nor the abs advertised. The cupboard under the stairs breathed a sigh of relief.

"Er, nice," said Fi, making no attempt to disguise the distaste in her quick assessment of Stell's battered, discoloured rugby shirt. "Yoda. Cute." Stell felt a bit smaller.

"We'll start with a warm up," Fi continued, "then abs, then we'll do a full upper body, some aerobics and a stretch. Wayne's class is after, so that gives us about an hour, maybe an hour 15 before it starts. Is that OK with you?" The question was rhetorical.

"Hey, no problem," Stell replied." This was a *bad* idea," she thought.

Already way ahead of her gym companion in the fashion stakes (black mini-top with red trim and matching black, spray-on cycling shorts), Fi was ready for business. As Stell trudged up the stairs behind her, surrounded by ceiling-high mirrors reflecting every aspect of her appearance to the outside world, Fi seemed to glide into the large, bright, open-plan first floor main gym area. Men turned to look, some making plans that when their bodies were perfect, they'd ask her out, others, just pleased to behold what they thought they would never get. Women either stared at her or looked in the general direction of their trainers, mixtures of envy, heroine-worship and self-consciousness flooding through them all at the same time: the queen had arrived in her realm.

One or two women, including Chloe, Fi's employer in her proper job, approached her with the excuse of asking inane questions, but more to bask in the reflected glory of being seen to know her. Stell could see Fi's back straighten and chest swell, her step become more assured, her almost smirk struggling hard not to break out all over her face. Fi deigned to talk to these minions, vaguely promising to meet them or rearrange their personal training sessions at later dates. The full focus of Fi's attentions, for this evening at least, would be Stell.

"Let's warm up first," she said, as matter-of-factly as possible. The cross-trainer was an ideal piece of equipment to get the heart going, as arms and legs would move in unison, in a similar action to cross-country ski-ing. Fi whacked her controller up to the maximum of 25, for a duration of 10 minutes. "We should set yours for say 10 – 15," she said to Stell, her "serious and professional" face firmly set so as not give off any signs of subterfuge.

"No, no, I can do 25 as well," Stell replied, not wanting to seem like a wuss.

"This is all too easy!" Fi thought, her first trick to run Stell into the ground already succeeding quite effortlessly. "Girlfriend, this is serious payback time!"

The first couple of minutes had been a bit of a struggle for Stell, as the pace she had started off at was a bit more than she would have normally, if Fi hadn't been there. The next say 5 minutes had been challenging, but not really that bad. Minute 7 was harder, as her legs began to burn but minute 8 was torture. Minute 9 actually lasted about 27 hours and by minute 9 and a half, the only thing that kept the burn in every muscle in her legs from actually bursting into flame was the thought that it would be all over in, 30, 29, 28, 27.....seconds.

When the machine started to slow down at the 10-minute mark, sweat pouring, chest thumping, leg muscles screaming, eyes stinging from sweat and dripping hair mousse ("Note to self, NEVER wear hair product in gym," she decided), Stell could think only of a hot shower and a thousand-year sleep. She looked over at Fi who had hardly broken sweat.

"Good warm up, let's now do abs before you get cold."

"Sure," a hoarse voice belonging to someone else emerged from Stell's mouth. She grabbed hold of the handrail to assist wobbly legs as she dismounted the first instrument of torture.

Fi led the way over to the matted area of the gym where people generally stretched and worked on their abdominal muscles. She knew about the burn in Stell's legs and pounding in her chest, but she also knew that Stell was a tough cookie and that breaking her was going to be more fun than she'd had in ages! Being strategically positioned in front of her Captain, there was no need to suppress the smile and a wide grin danced from one ear to the other. One of the ladies on the mats, sitting with one leg behind her head, the other bent on the floor, thought the smile was for her and proudly but sheepishly returned it. Fi quickly recomposed her face to the normal fixed grin and said, "Hi, how are you today?" The lady on the floor blushed.

The Abs Area in the gym is a tribute to the creativity and ingenuity of modern mechanics. The abs novice will commence his training with sit-ups, which will be quickly reviled and corrected by anyone who's been to more than one abs class, classifying simple sit-ups as the work of the devil which "injure the back and don't concentrate on the major muscle groups." Then comes the abs cruncher machines (a la daytime T.V. ads), then follows various machines where normally the victim sits, bends, rolls over against ever increasing, fixed weights. Next follows the ball stage. Big balls, little balls, heavy balls, balls with weights, kettle bells (balls with handles shaped like kettles!), the object being to lie on them, sit on them, roll them, swing them and generally use them to support the rest of your body while the abs do the concentrated work. The more balls you have and the more mechanically complicated way in which you combine their usage, the more accomplished an Ab-man you are. The advanced Ab-man though, the ultimate 6 (or even 8) pack guy or girl, having graduated up through all the previous stages, then goes onto an inclined benches and slopes stage. The idea is to use your own body weight to lift various parts of your body (legs, torso etc) in different ways so as to counteract gravity. If you wanted to get really serious, you could combine weights (and maybe a ball or two!) with the slopes, but as the slopes and Serious Ab-men are normally kept away from the main areas of the gym so as not to dishearten (too much) normal looking people, this only ever occurs when an Ab-man (or woman) wants to show off.

Fi had pre-arranged to have a couple of inclined slopes in the normal abs area, coupled with a mesmerising array of balls. Stell stared in wide-eyed apprehension.

The first exercise wasn't too hard. She had to lie on her back on one of the slopes, head higher than her feet, and hold onto a handle above her head. At the same time, her legs would be swung up together so as to form a right angle with her body. Ten times.

"Hey, this isn't too bad, I'm quite enjoying this!" she had first thought.

Then, the balls started. She had to repeat the exercise with first the small balls clasped between her feet, then the bigger ones, then the heavy ones then the...

Stell couldn't do it anymore and her legs crashed to the bench.

"Gottcha!" Fi almost leapt in the air, clapping her hands in pure glee. "Breaking point."

"Hey, no sweat," came out of her mouth. "Let's try something else."

By the time the two walked away from the mats towards the free weights, Stell doubled up in pain, Fi skipping and singing a tune to herself, Fi was starting to feel bored. The nurse-maiding had been fun, now she just wanted to ditch the monkey and do some proper training. Already thinking ahead towards the hardening in Stell's muscles that would occur over the next couple of days and the inevitable suffering that would follow, she called behind her, "Are you OK, does it hurt? Do you want to stop?"

"I'm fine, honestly," Stell smiled, hoping the words hadn't come out more like a grimace. "What's next?"

Fi stopped in front of the chest press machine which was being occupied by a huge old guy, probably an ex-boxer or bouncer trying to recapture former fitness. Turning directly towards Stell and looking challengingly into her eyes, she said, "Listen, this may be hurting now, but trust me, in a few days time, you'll feel great. We can stop anytime you want to." Only her lips were smiling.

"Feeling great already," Stell, unsmiling and exhausted, heart burning and lungs on fire, replied, staring straight back.

Chapter 38: Rochester Elms Away

Before the Rugby Football Union was formed in 1871 and the word "rugby" ever existed, there were a few clubs which played the game that would develop into the sport we now know and (ahem) love. These clubs are proud of their founder-member status and, in order to leave no-one in any doubt of their history, continue to call themselves football clubs, with the words (Rugby Union) attached almost as an afterthought. Rochester Elms Football Club (Rugby Union) was one of these illustrious few.

With the traditions and history that such a stalwart of the game possesses comes a sense of entitlement, a deep-seated belief that they have the right to win every time any team wearing their colours takes to the field. They will thus employ every means, fair and foul, to ensure the expected outcome, which normally means: they train more than every other team, they employ professional coaches, physios, doctors, SCOUTS (a gentleman wearing a red and white striped bobble hat had been seen lurking around a few of the Hammers ladies' games over the last few weeks. People thought he was just a new perv) and they even financially remunerate their best players. They also cheat.

Playing against Rochester Elms is like being the away team at Old Trafford. No matter how initially impartial an official may be at the start of every game, by close of play, the constant barracking by the crowd, the haranguing by the home-team officials and reproachful, malevolent questioning of *every single* unfavourable decision by the coaches would eventually wear down even the stiffest referee resistance and he would eventually be swayed in favour of the hosts, just for a bit of peace and quiet.

Rochester Elms players themselves were all too often the Big-Fish-In-A-Small-Sea hopefuls who had attended nearby Troubadours' summer training and were unceremoniously told to "Sod off back to Old Rubberduckians." Sometimes, like economic migrants who had left their homelands in a fanfare of hope, expectation and quite possibly a good deal of bluster, they couldn't face the ignominy of a return in failure and so, during the journey between Troubs and their home clubs, had made a detour to Rochester Elms Park. Relms teams thus tended to be unfriendly, unsporting and packed to the rafters with all those who never quite made it at the larger, more successful clubs, but still felt the sense of entitlement.

If Troubadors was the equivalent of Rugby Royalty, Rochester Elms was the Unfavoured Second Son, having all the pretensions of divine right but always being in the shadow of the heir to the throne.

The Relms Ladies' II team – the Valkyries - had big fast forwards and whippet-like speedy backs. They had half-backs who could spin pass farther than most male players and a refereeing and linesman team who could concoct reasons to award penalties, tries and put-ins to the home team that could baffle even the most committed conspiracy theorist.

In the mud and blood and general confusion that is forward play, it is much easier to give decisions against the away team as most of the action takes place at close quarters and is hard to spot.

The only way to beat the Relms is to spin the ball to the backs, where the play is more open and referees decisions are more easily scrutinised. Not that it makes much difference, as when a Relms ref gives a decision, it's unlikely it will ever change, unless it's against his own team. On a day like today though, where the wind whipped frozen rain into faces, thighs and numbing hands, spinning the ball wide was going to be significantly trickier than normal.

The Hammers had made the short trip over the river Thames to the leafy and green parts of south west London where it is no longer possible for any normal human being to be able to afford to buy a house. Stell had formed the pre-match huddle and was giving instructions to the team. She and Coach, (who was literally taking a back seat on this one: he had just undegone an arthroscopy on his worn knees and, armed with crutches and a comfy chair, was watching from the sidelines) had devised a strategy to cope with the expected officiating bias of the game and wanted to make sure that everyone was on the same page. Fi was back in the team in what would be one of the last games before Christmas and was looking leaner and fitter than ever. The girls were jumping on the spot, hugging themselves and doing anything they could to keep warm against the biting cold. The grey skies had momentarily ceased their downpour but were still threatening rain, which could, if the torrent commenced, change the whole nature of the game plan as rugby balls, doing their best impersonation of bars of soap, tend not to like being caught.

"Nobody uses soap any more, but "as slippery as a bar of shower gel" just doesn't sound right," Gwen thought to herself, drifting off from her close friend's rousing speech.

"Gwen!" Stell shouted, seeing her tune out for a moment. "This is serious. Listen up Ladies," she said. "We know what to expect." Everyone concentrated on their captain's next words.

"Relms cheat, we know this." A couple of nods from the girls who had played them before. Stell continued, "But we also know how they play." Again, more nods.

The previous season, as a friendly (Rochester Ladies II were in the division above but had been relegated), the Hammers had locked horns with today's opposition and were expecting to get smashed, Relms having much better facilities and, man for man, much better players. However, every Relms player seemed to be playing as if they personally had to score from every phase of play. A forward would thus pick up the ball and run straight into a Hammer and, if tackled, wouldn't go to ground to present good ball to her halfbacks but stay on her feet and try to wrestle free. Support players arriving would try to rip the ball from her and embark on a run of their own and the same would happen again. If a Relms player ever went to ground, the arriving support, as opposed to trying to form a defensive wedge to protect their fallen colleague, would simply try to pick up the ball and run with it herself, normally straight into the waiting Hammers' defence. "It was like playing against a team of Fi's!" Stell had thought to herself at the time.

If the ball ever reached the no. 10, rather than use her incredible pass to feed the rest of the lightning-fast girls in her back line, the preferred option was to either kick away possession (to demonstrate what a good kick she had) or occasionally run with the ball (to demonstrate what a good runner she was). The idea never occurred to her to demonstrate what a good passer she was... A couple of seasons before, a super-quick ex Relm Valkyrie 1st teamer[76] had turned up for training wanting to join the Hammers. She'd been on the wing for Relms and hadn't received a pass for *more than 6 weeks!*[77] The would-be Hammer had subsequently been dropped to the Relms 2nd team, where she described life as being a self-interest hell where nobody even liked, let alone would put their body on the line for, their teammates. The only motivation they had was to get into the 1sts.

She only lasted two training sessions at the Hammers though as nobody liked her.

"Too big-headed," they'd all agreed at the time.

Building on her past experience of Relms, Stell concluded: "We need to hit their single forwards hard and low and *make sure* we put them on the deck. We need to get the numbers there so we can win the ball back in the ruck as they'll be going in in ones and twos. Once we've won the breakdown, we'll concentrate on attacking the fringes[78] to suck their defence in, then we'll try to move the ball to our speed merchants," she paused to look at Leafy, Cisk and Katia. They felt a small surge of pride. Cisk smiled nervously.

"If it rains more, we'll have to keep passes short, so Fi," Stell looked at Fi who, gum-shield in, nodded her head in acknowledgment, I don't want you involved in the heavy stuff at the fringes, but I need you ready to support the backs."

Fi unlinked her arms from the huddle and took her gum-shield out to speak. "You mean, you want me to just stay out in the backs?" A reasonable question but Stell knew Fi knew what she meant. She had to try not to rise to it.

"No, Fi, I want you up with the forwards to secure the ball, but *only* commit[79] if necessary. As soon as the ball is in Katie's hands, I want to see you sprinting to where the next breakdown is likely to occur. Like we did in training," she added at the end.

"Right, gotcha," Fi said, putting her gum-shield back in.

"1 minute please Ladies," the ref interrupted. "And I must say, it's awfully cold to be playing today. Maybe I'll make the game a bit shorter, you know, so you can get into the warm showers earlier and enjoy the rest of your Sunday."

The ref for today was Catweazle.[80] He was so called because, well, he looked like an 11th Century Druid[81]. He was stick thin, not worked-out thin, more emaciated thin, with a wild mess of black hair, a bizarre, bushy black beard and a thick black moustache that the girls were convinced he'd waxed so that it curled up at the ends. He also had a huge soft spot for ladies' rugby but was so eager to convey his love for the players that he came over as, well, really creepy. He also smelled very strongly of onions. The good thing about him though was he was fiercely independent and wouldn't be easily swayed by the partisan crowd, coaches nor linesman.

"No, we're fine with the normal time ref." Stell replied. Turning her attention back to her team she shouted, "Are we gonna win?"

"Yes!!!" was the reply.

"I said, are we gonna win?"

"YES!!!!" even louder. This time, even Fi had joined in.

"A-ROO, A-ROO, A-ROO – HAMMERS HAMMERS HAMMERS!!!"

Soph kicked off towards the Valkyrie pack which, as expected, charged up towards the Hammers' defending pack. Sib crashed into the ball carrier who, momentarily halted, continued to battle to move forward. Mands hit her from the side and all forward momentum ceased. Also, as expected, the Valkyries tried to collect the ball from the floor which had been presented by their falling comrade, instead of forming a defensive phalanx, and their loan-prospective ball retriever was swept away by a red wave of Stell and Sib, who left the ball free on the wet earth behind their back feet. As again expected, the fallen Valkyrie illegally held onto the ball on the floor so her team could again attempt to retrieve it.

"Release it 4 white!" the referee called.

"What's the matter with you sir, Hammersmith and Fulham are holding on to her!" was the shout from the Relms Head Coach, a totally bald, short and stocky former front row forward.

Before the referee could remonstrate, Fi swooped down to pick up the grudgingly-released ball and was about to burst into a sprint when the Relms support forwards buried her under a pile of red and white hooped shirts.

"Balls not coming out of there," Catweazle said, "Scrum down white ball."

"About time too sir!" was the Relms Head Coach's riposte.

The referee groaned but, for the time being, kept his counsel.

The resulting scrum saw the Valkyries push the Hammers back the permitted one metre, before the largest Valkyrie at the back of the scrum picked up the ball and attempted to run to her right, in between Leafy on the wing and Mads. The Hammers stopped her break with Mads wrestling her to the ground but before she hit the deck, she was able to pop the ball to a support player. The support player turned her back to the Hammers and all her forwards piled in behind her, to protect the ball and try to drive forward in a maul. However, lacking the sheer bulk of the Stokie Bears and against a much more organised defence, the Hammers were able to stop the pile of players from making any ground.

"To me Hammers!" Caz called from the sideline, encouraging his team to change the direction of the maul so it was moving sideways and not forwards. He added a, "Ref, they're coming in from the side!" as the Relms, momentarily panicking to counter the sudden change of direction of their combined drive, broke off from the back of the mass of bodies and reattached themselves onto the side of the maul.

"Seems like your eyesight's as bad as your legs!" the Relms Head Coach called out to Caz. "Maybe you should go back to football where you belong?"

"Oh dear, fighting talk," Caz thought. "Here we go again...."

"Not as bad as your hairstylist though!" he shouted. Mrs T (and Fred), the only Hammers supporters who dared brave the icy chill (more from the infamous Relms' hospitality than the weather), winced and smiled at the same time.

"I'm playing advantage!" the ref shouted.

The ball emerged from the mass of players on the Relms side and one of their forwards ran into the "7 channel"[82], where Fi was conspicuous by her absence. The forward ran through the massive gap in the Hammers' line and had the speed to beat the hastily retreating covering defence to make it over the tryline, to much home crowd cheering. The Home Coach, brandishing his largest smile, looked over at Caz, who was now standing up on his crutches in exasperation at the shocking defence: 5 – 0 Relms.

"Come on girls, they shouldn't even be on the same pitch as us!" was the Relms' Coach's encouragement. The cardinal sin of boasting at a rugby game was obviously something the Relms Coach couldn't give two hoots about; if it were his team that was winning.

The Hammers gathered under the posts to receive the conversion kick. Stell was livid as she removed her gumshield and shouted at Fi, "Where the fuck were you?"

"I was out in the backs as you said!"

"Was this deliberate or did Fi really not know where she was supposed to be?" Stell thought, as the conversion kick sailed over to more delirious support.

"Forget that girls, let's get right back at them!" she said, jogging up to the halfway line for the restart. The other Hammers jogged back into position too, trying not to look in Fi's direction to avoid displaying how pissed off they were. Best forget and focus on what they could influence, which was what would happen from then on.

At the restart, Zoe was able to tap the ball back for the Hammers and they could mount an attack. Shouts of "She's in front of the kicker sir!" from the home support were ignored by Catweazle, who was starting to wish he'd never left the 11th Century. A few Hammers' forward drives, repelled in part by the Valkyries, had set up good ball for Katie to move to Soph at Flyhalf. Sophie was about to loop a pass out to Lara at Centre when, right on her shoulder, Fi rasped a: "Sophie, NOW!!"

Her path to her Centre being blocked by the Vice Captain, Sophie hesitated, caught in two minds. Reluctantly she popped a short ball to Fi who, from a standing start, caught the ball and shifted through the gears to attack at full speed.

Or rather, would have attacked at full speed if she'd managed to get past 2nd gear.

The hesitation in the pass, plus the fact that Fi was 10m behind the gain line[83] meant that the wall of hoops was on her almost as soon as the pass was made, the famous "Man and Ball" situation. The crunch of the tackle was audible and the ball spilled forward.

"Smash 'em girls, smash 'em!" The Relms Coach encouraged enthusiastically.

"Knock on Red, Scrum down White ball!" shouted the ref. He wondered if he'd brought any "Instant Muteness" spells with him.

"What the fuck is wrong with you?!" Stell yelled directly into her face this time. Fi said nothing as she was helped to her feet by Mel and Hannah. The other forwards made no secret of their growing frustration and were glowering.

As half time approached, the Hammers were down 12 – 3. Apart from Fi trying to pick up scraps and going on solo runs when outmanned and completely out of position, the only other thing to note from a fractious first half was the intervention of a definitely not "specially-trained to put off the opposition kicker" Bichon Frise dog who ran onto the pitch to yelp and bite at Sophie's ankles when she went to take a penalty kick at goal. Fred, who was bored with the constant stop-start nature of the game (he liked seeing lots of people running one way after a ball, then the other way: it was all very exciting!) saw the other dog charging onto the pitch as a challenge and had hunted it down for something to do. Mrs T was ever so proud.

"Can't you keep your bloody dog off the pitch?" the Realms Coach shouted.

"It's *your* dog who was on the pitch first, young man!" Mrs T protested in her sternest School Mistress voice. "If you can't control your animal, nor your manners, you'd be better off not saying anything at all!"

The Relms Coach was about to argue back, but hearing the whip-crack sternness in Mrs T's voice and the slightly unhinged flash of fire in her steel-blue eyes, decided against it. Being physically attacked by an older lady at pitch-side wouldn't do much for his street cred'. He opted for a: "C'mon girls, we've got this in the bag," making sure to concentrate his vision on his celebrating team and avoid any eye contact with the sole Hammers human spectator.

During the few seconds of doggy distraction, Stell took the opportunity to accost her Coach. One of the benefits of the near miss at the Duke of Monmouth was that team selection had become a joint process between her and Caz. The responsibility of mid-game substitutions though had been given over completely to him who, from the sidelines, was in a better position to analyse what was going on on the pitch and make the necessary changes.

"Caz," she said. "I want to make a substitution at half time."

"I was thinking the same thing," he answered, looking over to the Hammers lined up behind the penalty taker, where Fi was standing apart from the others, hands on thighs, bent over trying to catch her breath from all the pointless running.

"Do you want to do it or should I?" If he could spare her the potential uncomfortable situation of expulsing the Vice Captain from the field of play, it would be better for team morale.

Stell gulped. This was it. Only half a season ago, taking off Fi, their best player by far would have been unthinkable and the team would have been up in arms. However now, the Hammers *were* a team, they all struggled together to win and any one of them would have traded any number of Man of the Match awards if it meant the team would be successful.

"Wouldn't they?"

Stell didn't have to think twice about the answer to her own silent question.

She addressed Caz, "No, I'll do it." She gulped again.

The second half was a completely different affair from the first. Ball secured by the forwards could flow along the back line and Zoe, moving to no.7, was able to support the fast girls if they were ever half-stopped. The Valkyries simply could not get out wide fast enough and so the Hammers, without a Fi-shaped obstacle in their midfield, poured through the tiring defence time and time again. The renewed rain had limited the scoring though, but with only 10 minutes or so left, the Hammers were 30 – 12 up. The Relms Coach was now swearing openly at his players, calling them a "Disgrace to the shirt" and refusing to let a very clearly injured player leave the field.

"Come on Princess, you've done fucking nothing all game. Tighten up your bloody bra-strap and man-up for once?!!"

Catweazle put his whistle to his lips to remonstrate, but seeing the glare in the Relms Coach's eyes, put it back in his pocket.

Caz couldn't resist one last pop:

"Come on girls, they *definitely* shouldn't even be on the same pitch as us!"

The Relms Coach blew his top, "Right, that does it, I've had enough of you!" He continued, "I've got friends high up in the RFU and I'm going to report you! You're a disgrace to the game!"

"Yeah, and my Dad's bigger than your Dad!" Caz thought, but stayed silent.

Well, for a few moments anyway...

While the steam from the top of the Relms Coach's bald head dissipated in the cold air as he calmed down, Caz, whispering loudly enough for anyone within a 30-yard radius to hear, added sweetly: "Some people should never have been allowed to leave the football terraces."

The Relms Coach threw down his clipboard, pen and "Coaching for Dummies" manual[84] and marched over to Caz, rolling up the sleeves of his Relms tracksuit. His 2nd in

Command, plus one or two of his substituted players, dived in the way to stop him, as did Catweazle blowing hard on his whistle.

"Gentlemen, gentlemen, calm down, it's only ladies' rugby for God's sake!!" he shouted in mid-scuffle. He then again blew hard on his whistle, this time two short and one long blast to signal the end of the game. As the Hammers and Mrs T cheered their hardest-won victory yet, forming themselves into the winners' tunnel to clap off their defeated adversary and the Relms' Coach pushed away his restrainers and marched off in a huff, Caz allowed himself the smuggest of smug smiles.

Chapter 39: Cake!!!

Fi refused to let the tears welling inside her escape from the corners of her eyes, trying to ignore the negatives from the game and focussing on the positives.

Yes, she had carried the ball loads today against Relms Valkyries and *had* made yards. Yes, she had tackled her heart out and had covered every blade of grass. No, she hadn't scored any tries or even been on the shoulder of the girls who had scored the tries.

"That was a negative," she thought to herself. "Don't need that crap." She tried to continue her train of thought.

Yes, she had been awarded Dick of the Day and been substituted at the start of the second half!

"No, that's not what I wanted to think about!" she protested, but it was too late.

She'd only stayed at the Rochester Elms clubhouse long enough to be awarded the un-coveted medal of shame and to drink her "dirty pint" which was now rumbling uncomfortably in her stomach on the lone bus ride back to Fulham. She had slipped out of the clubhouse unnoticed, so as to not have to listen to the "Bye bye Fi" song, which would only further compound the obvious feeling of superiority that both teams now had over her. The thought: "Thank God Daddy wasn't there today," absentmindedly came into her head.

As the bus crossed the Thames into Hammersmith, only another 15 minutes to go until home, all those girls laughing and jeering *at her* - some with much more relish than was absolutely necessary (she made a mental note of who was enjoying themselves too much at her expense, for future score-settling) actually *hating* her - was proof, if any were needed, that people: women, teammates, were like that British Prime Minister's description of ("Was it the Germans?"): "they're either at your throat or at your feet."

The movements in her stomach, painful as they were becoming ("I think I'm getting a stitch") were nothing compared to a deep, deep burning right in the centre of her heart. She hadn't felt this feeling, well nowhere near as strongly as this, since *that* time, all those years ago....

The Stanleys had just moved to California from Zimbabwe and were still finding their feet in an alien environment. She'd just started her new school, Valley Falls and although the teacher was nice (a Miss Cardoza or Carloza, she couldn't quite remember), the other kids in class kept on laughing at Fi's strange accent, trying to impersonate it in the most inaccurate and simian of ways ("Like monkeys with potatoes in their mouths," she recalled).

However, she loved the house (big, bright, a feeling of finally being "safe") and was exploring the many rooms and semi-opened packing boxes: "It was like a big treasure hunt! Every new box uncovering toys and games and things from back home not seen in months, maybe years!" Fi allowed a tiny internal smile to lighten her mood by just a fraction as she stared out of the bus window.

Susie was still a toddler and was enjoying the treasure hunt too, unpacking box after box in the way that over-excited children tended to do (i.e. all at once, then discarding the contents and moving onto the next one) and the floor was fast disappearing under a carpet of shredded wrapping paper, ripped cardboard boxes and clothes, clothes clothes! Fi and Susie had suddenly come across a doll's house that had been Fi's but was passed down to her little sister, before she had really had much time to get full use out of it. It had also been transferred through every generation of Johnston infant girl for the last 150 years and was unbelievably precious to their Mother: a symbol of all that her family had lost. That's when the fight had started.

"It's mine, it's mine, Mummy gave it to *me*," Susie had squealed, clutching the toddler-sized house to her body as hard as her little arms, which didn't quite wrap round it, could.

"Mummy can't have given it to you as it wasn't hers to give! It's mine and I haven't finished playing with it so you just better let go or I'll *kill* you,"[85] she had replied. Sounded a fair enough threat between siblings of 6 and 3 and a half.

Their Mother, who was usually eerily quiet but today, possibly as a result of one or two mid-afternoon Gin and Tonics, had snapped and started screaming: "Ah've hed jusd'about enuff of you tew! Leave the fucking doll's huss alone, der pair'v you!"

Fi and Susie had stopped and looked up at her, momentarily shocked to hear their Mum swearing, but then the fighting renewed with even more determination, both girls suspecting that whoever won the turf war in the next few seconds was likely to be allowed to keep the spoils of their aggression. Fi tugged at the roof of the antique, dry, wooden house, Susie squeezed onto it for dear life. Then the inevitable happened.

With the "crack" of the roof separating from the base of the house, something in Penny Stanley broke. She walked calmly over to the key cupboard by the kitchen door, picked up her car keys and walked towards the front door.

"Mummy Mummy, where are you going?" Fi had cried out. Penny Stanley said nothing as she descended the front steps, got into her car and drove off.

Penny came back two hours later to find both her girls huddled together in the middle of the living room floor, amidst the discarded clothes and wrapping material, sobbing their eyes and hearts out. Most of the actual tears had long been exhausted, so all that was left was the dry, chest-wracking, hacking convulsing their tiny frames. They hadn't moved since she had left. Penny went over to her daughters to comfort them, but Fi refused any contact with her mother, pulling Susie tighter to her. When the two girls were eventually parted and put to bed, Penny Stanley trying to make amends by cooing baby-like nothings that one would to an infant, hugging them and making an extra effort to read a bedtime story, in a way she hadn't done for years, the incident that afternoon had not been and would never be mentioned again, not even to their father.

In her unfamiliar room, on her own that night, Fi, using her 6 year-old logic and remembering the feeling of total abandonment that had paralysed her on the living room floor and left her tiny heart torn into uncomprehending shreds, made herself a solemn promise: "Love is conditional and can be withdrawn. Never be on the wrong end of the withdrawing again."

Over time, this philosophy had evolved. One way to make sure you were on the right end of the withdrawal phase was to make people like you more than you liked them. This could be achieved by being perfect: hair, body, fitness. Another way though was to simply not care about anybody else. Fi found herself deliberately looking for faults in friends, family, potential partners, total strangers, thus preparing her "Reasons Why I Will Leave You First" list before they did. She had thought she was well on the way to mastering the art of being the perfect object of desire, while at the same time, emotionally, keeping all and everything at bay.

"Nothing can hurt me any more," she whispered to herself as she stared out the bus window. But something in her chest was still smarting.

The bus arrived at its designated stop and Fi got up and walked to the Leprince home, completely ignoring her posing mirror on the way. Letting herself in with her key, she walked past the open living room door where Chloe was watching television, her employer sensing that Fi was not in the happiest of moods, and headed straight for the kitchen. It was the twins' birthday the next day and Mme Leprince had ordered a huge, cream-laden chocolate cake to celebrate. Fi took the cake out of the fridge and laid it on the worktop. She opened the fridge again to remove a can of spray-on Chantilly foaming cream and reaching up to the kitchen cabinet that housed the jams, sweets and condiments, took out a large pot of chocolate spread. Finally, she opened the 2nd kitchen drawer and removed a basting spoon. Balancing cake in one arm (smearing her Hammers' t-shirt), chocolate spread and spraying cream in the other, with the round end of the basting spoon buried in the front pocket of her jeans, she made her way upstairs to her bedroom.

Chapter 40: Fi's Meeting

Stell was away on a work function, (Bet Now! conference in Brighton) so wasn't able to attend training. The Thursday night was bitterly cold and the pre-Christmas frost was likely to lead to most, if not all, of the games being cancelled for the weekend. Caz received an email from Fi that afternoon, detailing an alternative plan of action if training had to be cancelled as well. He hadn't spoken to her since the Relms game, so wanted to gauge how she was feeling. Caz read the email with growing morbid interest.

"Hi Caz, just wanted to say I'm really enjoying the training and the way the team is playing at the moment. If we can't use the pitch this evening though, I'd like to have a general discussion on the ongoing team tactics and strategy situation, if everybody feels we're pulling in the same direction so as to avoid conflictual outcomes during game time and possible off-field communal interaction. I think it's a great way to improve, develop and embrace the team building ethos and make us stronger going forward."

Caz didn't know whether to laugh, cry or just scratch his head until a bald patch appeared. He understood the words (well, *most* of them as he wasn't too sure if "conflictual" even existed), but he just didn't know what any of it *meant*. Then he remembered, "Ah, she's *American*!"

After the previous Sunday's debacle, Fi's stock was definitely lower. The Hammers had made their excuses at Rochester Elms clubhouse and left as soon as they could to retire back to the 'Sheaf. The final insult to injury, that Caz thought was rather appropriate, was for him to order a couple of bottles of the club's finest champagne, so he and the Hammers could toast their victory, plus silently boast of their financial and cultural superiority, at the same time. "Ah, it's like being back at Troubadours!" he smiled to himself as the team headed towards the bus stop.

Back at the 'Sheaf that evening, the girls were too embarrassed by Fi's definite and blatant ignoring of all pre-match instructions, which to be fair she always did anyway, to talk much about it. What had changed though was that rather than be willing to accept her "wilfulness" as per normal, there was a definite feeling of antipathy, as if a part of the team wasn't pulling in the general direction of the rest. Caz had noticed an infinitesimal shift in the girls' allegiance, not so much as anti-Fi but more pro-team. However, he couldn't afford for Fi to feel an outcast in her own team – she was too valuable, when (and if) she ever listened – so the offer of her giving a team talk, in order to get the other players back on her side, couldn't have come at a better moment.

"Besides, with Stell not being at training this evening, what's the worst that could happen?" Emails flew back and forth all afternoon announcing the alternative plans.

As expected that evening, Brendan the Groundsman informed him on arrival at the training ground that the pitch was frozen solid and couldn't be used. Most of the boys had already filed off but a small contingent of the ladies were milling around the entrance hall, a little curious as to what was going to happen next. Brendan, more out of devotion to Fi than duty, had arranged, following strict instructions, approximately a dozen chairs in front of a whiteboard, with a stack of A2 paper neatly attached to it, on the first sheet of which were the words "H & F Players' Meeting", then the date and then underneath, the words, "Fiona Stanley". The meeting area was positioned towards the back of the hallway, away from the icy blasts whipping through the double doors at the front whenever a newcomer entered.

Fi was waiting by the whiteboard, trying rather unsuccessfully to hide her impatience at the latecomers, like a teacher with a less than respectful, but nevertheless fearful, bunch of naughty schoolchildren.

"C'mon guys, we should have started 10 minutes ago," she tried not to hiss impatiently. Everyone, including Caz, sidled into the nearest chairs.

"Right, as Vice Captain, I wanted to start by saying well done to everyone who's contributed so far this season." Various slightly miscomprehending groans followed.

"Where was this leading?" was the general feeling of the group.

Caz hadn't made up his mind yet what this was all about: a genuine attempt to improve team performance or maybe just Fi wanting to show she was still an important member of the team? He remembered stories of American D-Day veterans who, after being injured for a short period, had rejoined their units. They felt the bond had been broken between them and their comrades-in-arms and they needed to do something, often a foolishly brave act of heroism, to re-establish the link. Maybe this was Fi's way of being re-accepted back into the group and re-establishing her status?

"Or maybe she just likes talking bollocks!" was another perhaps more plausible explanation.

"What we gotta do though, if the present momentum is to be maintained, is to be more focussed on tactics and game plan."

"That's rich coming from her," everyone thought, but continued their silence.

Fi tore off the first sheet of paper, folding it neatly onto a small table behind the whiteboard and continued. No-one heard the next few words she uttered as their total attention was transfixed to the next sheet of paper.

Caz could more or less make out 8 stick men in a scrum formation. These were in solid lines of blue felt pen. There was also a three-quarters line of stick men (the backs), numbered 9 - 15. They were also in blue felt pen. This is where he then got lost.

The solid blue lines seemed to morph into broken blue lined figures, which then changed again into dotted blue line figures. These were supposed to represent the same group of players but at different times. There were red lines, dotted, solid, broken, starred, all indicating movements of the blue figures, plus green lines with great swirling arcs and massive arrows, indicating alternative movements. There were also black lines (solid, hashed, starred, broken, some part broken-hashed-*and* starred!) indicating the movement of the ball. This wasn't so bad until you introduced opposition stickmen, also numbered from 1 – 15 but in pink ("Ooh, fuschia, my favourite colour!"

Gwen wanted to interject. Seeing the concentration on Fi's face, she thought better of it).

Fi attempted to explain what the diagram was and how it functioned. After a minute and a half, it was quite clear that she was lost and had to restart. The more flustered she got, the more her Rhodie accent popped unexpectedly into her sentences and the conference delegates, fidgeting in their chairs now and looking at their watches while thinking of what they had in the fridge to eat when they got back home, were getting restless. Caz, under the pretence of going to the loo, collared Brendan in his office, whilst he was watching a Gaelic football game on his miniature black and white tv.

"Brendan, please," he begged. "Could you come along in 2 minutes and say that, as there's no training tonight, you have to shut off all the lights early?"

"But Oi don't Caz, everytin's fine!"

"Please Brendan," Caz implored. "It's for Fi. She's dying out there." He was trying to appeal to the groundsman's obvious crush on his Vice-Captain.

"Oh, Oi don't know," he shook his head. "She'll be pretty mad."

"Brendan, take a look for yourself!"

Brendan poked his head around the corner to hear Fi's wavering voice, confidently declaring: "In order to be the Best of the Best, the Best of a Breed and really be the Big Hitters in this league, we need to develop bespoke solutions to the ongoing problems we experience in game time, which is why I'm proposing this Brain Dump and really Brainstorm this thing. Our Core Competencies are up to scratch, but to give us the Cutting Edge, we need to be more Player-Centric by visualising the process end-to-end. Going Forward and by Joined Up, High level analysis, we can remove some of the Low Hanging Fruit from our team and from our gameplay, but at the same time Managing Expectations from some of the Big Fish, so we don't get Betamaxed by other teams who are thinking more Out Of The Box than us. It's absolutely Mission Critical that we are pro-active, but still focus on the essential so that not only do we achieve the Quick Win, but that we achieve a seamless transition to a Win-Win situation."

She paused for breath. No-one said a word.

"C'mon guys," she encouraged. "We're all Team Players here. If we Take Ownership now and see the Big Picture, we can all Upskill and be part of the future of ladies' rugby at this club!"

"Fockin' hell!" exclaimed Brendan, "it's worse than Oi thought!" Recovering slightly and now totally complicit, he asked Caz, in a conspiratorial whisper, "When do you want me to kill the loigts?"

"Wait till I get back to my seat, then give it about a minute," Caz whispered back.

"No problem," he replied, his shock at the flurry of meaningless words being replaced by the chivalric desire to save the object of his affection from further verbal self-immolation.

After Caz had returned to his seat, Fi was in mid-"Back Of The Envelope Bag of Snakes Blue Ocean Opportunity" when the whole building went black.

"Sorry ladies, Caz, but we have to close up early. Council regulations when there's no training." Then he added a heart-felt, "Sorry Fi." Without adding the, "It's for your own good," that he wanted to.

"It's alright Brendan. We can carry this on over at the 'Sheaf."

"Either she was completely insensitive to the mood in the room or she was just bonkers." Caz wondered.

But, by this time, all the girls had taken advantage of the darkness to scarper into the wordless peace of the south Fulham night.

Chapter 41: Christmas Cheer

When training resumed after the Christmas break, Stell had already had residing in her inbox for over a week, an email from her Vice Captain announcing that she was leaving the club with immediate effect. If this had happened only weeks earlier, Stell would have been panic-stricken and done all in her power to try to change Fi's mind. Now though, all she felt was relief.

The mood at the first training session after Christmas was one of apprehension for the beasting[86] that they knew awaited them after their likely gastronomic indulgences of the holiday ("But Caz doesn't believe in fitness!" was their unconvincing attempt at reassurance) and sadness at the departure of their Most Valuable Player of the last two seasons, which some had suspected and had made bets on during the holidays, especially after her pre-Christmas "meeting". However, there was also a sense of progression. The club was growing (25 at training for the first time ever!) and it was inevitable that at some stage, people would move either on, up or out.

The holidays had brought with them the usual mixed bag of news and gossip, with family members who normally never spend more than a few hours with each other *a year* electing to share the same space for days on end, whilst over-eating, over-drinking and, most importantly for rugby players, not having the opportunity to release any build up of tensions by running, lifting weights or hitting something!

Long-running arguments, family disputes, "put to bed but only for the time being", disagreements would find their way to resurface, between the hugs and genuine warm welcomes of the Christmas Eve and the frosty and impatient goodbyes on Boxing Day, tinged with relief at the lifting of the siege and silent vows NEVER to do this again. Until next year.

The Theakston Mansion had been relatively quiet. Jake and Huggy had come to visit, Huggy with a new girlfriend in tow (Stell would have loved to befriend at least one of his ever-changing stream of young ladies, but they just weren't around long enough for it to be worth the effort) and Jake tactlessly constantly enquiring why she still lived at home ("Cos London's bloody expensive! We can't all be Investment Bankers like YOU!")

Most irritatingly though, he kept on trying to mention what Dad was doing, at which point, Huggy always found an excuse to leave the room. She was mildly interested, but not enough to actually ask about him.

Matt from home (she still, deep down, referred to Milesborough as "home") also paid a visit. Working in London now, he still hadn't got over his childhood crush on her. "Why not flirt just a teeny bit," she'd thought to herself. "After all, there's no reason why not...."

Carlton Edwards' Christmas involved flying to Denmark to spend some time with his children. Britta had been cold and detached ("No change there then") but somehow had managed to convey that she was willing to consider a reconciliation (if he'd come to live in Denmark, obviously). He somehow managed to leave with him being committed not to move to Denmark and his future-ex-wife convinced he was definitely going to. "The old Anglo-Scandinavian communication skills were thus working as per normal," he thought as the plane left Copenhagen Airport.

Gwen and Ily's wedding plans were in full swing and she had chosen not only *the dress*, but the bridesmaids' dresses - as Maid of Honour, Stell had to be head-locked into agreeing to allow herself to be bedecked in pink (Hollywood Cerise) - the matching flowers on the tables for the reception, the co-ordinated decorations for the room, and 103 other things. There still remained a further 761 assorted items that needed to be attended to (Ily had made a list) so spending the 25th with his family in Whitebeach was hardly a chore at all. For her, the holidays literally flew by.

Talk of weddings though had definitely hit a sore spot for some.

One of the former players, an Aussie called Olivia, had finally decided to make an honest woman of her long-term partner (a Psycho turned Hater) who, after many years alternatively scowling and not watching from the sidelines, had convinced her to stop playing. They had organised a Civil Partnership service to be held in nearby Kensington during the off-season summer months and all the long-serving Hammers, who had played alongside Olivia two seasons before, were invited and looked forward to what offered to be a huge, posh-frocked, summer piss-up.

Larry and Siobhan, spending Christmas in the bosom of her family in South Wales, were of differing opinions towards the forthcoming wedding.

Her sister Caitlin was too busy fussing over the new baby ("A girl!" Sib had congratulated herself) to spend much time fawning over Larry as usual. He had tried to bond with Caits' husband Peter, but the combination of pompousness, superior-than-thou sarcasm and physical weakness that he often found in the English really stuck in his craw. "If you're going to say something, why not just come out and say it!" he had thought.

He'd run out of games to play with Dylan, Sib's 3-year-old nephew so now, he was bored. It didn't help that one or two of the visitors to Sib's parent's huge house, set in acres of green, exceptionally wet fields, made no secret of the fact that he was a foreigner not welcome in these parts[87], but at least he wasn't English so hostilities were kept to just the odd glower or two.

It was on Boxing Day that the subject of Olivia's impending wedding had come up. For once, he and Peter seemed to share the same opinion: there was something innately "not normal" about people of the same sex getting married. He'd made the mistake of expressing this in front of Sib, who, after three days of being confined to home with her increasingly frustrated Australian and not being able to hit anything, snapped, in the cold, calculated way that only she could.

"Darling," she said. This was always a bad sign. She never called him "darling" apart from to lull him into a false sense of security before the onslaught commenced. He didn't answer.

"Do you know in how many species homosexuality is found?" Peter's ears pricked up, sensing a bit of sport at the expense of the Australian. Sib's Dad and Caits, knowing full well this tone of voice from arguments of old, shook their heads in despair, Caitlin suddenly busying herself with tiny Rhiannon. Rhiannon pushed her away; she wasn't going to miss the next bit of action even for breast-milk. Sib's Mum was going to cut her daughter off, but Larry answered, "No, how many?"

"Oh dear," Mrs Owen thought. "Here goes....."

" 450," Sib answered. Nobody knew this. Attention was sharpened.

"Darling," she continued. "Do you know in how many species homophobia is found?"

Sensing a trap, Larry didn't say anything. His head made a shaking movement though to betray his answer.

"Only one." Sib allowed this statistic to sink in. "Which of the two would you say is "not normal" now: homosexuality or homophobia?"

This wasn't fair. She was trying to portray him as a raving homophobe; he'd lived in Sydney (for a short while) for Christ's sake!

He floundered for a response. "People are supposed to be together to have children!" he protested. "Gay couples can't have children!!!" "Good point, well made," he thought to himself.

"Do you want to have children, Dearest?" Sib asked.

Larry thought back to the conversation they had had weeks before, when he'd made a statement the equivalent of: "If I mess my children up as much as my Dad has with us, I wouldn't want to have any." He knew that Sib had filed this conversation for future use (when most women get hysterical in an argument with their partners, Sib just got historical[88]). Not wishing to incriminate himself, he managed an, "Er, er..."

"So," the enemy infantry were in retreat, all that was left was for Sib's cavalry to give chase and hack them down, one by one, "are you normal, Larry?"

"Hell yeah!!" He could answer that one. However, he felt another trap had been sprung.

"So, if having a percentage of gay is "normal" in most species, and we have established that you are normal, correct?" she didn't pause for an answer, "and all species are comprised of individuals, then logically, all individuals in a species should contain elements anywhere between 0% and 100% gay."

Larry was just about following. Sib's Dad wanted to leave the room to spare his future son-in-law's blushes, but it was fascinating! Caits and Mrs Owen were pretending to be busy doing other things, but didn't leave the room either. Peter and Rhiannon though were lapping it up and couldn't wait for the next word. They weren't disappointed.

"What percentage of gay are YOU Larry?"

"What?!!!" All were shocked, Sib was really going for the jugular and she had the "take no prisoners look" in her eye. She pressed on.

"Have you ever been turned on by the thought of another man naked? You know, when you're in the showers with your team mates, have you ever wanted to just reach out and grab another man's bum? Or even checked the length of your team mates' c..."

"Siobhan, I REALLY THINK THAT'S ENOUGH NOW!" Mr Owen interjected just in time. As her Dad *never* raised his voice, when he did, shutting up was the best policy. Peter stifled a chortle and Rhiannon, not understanding a word but sensing the heightened tension, virtually clapped her hands with glee.

"Look, she's smiling," Caits said, to change the subject, only just realising that this probably wasn't the best conversation-changer she'd ever come out with. Nevertheless, all turned their attention to the 2-month old, except Sib and Larry. Sib reached over to her glass of red wine and took an elegant sip, as if nothing had happened. Larry's whole face burned with thinly-concealed fury and humiliation.

"This is not over," he vowed, still smarting.

Chapter 42: The Curious Case of Megan Mendez

The post-Christmas sense of loss that the Hammers felt with the departure of Fi was more than compensated for by the arrival at training of a few new players, one being a former Argentinean rugby international by the name of Megan Mendez. Tall, slim, blonde? ("How do you get blonde from Argentina?"[89] Gwen had asked), Megan looked super-fit, extremely athletic, spoke fluent Spanish, Welsh and had come to London, on her own, to improve her English, plus of course, get a job. She had a Latin American cool, sexiness to her whole persona that re-ignited some of the feelings of envy that Fi had amongst the team.

"Oh no, not another one!" Stell had initially thought. However, Megan was open and friendly and completely different to Fi, in terms of character, in every way.

On reflection, the fact that Megan was from Argentina was the only thing that could be verified about her (Stell having seen a copy of her passport for club registration purposes).

Suspicions started to arise, firstly from Caz, when he saw her train. In fact, she didn't train at all. Megan was introduced to the girls, her future teammates, and even though she had her kit on, she stood around talking for pretty much the whole training session.

"Funny," he thought. "If I'd joined a new team, and was quite clearly a good few leagues above the level of my teammates, I'd be eager to show them exactly what I'd got." He put it down to the cold, or maybe post-Christmas rustiness.

The first game of the second half of the season was at home to the Masingford Dragons and the much-improved Hammers were expecting a comfortable win over the bottom of the table club. Caz and Stell were eager to see their most recent acquisition in action and with Siobhan ringing up to say she would be late (after an extensive and fruitless search for her kit, again. She had to wait for the clubhouse to open to buy new), they had selected the Argentinean to cover for her at no. 7 in a re-arranged back row. When Sib turned up, Megan would move to the wing (in Katia's absence, who hadn't returned from Christmas back in Germany), her favoured position and the one at which she'd been capped for her country.

It was obvious that Megan was no no.7. She was always in the wrong place at the wrong time and even though apparently quite fit, she couldn't keep up with play. By mid-way through the 1st half when Siobhan arrived, the Hammers were already 20 points up and Megan had not touched the ball.

Caz called his captain over for a mini-conference. In order to bring Megan more into the game, they switched her to wing in place of another newby, Christy. Coach and Captain had been working on a move in training that would put the winger into acres of space and then all would be able to see her roast her opposite number, leaving her for dead in the wake of her searing acceleration.

When the ball eventually worked its way to her, Megan *did* catch it, after what seemed like a deliberate comic juggle (she was standing too far forward and had to reach behind to take the pass), but when all were expecting a burst of devastating speed on the outside of her opponent, Megan stopped, cut inside and looked to pass the ball back from where it had come.

"Eh?" Caz and Stell thought simultaneously as they exchanged puzzled glances. They then looked sheepishly away, realising that they were staring at each other for too long...

The rest of the game followed a similar pattern. Virtually all the Hammers were able to pour through the gaps which appeared everywhere in the Masingford line and chalk their names on the scoresheet.

All except Megan.

When she did catch the ball, preceding comic juggle being standard performance by now, she never even attempted to beat her man, preferring to always pass back inside, sometimes even having to run sideways or backwards in order to find someone to pass to.

It was getting beyond a joke now and Caz (refusing to substitute her as he just *had* to see how this was all going to end) and the other spectators: BAGS, men's team players, friends and a slowly growing army of parents on the sidelines began to shout, "Run Forrest run!"[90] whenever the ball came anywhere near her.

With only seconds to go until the end of the game, Megan was presented with a golden opportunity: only 40 metres out with one defender to beat. The crescendo of more Forrest Gump shouts from the sideline had now built up so loudly (probably even being contributed to by the Dragons' travelling support) that, unable to ignore them any longer, Megan finally decided to put her head down, pin her ears back and sprint for the corner.

Up until that moment, very few people had ever witnessed a fellow human being running through treacle before.

Megan Mendez was so slow that time seemed to be not standing still, but running backwards. Really, really slowly.

The defending Dragon, a front row forward completely out of position as she was just too exhausted to keep up with play, initially had not even bothered to attempt to give chase, her team being so far behind and her opposite number being so much more athletic-looking that it seemed pointless. Suddenly though, given the distinct lack of speed of the girl attempting to race around her, she was filled with renewed hope. This was a race she could possibly win and restore some dented pride to her outclassed team. Sucking in a huge gasp of air, she fired up her short, chubby legs and catapulted herself forward in the direction of Megan Mendez.

Later that evening, the crowd would crown the "Snail Race" between the Megalobulimus Oblongus (large, rather attractive South American) and the Helix Pomatia (short, fat, British) as being the highlight of the match for entertainment value.[91]

Both teams, rather than trying to participate in the slo-mo action unfolding before them, had cheered on their respective teammates as they both crawled to the corner flag, the red-shirted Megalobulimus reaching out a tentacle to ground the ball over the tryline just before the dark purple and green clad

Helix brought her to ground. Even the exaggerated cheers of team Megalobulimus seemed in slow motion.

In the clubhouse afterwards, Megan Mendez was awarded Man of the Match by the opposition, which she accepted with good grace, downing her dirty pint with aplomb. At least she'd done *that* before. It was clear to anyone who'd ever previously witnessed a game of rugby being played that seeing one was all the new Hammers' winger had ever done. And even that was doubtful.

The thing that the Hammers were curious about was *why* she had tried to convince everyone she was an international rugby player, when it would be so easy to spot that she wasn't. If she wanted to join a rugby club, all she had had to do was tell the truth about her abilities and experience and she would have been accommodated like all the Newbies were, starting at the appropriate level and when she was good enough, getting a run out in the last few minutes of an unimportant game.

It was only later on that evening, after the drink had begun flowing and bruised warriors from the previous evening were being comforted by camp followers and players of today that Megan Mendez' true reasons for joining the Hammers became apparent.

Gwen had tried to find a relatively secluded corner of the pub so she could text her Ily in peace and quiet; he was on manoeuvres with his unit so hadn't been able to attend the game. In the back entrance to the 'Sheaf's kitchen, barely hiding behind the partially-closed door, Megan Mendez was on her knees, head bobbing back and forth, in front of a paralytic Larry Mitchelle, who was groaning in what could have been either pleasure or the discomfort of the gassy dry-retching that heralds a serious bout of vomiting. Gwen could make out Megan's hands fondling Larry's testicles which were visible outside his open fly as her head enthusiastically buried itself in his crotch.

"Ah, so that's where she gets her ball-juggling skills from then!" Gwen thought, on her way to report the cardinal sin of BAG-swapping (punishment: immediate excommunication) back to Siobhan. "Thank God I've got Ily."

Chapter 43: Gwen's ILY Part 1

From the moment Gwen arrived at the training ground, the other Hammers knew something was wrong.

She'd obviously felt guilty for having to report Larry's infidelity to Sib that night, but after the screaming shouting match between them outside the pub (Sib's cool disappearing along with Megan Mendez, who was never to be heard from again) and the girls' commiserations with a trying-to-be-strong-while-wailing-like-a-banshee Siobhan Owen ("He's not worth it", "There are more fish in the sea", "I never liked him anyways"), not really helping to stem the sobs. In fact, they seemed to have had the opposite effect). All seemed to have been forgotten over the last few weeks (except by Sib).

Gwen's obvious distress tonight was for another reason entirely.

For many years now, Gwynth Evans had been waging a one-woman war against the popular misconceptions often associated with Women Who Play With Oval Balls[92]. She had set out to prove that it was possible to be a rugby girl *and* be feminine at the same time and had cunningly chosen a subtle way to subliminally influence all she encountered and convince them that she was indeed the embodiment of the two apparently diverse positions.

Gwen thus chose to adorn her life with the colour pink whenever it was humanly possible! Clothes were the easy part, it was things like a pink toaster, pink armchairs, pink beer mats and a pink car (a tiny Fiat Cinquecento – "Thank God for the Italians and their strange ways!" she thought) which were the real challenges. Work colleagues, team mates, family members alike were now unsurprised to find Gwen bedecked in dizzying arrays of amaranths, fuschias, cerises, roses, salmons and magentas. Even when attire did not allow for her colour preference, such as in the heat of battle on the pitch or at training, bright pink-hued lipsticks, with eye-shadows and mascaras of similar and sometimes un-matching shades were always in evidence, so Gwen's pretty face, sparkling eyes and constant smile gave her the permanent look of a cute and, despite her growing reputation amongst the boys' teams, innocent little girl. The Gwen who appeared at training that evening looked anything but.

Her face was red and swollen with crying. Any attempts of mascara from the previous evening had long been partially washed away by the tears, leaving dark streaks over cracking skin where eyes and nose had been wiped too hard by first tissues, then toilet roll and, once the others had run out, rough kitchen towel. The pink of the eye liner had mingled with the salt of the tears to further sting the blue eyes which seemed to shine out even more brightly than normal. Silent as she approached the changing room doors, Gwen trembled.

Stell was the first to see her and rushed over. "What's happened?" she said, her voice louder than intended through worry and shock. Gwen fell into her arms and began to sob deeply. The other girls just stared, not knowing what to say but all pretty sure of what they'd been taking bets on for a few weeks now.

Eventually, through the tears, Gwen was able to let escape the words, "He's left me."

Gwen's ILY was a nice guy. An officer and a gentleman, he had been brought up in mostly male environments (boarding school, university, Sandhurst, then on deployment) and had never really had much time for the fairer sex. They were alright, he supposed, but they seemed almost like an unfathomable and strange breed. There were the examples of his Mum, his older sisters, fellow students at Uni and the like but, since the rejection of his advances by one of his sister's friends (he was 11, she was 13, she just laughed, kissed him on the head and told him to "run along like a good little fellow") he really hadn't thought too much about them apart from for the obvious (looking nice, making the tea, good for a shag and producing children). He'd also never been into dancing and couldn't really see the point of small talk, so his teenage years of attending discos and trying to "cop a feel" of whichever young ladies were left at the end of the evening, after boosting his confidence with considerable amounts of Dutch courage, were a nightmare from which he couldn't wait to escape. Besides, it always seemed to be "other" blokes who got off with the best girls anyway. He didn't really mind though, as he and his mates were quite used to "trawling the bargain basement" for any women that the flash gits hadn't already reeled in. The best bit of advice he'd received was "always go for a fat bird; they're more grateful."

After one or two uninspiring attempts at relationships and at about the time when his old trawler mates were, one by one, getting hitched, he had the tremendous luck to meet a "Prime A bit of Totty" (Gwen) at a good friend's wedding and, over the course of a few short weeks, the future was looking bright!

He thought Gwen was amazing. Compared to his normal fare, she was really beautiful, had gorgeous, wavy blonde hair, was enormously clever, well educated, great tits, was a super sportswoman (played rugby), had a brilliant body (for a prop, that is) and was everything that those really fit women who got off with the flash blokes were: all that he'd always wanted. He literally couldn't wait to get back to his army pals to tell them whom he was dating and the phone-load of pictures he took of her were sufficient to whet their appetites for when they would finally meet her.

The presentation of future Mrs ILY passed like a triumphant return of the King and Queen-to-be. His Mum got out the best china (he didn't know his Mum had *any* china), his brother tried to flirt a bit (would be bad form not to, obviously), his sisters looked on approvingly although initially, keeping a bit of a distance and when he took her to the local pub, none of his mates, nor any of the women who frequented that establishment, could believe that *he* had pulled *her*! "Stick that in your pipe and smoke it, boys!"

ILY was now a happy man. He was walking with a spring in his step as, irrespective as to what happened during his working day or when he was on deployment, he knew that, waiting for him at home, was this angel who was (as a result of, again unbeknownst to him, copious amounts of practice) unfathomably good in bed!

And boy, how good was good!

The first time they slept together, ILY was not drunk as had become a custom with his one-night-stands-but-hoping-for-mores. He wasn't even slightly tipsy. It was in late afternoon, at her flat in Hammersmith and Gwen had gone to the enormous effort of lighting huge candles (French rose), with silk drapes (in Spigelia marilandica or Indian pink: one of her friends had recently returned from Goa) and cushions (lavender) over the 1½ sized bed in her tiny shared flat. The blinds (coral) were half-closed and the lighting (Thulian)) was dimmed, with the light aroma of agarbathi incense giving the room the glow and smell of a mystical, magical, maharajah's tent.

Gwen had taken him by the hand and led him over to the bed, kissing him gently on the cheek, then lips, then lowering herself onto the bed before beckoning him to join her. She then laid him down, on his front, and softly, lovingly, kneaded his shoulders, working her hands down his back before caressing his buttocks.

"Fucking hell," he thought as his hard-on pressed into the bed. "Thank God I made myself come beforehand or I certainly would now!"

When they eventually made love, which lasted not as long as Gwen would have hoped ("Not bad, but definitely can be improved," she thought), ILY could not help himself from thinking that it was all a dream, that this sort of thing never happened to him, that she would eventually wake up and realise she'd made a horrendous mistake. He lay on the bed, head nuzzling into the back of her neck – "Man, she smelt so good," he thought – nervously expecting her to be disappointed, to be riddled with regret, to get up, get dressed and shoo him out of the door as quickly as she could. Gwen turned round to face him.

"Here goes, I knew it was too good to be true," he thought. ILY braced himself for the inevitable rejection.

Gwen kissed his chest and reached for his now satiated penis, holding it gently but firmly in her hand.

Looking deeply into his eyes, Gwen whispered, "I really love you."

A man is marooned on a desert island with a beautiful model. After weeks of platonic survival, needs must and an amorous relationship begins. A short while later, the woman turns to the man and says, "Darling, you don't seem happy. Is it me?"

The man says, "Would you do one thing for me?"

"Anything," comes the reply.

"I've made a wig, a false beard and some men's clothing that should fit you. Could you pretend to be my mate Billy? He's from Ireland so could you put on a strong Dublin accent for me as well please?"

Perplexed, the woman does as requested.

The man pretends to make a phone call and the woman answers. "Hello," she says in a strong Dublin accent.

"Hello, Billy," the man says. "Is that you?"

"It is," she says. "Whatdyoo want?"

"You'll never guess who I'm shagging!"

"So, how was it?" The entire table in the Officers' Mess hall went quiet in anticipation of ILY's bedroom tales.

"She is A-M-A-ZING!!!" ILY replied. "I mean, WOW!!!"

"Did she do anything kinky?" asked one of the juniors. Someone threw a scrunched up napkin at him.

"Now, that would be telling." Disappointed faces, so ILY continued, "Actually, she did EVERYTHING!"

"You're joking, right?" came another voice.

"Absolutely not! Bloody hell, THIS is definitely what all the writing and fuss is about," ILY blurted out. Then, realising that this might make it seem as if up until that point, he'd only ever had rubbish sex with people he didn't really fancy or who didn't even fancy him but were just desperate, he added, "She's not as good as that stripper in Hamburg though, remember?"

"You did NOT shag that stripper mate! The state you were in, you would have needed a flag pole to keep it up!"

"Yeah, a very small flag pole!" said another colleague.

"It's not the length that's important," retorted ILY, "It's the width, plus what you do with it! And remember boys, the best fillies only let the best jockeys ride them!"

"So, when Gwen eventually bucks you off, bagsy I go next!" A chorus of "No, me's!" followed.

"Please form an orderly queue, gentlemen!" ILY conducted, smiling as broadly as he ever had during the whole course of his life. He felt a renewed respect emanating from this little band of brothers as he now had something that they wanted.

The evening continued in light-hearted banter mode, with the topic of conversation swinging in all directions. Despite all the pleasantries and good humour, ILY *knew* that, the one thing linking the thoughts of all the officers around the table, if not at the forefront then at the very least lurking around in the darker corners of their minds, was Gwen.

He now had the thing that he'd always dreamt about: a good-looking, presentable, sex-maniac GIRLFRIEND on his arm that the other blokes wanted. No more "plus ones" for him on invites! Maybe it was a bit soon to be discussing wedding plans - "if you like it then you gotta put a ring on it!" – but ILY's whole attitude to everything began to change. The "Desperate: Please Avoid At All Costs!" sign that had been branded onto his forehead ever since his discoing days was slowly disappearing, along with its "Fear of Rejection" and "I'm Not Worthy" mates.

Problems at work which before had seemed almost insurmountable suddenly were of miniscule importance, as the most important thing was waiting for him at home and solutions became a relatively straightforward (and slightly boring) chore. His superiors noticed a change in the man and the buzz of promotion talk filled his working environment.

ILY even looked at women differently now. Before, there was almost an antipathy, an innate sense that they knew they had something that he wanted to play with, but they wouldn't give it to him out of spite, taunting him and goading him with the proximity, but inaccessibility - to him at least - of the toys they so openly displayed. Once or twice, when the frustrations had grown in him to fever pitch, he could even imagine *taking* their toys away from them...

Really attractive women usually aroused in him conflicting emotions of desire and jealousy, especially if they were with another man whom he considered was no way near as good as him. Now though, he simply didn't care! If a woman looked great, he could appreciate how great she looked, openly and without rancour[93].

He could now have conversations with women without thinking of anything other than what they were actually discussing, the almost perma-sexual frustration having completely disappeared as well and, with a Gwen-accented change in dress sense (pink shirts were introduced but he made a desperate, even though ultimately futile stand over pink foulards), the confidence of the well dressed and well-serviced man made him much more interesting to the opposite sex. Women before who wouldn't have given him the time of day, now stopped to talk, possibly because he looked at their faces as opposed to a few inches lower, but also, after they had met Gwen, the ancient female rivalry seemed to kick in. ILY let slip once to his mates, "Before, when I was desperate, I couldn't shag for love nor money, now that I have a fiancée, women are throwing themselves at me!"

"I'll be your wingman, if you don't mind: sloppy seconds is my style!" was the unsympathetic reply.

ILY was in love and in awe and life was great. There was only one teeny, weeny problem though...

The rugger bugger girls *really* did not like him. He loved seeing his Amazonian on the pitch, flying into tackles, pushing for all her life in the middle of that scrum thing. Once or twice, he'd even seen her run with the ball! However, when he was there on the sidelines, or in the pub afterwards, some of the girls were even bigger than him! They all had their in-jokes and funny stories and all had so much history on and with each other (the phrase "Bournemouth 7s" always brought forth huge guffaws of conspiratorial laughter) that he basically would never be accepted by any of them. Even the nice ones looked at him with a sort of thinly-veiled contempt.

The only other blokes there were either coaches who were former rugby players themselves or current rugby players, thus they were normally all quite big with bulging muscles and egos to match. Again, all seemed to share a real disdain for anyone who hadn't spent half their life covered in mud while being sat on by other rugger buggers.

ILY had never really been particularly big nor sporty, and basic training in the army had nearly killed him. Sat behind a desk intercepting enemy communications was what he did and he enjoyed it, but once, when he was talking about work to the beautiful American one, she quite unashamedly actually *did* close her eyes in sleep.

ILY knew he would never be one of them and that, as close-knitted as they were, Gwen would choose them over him every single time. In fact, he was convinced that it was only a matter of time before Gwen woke up, looked across the bed at the skinny, nerdy officer lying next to her, punched him in the face and kicked him out of her life forever.

The more that emerged about Gwen's "colourful" past, most of which was either invented or exaggerated by her team mates, just to wind him up, the more uncomfortable he became. "She's normally only ever gone for people like *them*. Why is she going out with *me*?" he found himself asking more and more. At particularly insecure times, he imagined that Gwen was only seeing him as she'd gone through most of the rugby boys at the club and just needed new meat. "All four teams, probably."

He drained the last of his beer and looked out of the window of his local towards the little village square. The early spring day was bright and clear, although still cold, and he was participating in a late afternoon, day-off tipple. He stared down into his empty pint glass.

The barmaid came over to clean the table. She was short, enormously curvy, with black hair, blue eyes and a rather naughty little inflection to the corner of her lips. "Don't usually see you here of an afternoon," she smiled. "Can I get you anything else?" She lingered over the table, lips slightly parted, her large breasts casting a shadow over the empty glass in his hands. ILY had been trying it on with her for as long as he could remember and, if anything, had made *minus* progress. After he'd given up his pursuit as a Mission Impossible and, coincidentally, after she'd met Gwen a few weeks earlier, the barmaid's attitude to him had thawed and he hadn't even noticed. Until now.

The world of opportunity seemed to be opening up and here he was, thinking about getting married and slamming its doors firmly shut. Forever.

"Gwen would probably end up leaving me anyway," he tried to convince himself. "I think I'll have another one please Betty. And have one yourself."

"Ooh, you're a bad influence you are! I knock off in half an hour. I can have one with you then, if you like," Betty smiled, and twirled away triumphantly.

Things were definitely looking up.

Chapter 44: Gwen's ILY part 2

Gwen was useless at training that night. She tried to participate but mentally, was in a totally different place. Caz had been told about what had happened so was nowhere near as harsh to her as he would have otherwise been and when she said she'd finish early and retire to the 'Sheaf, after the 15th dropped ball, he breathed a sigh of relief. She couldn't face the hour and a half journey back to Whitebeach where she'd moved in order to be with ILY, so was going to kip on Stell's floor in the Theakston Mansion round the corner.

Back in the 'Sheaf, pint of Snakebite and Black in hand, Gwen had a few minutes to herself before the other girls finished training and came back to commiserate - and probably gloat - in equal measure. All these break-ups occurring at the same time, miraculously coinciding with the team finding its confidence both on and off the pitch, they could lead to players just not bothering with anyone outside the close-knit band of sisters at all.

She remembered the original conversations with the girls all those months ago after she'd first met her ILY at the wedding.

For weeks after she'd met him, ILY had been sending texts, making phone calls, sending sweet, even though a bit soppy, cards and generally behaving like the true gentlemen he was purported to be. She had told the girls that she had had a drunken snog at the wedding ("As everyone does, right?"), but hadn't really expected much to come of it afterwards, so the fairytale courtship thing was a nice surprise and something she could impress her teammates with. Gwen may have possibly been guilty of boosting him up a bit too much, for maximum self-esteem effect, as it was very unlikely they'd ever get to meet him, so when the relationship began to take on the appearance of something more permanent and she had to get out the pictures, they were definitely underwhelmed.

"He's not very cute?" said Mads, subtle as usual. Sometimes, the logic that accompanies an IT Development Consultant of "telling it like it is" can be hurtful.

"He's lovely though!" Gwen heard herself protesting.

"He's not very big either," observed Mands. "I could snap him in two with one bite."

"To be fair Mands, you could snap anyone in two with one bite," Caz quipped.

"Nah mate," she responded, "with YOU, Coach, it'd be one and a half."

"You should see him in his uniform, Richard Gere eat your heart out!" Gwen pushed further, already starting to feel as if she were protesting just a bit too much. The other girls felt it too.

"I thought you'd be more interested in seeing him *out* of uniform," contributed Fi. Unusual for her to participate in the banter, but when such a clear-cut opportunity presented itself to score a few easy points, hell, why not?

The slight pause before Gwen replied with a, "Seeing is believing!" and the almost imperceptible hollowness of the cheery smile accompanying the line was all the girls needed to convince themselves. Individual mental notes, soon to be made into a public (minus Gwen) sweepstake on how long this particular ILY would last, were made, some gleefully with more relish than a super double tower burger with cheese, others with regretful familiarity. If that were not enough, Stell changed the subject of conversation a little too swiftly in order to spare her friend any further unconvincing defence of her choice of bloke but, the truth, although for now unspoken, was out there: after probably the umpteenth time of going for a rugby-playing Mr Right, Gwen was settling for a Mr Right Now.

The girls chatted about the upcoming games and how, with present performances, there was even a chance of winning the league and gaining promotion. Enthusiasm for the topic grew and all, except Gwen, seemed to have forgotten the uncomfortable conversation of a few moments earlier. The smile was transfixed but her ears burned. "Why oh bloody why can't they just be happy for me?!!" she protested silently. "They know that all I want is to be happy and find someone who loves me. Why don't they think I love him, 'cos I do!!"

However, even she knew this wasn't quite true.

She'd grown up in a tiny corner of South Wales where men played rugby. In fact, as there was little else to do in her community, women played rugby too. Children played, babies played and, it wouldn't go amiss to see a few sheep tossing the ball around before getting in some serious grazing. In short, if you didn't play rugby, you were probably a closet footballer and should relocate to North Wales. Immediately.

So, the fittest and most fancy-able blokes in Galwick were to be found at the rugby club. As there was very little else in the way of permanent employment (mines closed down ages ago, most of the youth, the very second they were old enough, pushed off to the bigger cities to study or find work), young hopefuls from the age of Walking Upright prayed and trained for the day when one of the frequently visiting scouts from a bigger club, or even the mighty WRFU, would reach down from on high and yank them into the world of superstardom.

Once a professional rugby player, the Young Hopeful would hardly ever grace the likes of Galwick RFC again, at least not until well after he'd finished playing, or if he did, he would be virtually untouchable, being surrounded by super-skinny Cardiff or Swansea WAGS[94].

The only chance then of being with a rugby star of the future was to identify their potential well before the coaches did and get into their heart - and their pants - before others cynically tried to get into their wallet (and their pants). Before the age of 16, Gwen had fallen in love with and subsequently lost, to Neath or Pontypridd RFCs or Marks and Spencers Swansea or Bristol Uni, far more potential "Loves of her Lives" than she cared to remember. However, she remembered every single one and each one had taken just a tiny piece of her heart with them.

And, she really had fallen in love.

Being fairly short and of a sturdy (definitely NOT thick-set) build, she was automatically selected to play front row from the age of 5. Taking a keen interest in players in her position from games on the telly or at Galwick RFC, there was something about the men front row players that she found magnetic.

Firstly, they looked like bears.[95]

For every heroic (although in modern warfare, totally pointless) cavalry charge, for every sweeping "Shock and Awe" tank attack, for every aerial and artillery blitz, at some point in the proceedings, there will have to be a hand-to-hand, front line, knee-deep-in-mud infantry struggle in some godforsaken trench or bombed-out building where bayonets, knives, shovels, teeth, bare-hands, everything and anything is used to kill the enemy or be killed. This was the front row.

Indeed, so much went on in those few murderous and fetid inches[96] that often these frontline warriors didn't give two hoots about the actual result of the match and, with the opposition fellow members of the unofficial Front Row Union (positions 1 to 3), talked about "the real score" i.e. how many scrums they won or lost. They were almost smug in the knowledge that having a good scrum doesn't guarantee the team victory, but having a bad scrum will certainly guarantee the team defeat.

The raw combination of the power and the bravery necessary for their role (which, consequently led to facial scars, broken teeth and noses, cauliflower ears and sometimes "Props' Lump"[97]) meant that, to Gwen, they were *far* more manly than the prissy, forever-dieting, pretty boy "conventionally attractive" backs. Not for them the salads of the self-conscious as the more they ate – and boy, did they love their food and drink! – the more muscle they could build on top of the bulk and the more potent they became on the pitch.

And in bed!

Physicality, brute strength and pleasure was what they were all about and there would be no self-obsessed soul-searching as this great, hairy ape-like man would eagerly lap at every part of your body before (and after) jumping on and giving you the sort of rogering that could (and often did!) leave your head spinning, your heart fluttering virtually out of your chest and your nether regions tingling in excitement for days!

They also had big hearts to go with their laughing, prankster, devil-my-care attitudes and thus could be much more fun than most other men; rugby player or not.

Gwen wasn't a "slut" as such. She just knew what she wanted and loved and couldn't see why if she wanted to sleep with someone who she fancied the arse of (just like the rugby boys did), she couldn't just shag and be done with it. The body is said to remember feelings, good and bad. Perfumes can often remind you of certain people, the smell in the air of certain situations, one familiar scene could remind you of a time and a place when you were happier, sadder, lonelier. For Gwen, Front Row Forward reminded her of sex. And bloody good sex at that!

She also got a thrill from the fear that some of the other girls displayed when asked to prop and she positively LOVED the feeling of power that being right in the thick of the action gave her, especially when her front five were steamrollering over the opposition front five.

The cuts, bruises, sore knees, necks, shoulders, back and shins and the black eyes were all worn as badges of pride on the Monday morning at the hospital where she worked as a Rehabilitation Physio. Now that the Hammers were winning virtually every game and by big scores as well - ("Won 8 out of 10 of our own scrums last week and 2 out of 5 of the oppos!" Gwen congratulated herself on the tube into work. "Oh, and the team won") - the local Hammersmith and Fulham Gazette had started covering the games, with a view to probably doing a front (or rather back) page end-of-season spread, with photos of the team lifting the much coveted Rugby Football Union Women's South East West League 2 cup! Wow...

Colleagues before would ask how the team had got on the previous day, but now they would have read the result, either in the press or on the internet, thus rendering any announcement, slightly disappointingly from Gwen's point of view, redundant.

"I see you guys had another win yesterday." That was Brian, a junior nurse and right Know-All. He had first started out, many months previous, by saying that women shouldn't play rugby, but a headlock (playful but just a bit harder than absolutely necessary), plus the increased interest from other staff members, soon got him to change his tune. As rugby was now a standard Monday morning conversation piece, he had decided to take the lead and try to find out more than anyone else. "That should put you second in the league with just about half the games to go."

Only thing for Gwen to do now was fill in the details. It felt a little bit less fun than answering the initial, "How did you get on?" bated breath question as soon as she stepped into the staff room but, if anyone were interested in the minutiae of the game, a little embellishment here and there about how evil the opposition front row were or how ferocious her tackling was would make up for it.

After those few minutes rugby talk, the other staff – nurses, junior doctors, clerks – would filter off on their various duties, the ladies in general muttering about how they couldn't do it, some harbouring desires to "give it a go" themselves, the men with smiles of approval, some reminiscing on playing at school and how they'd like to take it up again, some on how they'd always liked the game but had never got into it. Over the last few weeks, there was a growing feeling that they should organise a trip to see Gwen play one Sunday. Gwen almost wet herself with pride, whilst trying hard not to get lipstick (Persian Rose) in her ears.

It was during a similar moment of self-love that Gwen had made the decision. Pleasures given too freely are rarely appreciated and she felt that, even though she was a strong, confident, independent, successful woman, why did she have to keep on getting into relationships, (or was it just shags?) with the wrong blokes (rugby boys) and end up with her heart broken every other Saturday night/ Sunday morning? And, often only days later, whatever brief relationship she had enjoyed with that particular rugby boy (and she was sure that some of them even really liked her), he would be seen with, in tow, a hyper skinny, fake blonde Barbie-lookalike GIRLFRIEND, teetering on high heels like something straight off the pages of "Who do you do: magazine of the stars!" She was always, "Good old Gwen, alright for a laugh but you'd never introduce her to your parents!"

The amount of times she, with the help of her teammates, had put her heart back together again, she could swear that bits had fallen between the cracks in the floorboards or had gotten lost behind the sofa so that now, it just wasn't all there anymore. If she carried on like this, she'd be completely loved-out and turn into a bitter and twisted old cynic.

She looked in the long, rectangular mirror in the strangely shaped NHS toilet. She had just finished with Mrs Anderson, an amputee whom she was trying to get to use a prosthetic leg and had 15 minutes breather before she would see Ms Marsh, a 93-year-old spinster, with only seconds of her life left before she expired of cancer ("Fuck, can't be late for *that* one!" she thought).

In conversations the previous week, Ms Marsh, with no family members in whom to confide before she departed this mortal coil, had explained to Gwen why she had never married.

"I was waiting for the right man to come along. By the time he did, I was so old, he didn't fancy me!" She had given a little cackle when she recalled, "You see, I still saw myself as a beautiful young maiden, fresh and lovely, like an America: full of promise and hope! He saw me more like Antarctica: everyone knows where it is but no-one wants to go there!" The laughter gave way to coughing and Gwen had to lay Ms Marsh back on the bed, rubbing her back gently to ease her breathing.

All of a sudden, the patient seemed to focus completely on Gwen and said, with the utmost clarity: "You're lovely Deary. You remind me of myself when I was your age. How old are you?"

"Er, 25," she replied, a bit taken aback.

"The love of my life was well over 30 when I first met him," Ms Marsh said, her eyes dulling in reminiscence. "He was perfect, he was, all I'd ever wanted. But he didn't think it would work out."

"Er, how old where you when you met him?" Gwen asked tentatively.

"86!" she joked. The renewed cackling could be heard all over the ward.

ILY had ticked all the right boxes. Despite the faded jeans that were a tiny bit too short revealing white towelling socks, the yellow t-shirt (Gwen *hated* yellow) and regulation haircut, Gwen considered him like a new dress: once I get it home, I can alter it to fit perfectly! He was nice, polite, educated, came from a nice family, dependable *and* he was getting better at sex!

"I mean, what's not to love, right?"

All of a sudden, the moment after they had first made love, when they lay on her bed and he looked like he was going to cry, sprang into her head. There was something so sweet, so desperate, so *vulnerable* about him that instead of asking him to leave, she could hear the words being uttered, as if by someone else: "I really love you." She felt as if she were going to be sick.

The girls started filing back into the 'Sheaf after the night's training, scanning the almost empty bar for signs of their fallen comrade, their expressions a mixture of concern and "Tell us all about it" anticipation.

"Aw Gawd, I am NOT looking forward to this..." she groaned.

Chapter 45: Would you allow your daughter to play rugby?

The next few weeks were fairly uneventful in rugby terms. Sib and Gwen had formed a Union of the Dispossessed, comforting and depressing each other in equal measure over: their new-found single-dom, the very dreadful nature of men and why spinsterhood or lesbianism were the options of the enlightened. Katia, whose relationship with Josh seemed to be undergoing similar upheavals, also occasionally joined them on their binges of either drink, food or, when the guilt of what they were doing to their bodies got to them, amends-ridden gym binges.

The Hammers' reputation on the pitch had preceded them. Opposing teams on the Sunday were adapting their tactics to try to cope and contain their free-flowing and open style of play rather than actually trying to compete. Every new opponent tried to hold onto the ball in the forwards for as long as possible, in order to deprive the speedy Hammers' backs any possession, which was a tactic that had only limited success as the Hammers' forwards just wouldn't let them settle; the new back row of Mands, Zoe and Sib-the-Abandoned doing all in their power to disrupt. When an opposition drive did break down, the Flyhalf had no option other than to kick the ball long, hoping to reach touch and gain her forwards yards, plus a very welcome breather. If a kick missed touch, it would be caught by the eagerly waiting trio of Leafy, Cisk and Katia, who would take great pleasure in running the ball all the way through or round the approaching defence.

One thing the Hammers were still not very good at though was the lineout. The basic premise of this phase of the game is that when the ball goes out of play over the touchline, the team not responsible for it going out must throw the ball back into play, between two parallel lines of theirs and the opposition players. Traditionally, the players who could jump highest would normally win the ball back, but with the change of rules, it was possible to "lift" a player so they could now be twice normal height. The shorter, stronger girls would normally lift the bigger, taller ones, but as the taller ones generally tended to be heavier, lineout lifts were always a bit of a lottery, with players not being lifted properly, or straight, or sometimes not getting off the ground at all!

Stell and Caz', working like a true coaching team, saw the chink in the Hammers' armour and had thus perfected the quick lineout. The back trio had been taught to not wait for the lineout to form, if they were nearest to where the ball went into touch, and simply throw it to themselves (as long as the ball travelled 5 metres from the sideline) and recommence play. Now, even opposition touch-finder kicks were not safe.

Victory was almost assured against virtually everyone, even Relms in the return home leg, despite much shouting from their Head Coach, meekly submitted to the inevitable defeat, consoling themselves with a probable third in the league for that season. Numbers on the touchline increased as well, coinciding with an improvement in the weather now that the cold, dark, short winter afternoons were giving way to the first approaches of spring.

The only game to really look forward to would be the rearranged final game of the season: away to Kingston Tusks, who had, after Christmas, put together an impressive winning streak of their own. The winner would be crowned champions of the WRFU South East West League 2 and guaranteed promotion.

In the final week before the most important match in the history of the Ladies club, the mood was one of eve-of-battle campfire talk[98] where hushed voices often disclosed hitherto unspoken inner truths[99].

"So Caz," Stell asked after the Thursday evening session before the final game. Caz had wanted the team to spend some time on defence and the only way to do so was to organise another session on the Tuesday. Including Stell's party the next day, they would thus be seeing each other virtually every day this week. Caz gulped. "Would you let your daughter play rugby?"

No words had been spoken between the two, of a non-rugby nature, since their "incident" now months before. Caz had attempted to write an email on many occasions, but didn't quite know *what* to ask or where any relationship would lead. His Drafts folder was getting clogged up with unsent messages, all of which were about two lines long. It was nice to be able to talk to her, finally, about anything, but since he didn't have the words to talk about the "incident", this topic of conversation would have to do.

The "would you let your daughter play rugby" question was probably a trick one, but the pre-battle mood lent itself to telling the truth. "Yes," he had said to the combined audience of 5 players, hanging about in the 'Sheaf after training. Sib, Katia and Gwen would be joining them slightly later, having stayed behind at Fortress Hurlingham to doll themselves up for *another* evening out.

"And no."

"What are you talking about, Coach?"

The "yes" bit was easy. "I love the way it makes you guys feel about yourselves. One of the best sounds in the world is to see you guys in training, with steam rising over your heads as you've been working really hard, but laughing and joking, like you're having a good time."

"We're not Caz, honest." That was Mads. Undaunted, he continued.

"I also love the way you react when you do something really well for the first time, like when you beat Masingford at their ground and were climbing all over the scoreboard." They all tried not to smile at the memory.

"It also gives you massive amounts of confidence as you know that nothing is beyond the scope of your capabilities, as long as you're willing to put the work in."

And this was true! He couldn't put his finger on exactly what it was about the sport: possibly the intense training, the making instant decisions under pressure, the increasingly complicated laws which meant you had to play them, and the referee, to your advantage so as to skirt the very borders of what was acceptable, or the camaraderie that playing in the largest team sport in the world would generate, but for him, as well as for every other *proper* rugby player he knew, once you'd put yourself through that particular mill, testing the very limit of your mental and physical capabilities, you gained an inner confidence, an acute knowledge, of what you were capable of achieving.

It was no coincidence that, from occupying the higher echelons of the boardroom, to winning a Celebrity Dancing On Ice game show, former rugby players were willing to put the work in, no matter what the field of play, and generally succeed as a result.

Feeling as if he were "protesting too much," he added, "Plus, it keeps you out of mischief." The girls sensed he was too and rounded on the obvious omission.

"So why the "no" then?"

This one was more tricky. Eve-of-Battle etiquette dictated that he should tell the truth, that he should say, "It's because you tend to shut out the whole world apart from your team and anyone who doesn't play rugby. Because with many of you, you're using the game to settle scores against people who were in your lives but have either long departed or just simply shouldn't matter any more. Because you become insular and act as if you're front-line troops in the battle of the sexes, the flip side to your increased confidence and strength being you start seeing men as pathetic and weak and treating them as such, but at the same time wanting a strong man to stand up to you and tell you to shut up when you're being bonkers. Then, when he doesn't put up with your bonkers-ness, you call him a bastard and give yourselves even more reasons to hate all men, but then you still seek their approval anyway."

He suddenly realised he was probably talking more from personal experience with a certain person than on rugby girls in general.

"Sod etiquette," he thought, "I'm going to lie!"

"Cos drinking too much makes you fat!"

The collective groans were curtailed by the arrival of the Foresaken Three: Las Abandonadas of Gwen, Sib and Katia, dressed to impress[100].

Tonight was Ladies' Night at Varaderros and the Abandonadas were intent on drinking half-price cocktails all evening (with no intention whatsoever of paying for any themselves), dirty dancing with the fittest blokes in the bar and, who knows where the night could lead?

Caz wanted to say something the nature of: "Don't you think you should maybe be taking it easy? We do have an important game at the weekend," but it sounded too much like the stern, sensible instruction of a Father rather than a "hip and happening coach" so he thought better of it. Plus, he didn't want to upset the Abandonadas too much: they were still hurting from the rejections and infidelities of the last few weeks and were probably just in "anarchic rebellious misandrist" mode, needing to let off some steam against all men in general.

"Erm, like, what do you think you're trying to achieve dressed like that?" This was Hannah the trainee solicitor and 2nd Row. Very tall, slim, with large-rimmed red glasses (to match the wild red hair, usually tied up in some way or another: today in a bunch with a pin holding it in place), she always came to training straight from work so usually wore a conservative blouse under a grey, black or blue business suit. Hannah hardly ever spoke and didn't often socialise with the girls for too long after games, her incredible work-load, and devoted boyfriend, taking up much of her free time.

"What do YOU know about pulling men, Hans? You've been going out with yours for about a century now."

"Men want to feel *you* like *them*, but then want to do all the chasing around after you, so they know you're not just easy. They like being in control, or at least feeling that they are."

"Where's all this coming from?" the group collectively thought. Intrigued, they let her continue.

"You all look too, er, "aggressive," and, if you don't mind me saying, a bit "obvious"."

The Abandonadas didn't like this. Caz tried to surpress a snigger, Mads and Mands didn't bother with the surpression.

"Yes, that's it," Hannah continued. "Best thing is to whet a man's apetitite, then back off and watch them come running!" Out-of-character outburst concluded, Hannah reverted her attention to her drink.

Gwen, still smarting over the cancelled matching bridesmaid dresses and wall decorations, was hurt. "Go on then, prove it!" she challenged.

"Yah," Katia added. "You see zat man over at ze bar?" She motioned to a late-twenties/ early thirties man in plain suit reading a newspaper. They all looked. He wasn't too bad looking, just a bit boring. Dramatically exaggerating her Hamburg accent for comic effect, she continued: "Your mission, if you choose to accept it, is to get him to buy yoo a drrink? Zis message vill self-destruct in 10 seconds."

All joined in with the exaggerated, "Tick, tick, tick.....," but by the time they had reached the "Ker-boom!" Hannah had arisen silently from the leather armchair, challenge accepted.

In one movement, she removed the pin from her hair, bending her head forward so her mane draped down to completely cover her face, then shook her tresses free. The spectacles were whipped off with one hand before she completed the famous "bend and snap"[101] move, her head back up, releasing a mass of red waves to cascade about her shoulders in a way of which Mermaids of legend would have been duly proud. Undoing two buttons of blouse to reveal the top of a peach-coloured lace bra and pushing her smallish breasts together, she turned her deep brown eyes towards the floor, for just a brief moment, before returning her gaze to an eye-level, "Come get me!" stare, deep into the eyes of all three Abandonadas at the same time. A wicked smile curled one corner of her mouth as a tube of bright red lipstick appeared in her hand, as if from nowhere.

"Watch and learn girls, watch and learn," she said whilst applying the lipstick as provocatively as a chocolate bar advert, and shimmying, on suddenly elongated legs, over to the identified target sitting at the bar.

"Hi," she gushed, tossing her head from side to side, while fiddling with the remaining blouse buttons. "You look like you play rugby! Are you with the local team?"

"Er, no..." replied the stunned off-duty Accountant. "Whoah, she was GORGEOUS!!!" he thought. "But I play football though!"

"This sort of thing never happened to him (and probably still wasn't. But if it's a dream, I don't want to wake up!)" he concluded under his breath. A slight pang of guilt shot through him, as he remembered that he actually *did* have a girlfriend already.

("But Mavis the Secretary and this *Amazing Creature* were entire species apart, so it's not like he was being unfaithful or anything"). Nope, the justification was totally unconvincing, but he didn't care! He would have to think quickly if he were going to keep her interest for as long as possible though. Before she found out he was an Accountant...

"I *thought* you were a sportsman. Do you do it for a living?" Another toss of the head. The masses of hair flicked to the side. ("The same way it would if she were on top, biting her lip and moaning "Yes, YES!!!" he thought). Hannah bit her lip, waiting for an answer.

"Er, no."

("Oh no! Wrong answer. Bugger!") He could feel his heart pounding away in his chest.

"But we are pretty serious!" ("Better, better.")

"I just *knew* you did sports!" Hannah enthused, invading his personal space so the tips of her nipples were within inches of his chest. She squeezed his bicep. She thought about adding, "I love a strong man," but judging by his reactions: the fascinated eyes straining to not look down her cleavage, the heaving chest and the fish-gape mouth, she deemed it unnecessary. She bit her lip again and waited for him to pursue. She'd shown him the goods, now leave it up to him to seek and conquer.

("I'm going to have to tell her eventually, I suppose. Here goes....")

"Actually, I'm an Accountant," he half-mumbled, the final "tnt" syllable disappearing with his hopes of further developing the relationship.

"Not much of a conquering stud, is he?" flashed through her mind whilst a high-pitched and excited, "REALLY!" like he had just announced he was a Formula 1 Racing Driver, passed her lips.

Accountant man brightened! This gorgeous creature was interested in *him*! All the legal steps required for the eviction of "all thoughts of girlfriend Mavis" from his consciousness were circumvented and the bailiffs were there in force. Meekly, in their sensible shoes, sober work clothes, unmade-up face, practical hair and clutching their unremarkable handbag, "All Thoughts of Mavis" opened the front door and walked out of his heart. "Er, my name's Mark, can I get you a drink?"

"Bingo!"

While Mark was ordering her Gin and Tonic (she'd asked him what he was drinking first (beer), then requested something slightly upscale[102]), Hannah took the opportunity to turn towards the fascinated and open-mouthed Hammers only metres away in the corner of the 'Sheaf.

She tilted her head to the side slightly, raised both eyebrows to the heavens and, with an exaggerated smug smile, had no trouble in conveying her meaning: "And that, Ladies, is how it's done."

Chapter 46: Stell's Party

The evening started slowly. In ones and twos, the various Hammers arrived at the Theakston Mansion, a general feeling of subdued excitement and anticipation for the festivities ahead hung in the slightly chilly spring air.

After a free and frank exchange of views, Stell had persuaded an extremely reluctant Mrs T to vacate the mansion for the evening so she could entertain the rugby team in a pre-last game of the season celebration. It wasn't often that Stell won these arguments and this one hadn't been as animated as they had been known to in the past, but this may have been because Mrs T had grudgingly accepted that the girls' efforts over the course of the season had merited an evening of communal "letting down of one's hair."

Stell had come to realise that the thing that really bound the team together was not the game plan, tactics or even individual ability, but the feeling of not wanting to let your mates down. They had sweated together, shed blood together, fought, cried, shared physical pain, got drunk together, thrown up in lots of different and colourful places (a little more colourful after the throwing up) and had even been shouted at by that bastard Caz – whom they grudgingly loved and simultaneously and unanimously hated - whilst he tried to run everyone into the ground but pretending he wasn't. Speaking of which, he was supposed to be turning up this evening...

The main reason for the get-together though, was so she could make sure they didn't get too drunk just before the big game in two days time. Or get up to any other unsavoury mischief, as the steadily growing band of Abandonadas had a bit of a reputation to do, excluding her, of course. Her mind turned to Caz again. He was a bastard, undoubtedly - definitely a scoundrel of the highest order, even though nothing had *actually* happened between them - which in itself was weird. "Not that I want it to as after all, he was married and although technically separated, two children was just too much baggage... "

The doorbell rang and Stell's heart performed a little jump. Zoe went to answer it and when she came back, the unmistakeable face of the coach appeared around the corner of the door.

"Can I interest you ladies in these?" Caz said, producing two bottles of rather good champagne from behind the door, so all you could see were head, arms and bottles.

"Ridiculous man," she thought, but still couldn't suppress a grin.

Gwen, the Mistress of Ceremonies and Social Secretary, had put her Adondonadas membership to one side for the evening. She took the floor amidst the 12 or so girls lying and sitting around the large living room, perched in various positions on the worn furniture. "In celebration of our rather glorious season and in anticipation of our forthcoming victory, I would like to propose a toast in honour of Kingston Tusks." Slightly puzzled faces turned towards her, their attention captured.

"The toast is, "I hate Kingston because..." and I'll begin. I hate Kingston because they beat us by one point last year and we should have so won that game."

Mads chipped in, "I hate Kingston because they don't play proper rugby, but just stick the ball up their jumper and trundle forward like Mogodons."

Stell: "I hate Kingston because Fi plays for them." This was met with long, rather loud boos of agreement that the MC had to eventually call to order. Only days before, whilst on the tube on their way to their respective trainings, Mands had bumped into Fiona Stanley. She was wearing the unmistakable blue and yellow tracksuit top and bobble hat of the hated foe. They had exchanged sheepish, "Alrights," but nothing more; once an outcast, you stay an outcast. Mands had, as was her laconic manner, matter-of-factly let the information slip towards the end of the session, telling everyone, "Yeah, we're likely gonna have to play against Fi on Sunday. Saw her on the way to training at Kingston t'noight?" This had definitely added extra spice to the weekend's game.

The "I hate Kingstons" continued for a while, each new affirmation being significantly sillier and less relevant to rugby than the previous. It was Caz turn.

"I hate Kingston because blue and yellow are so last year." Collective groans, accompanied by the odd, "he's sooo gay" from Stell filled the room.

The round completed, the next affirmation was a round of "I love the Hammers because," then a game involving fines for not saying certain things in certain orders. Another drinking game followed in which various number combinations were acceptable whilst others were not and as the drink flowed, the original purpose of the evening – not to get too drunk – seemed to be forgotten.

"Right," said Stell, "Pictionary Challenge!"

The girls, plus Caz and Danish John (he worked in the 'Sheaf and had just become so fascinated with ladies' rugby, had started coming to all the games and accompanying Mrs T wherever she went) split themselves into four teams of three and began a highly competitive and alcohol fuelled session of drawing, acting, shouting out answers out of turn, cheating and generally poor but extremely good fun behaviour. There were a few awkward moments when Katia and Sib turned up, completely paralytic and reeking of spirits, the former slunk immediately onto an unoccupied bit of sofa and fell asleep, the latter texting away ("Uh-oh, drunken texts, always a bad idea") like fury until Stell had to tell her to "stop or the phone goes into the fishtank." From then on, whenever the muffled beep of an incoming vibrated her handbag, Sib anxiously looked at her bag then nervously at Stell, who managed to break from whatever expression she was wearing at the time, meet Sib's gaze with a warning glare then exaggeratedly look towards the fishtank. If there were only one thing she'd inherited from her mother, it was the Mrs T version of the Paddington Bear Hard Stare. Sib left the phone alone.

At one point Caz and Stell found themselves waiting outside the loo together. Something had definitely happened between them, but no-one knew what. On the one hand, they were combining so well as Coach and Captain in training and during games, but there was a tension in the air, an unspoken armistice, like enemies exhibiting all the diplomatic niceties while their armies stared with hostility at each other over no-man's land. "Oh I wish they'd just shag and get it over with," Mads thought, looking on.

Taking courage in both hands, Caz ventured: "Stell, I wanted to talk to you. Are you OK?"

"Why wouldn't I be? Just leave it, OK, we've nothing to discuss. Now if you please, I'm going to do a crap."

"God, Woman, can't you just be normal for five minutes and stop being such a foul-mouthed bloke?

But, a very wobbly and pale looking Katia had just emerged from the loo and Stell took the opportunity to slip in quickly so she wouldn't have to talk about feelings and pain and how she wanted to lick Caz' face and knee him in the groin at the same time[103]. "Biting was always an option as well," she pondered, as she sat on the loo.

Caz leaned against the wall outside of the toilet and let out a loud sigh, which must have been audible to anyone within ten metres. "Completely bonkers, definitely. No question," he thought to himself. "Had I known this rugby coaching thing was going to be so draining, I would never have given up hara-kiri. Blind bungee jumping has its plus sides as well..."

The evening ended with karaoke, Mrs T having been persuaded to purchase a do-it-yourself home model to facilitate such evenings. When Jake and Hugh occasionally stayed at the house, which was becoming an even rarer occurrence, and had friends over, it provided hours of family entertainment from which Mrs T was only too eager to escape.

The highlight of the evening, apart from the compulsory conga line in which the walking in a straight line skills of Siobhan and Katia were tested to the limit; must have been when Stell and Caz were chosen to sing "You're the One that I Want" from Grease. Throwing personal enmity to one side, they embraced their respective roles with so much commitment, the calls of "Get a room!" (from Mads) didn't seem too inappropriate.

"For fucking Christ's sake, just shag her and be done with it!" Mads felt obliged to add.

All in all, it was a fairly uneventful evening.

A few hours earlier, in a small town some 10 miles to the west of London, a door opened from a darkened corridor. "You can go in now, but only for a maximum of five minutes," the Nurse said quietly." She needs all the rest she can get."

The two women and one man entered the Kingston hospice room nervously. They had known Jen for years, well before her England days and would always remember her as big, tough, with a permanent gap-toothed grin and an occasional evil word. The girls had last seen her less than a month ago but now that the illness had effectively won, they didn't know what to expect.

The room was small and dark. A portable pump on a chrome stand fed a tube into Jen's arm and on the bedside table stood two vases, one yellow the other white. Imogen recognised the flowers that the girls had sent a few days earlier. There was an assortment of pills, in different sized jars and bottles, as well as an open but barely touched packet of crackers. Two plastic cups, one semi-filled with water and the other with what smelled like a large brandy, waited seemingly out of place, closest to Jen.

Don't Let Them See You Cry

The first thing they noticed was Jen's colour. Normally, she had a pale but reddish complexion, spending so much time running herself to exhaustion on the training pitch. Now though, she looked grey. "Grey and incredibly thin." A rounded belly could be detected under the bed sheets ("Jen was such an abs freak, she never would have let that happen"), from which you could just about make out a catheter, leading into a colostomy bag which lay to her side. You often hear people speaking of the spark of life that some call the soul – the difference between being alive one second and dead the next - as something which departs from the body at the moment of death. Jen looked as if this soul had already left, or was at least hovering by the door looking at its watch while searching its pockets for its car keys.

Jen coughed.

"Already on the brandy then," Martine quipped, lifting the cup of alcohol to her nose and taking an exaggerated sniff. Rick the Coach just stared. He had been new to the Tusks last season and if it weren't for Jen's expert guidance, being one of the ex-internationals, he would have been completely lost. In return, he'd been partly responsible for her extending her career for one more year and, even though he knew that the cancer had nothing to do with her continued playing, he couldn't help but feel somehow it was partly his fault. He put his hand gently on top of Jen's and left it lightly resting there.

"Beer's off," wheezed Jen.

Imogen thought the situation would be less grim if she tried to be practical. "Right, my girl, as Julie and Lukes' Godmother, it's my duty to make sure the little cherubs don't follow their

Mum's example and ensure that they stay away from alcoholic beverages."

"At least until they're twelve," Martine chipped in.

"Failed already there then," whispered Jen, followed by a bout of coughing. The door flew open and the nurse rushed in towards Jen, sitting her bolt upright, fluffing the pillows behind her back and reaching for the water in what seemed like one movement. Suddenly, Jen appeared twenty years older. She slumped into the pillows and looked as if she would throw up.

"I think that's all for now, she needs to sleep. You'd better all go for the evening."

Rick let go of his wife's hand and, as all three slouched towards the door, he managed to speak for the first time, almost in a whisper, "Is there anything we can do?"

Jen seemed to regain focus and her eyes burned with the familiar intensity that they had come to know over the years, just before she went into the "hit". The words did not come out anywhere near as strongly as they were used to, but they all knew what she almost inaudibly mouthed.

"Win it...."

Chapter 47: Hammersmith and Fulham Combined 1st and 2nd team (Men's) vs New Quay Ironsides: Friendly

Spring in England, especially April, has the ability to deliver all the extremes of weather that the planet Earth can muster and combine them into a single afternoon. After the earlier torrential downpour of windscreen-breaking balls of hail large enough to play marbles with, the sun had decided to emerge and bathed the green playing fields of west London with a warm, almost mid-summer heat.

The Hammers Men's First team had no game that Saturday, so a combined Ones and Twos team was playing a friendly against New Quay Ironsides. As is usual for a friendly game, the play was fast, loose and a lot more fun than the boring kicking duels that rugby matches can sometimes be. A few of the First Team boys who were not playing, some of the ladies' team, heads slightly sore from the previous night's "sensible night in" but under strict orders NOT to drink before the all-important game the next day, and a more than normal sized crowd, including Mum's-day-off Fathers pleased to be able to escape from the house with their adorable darlings after the morning's downpour, were enjoying the newly re-surfaced sun. Some of the children were passing rugby balls to each other and Dads, having spent the past week behind desks in stuffy City offices, made attempts, with varying degrees of success, to show their offspring "how it's done," in memory of a time when they too were young and fit. The game continued alongside them and every once in a while, when paying attention, the spectators would applaud some piece of especially good play, but more often bemoan the referee, in the most polite of terms, "Who had, the poor fellow, simply got it wrong."

"So, if you had a choice of marry, shag or kill, between Josh (not playing today, slight shoulder injury), Ben (playing, currently on course to be re-crowned Player of the Season at the annual Dinner Dance awards) and Larry (playing but also nursing a hangover – I wonder where Sib went to after the party at Stell's?), who would you choose?"

Mads was surprisingly on form, considering she'd only slept for three hours since the party. The sun always gave her body this little boost of energy, to be usually quickly followed by a mini-depression as she once again wondered why on Earth she'd left her native Sydney for the constant drizzle of London. "And that question goes to Gwen."

Gwen thought hard. "Shag Ben, kill Larry," to unconvincing cheers from Siobhan, "and marry Josh."

Katia smiled her approval of the joke, while a little knife twisted somewhere inside her.

"OK", said Gwen, "Caz..." ("Oh no!" he thought), "shag, marry, kill – Your Wifey, Katia, Stell," and even before the last "l" was pronounced, a shrill chorus of "Oos" and "Get a room!" could be heard from the girls.

Caz shifted uncomfortably from one foot to another. "Er," he said, trying to stall as long as possible, but before he could give an obviously self-incriminating answer, he was interrupted by a call from the pitch.

Barry, a six-foot four second row, was looking very earnest. "Could someone call for an ambulance, Ben's been hurt." The "Shag, Marry, Kill" game stopped suddenly while those on the sideline tried to take in what was being said. Barry shouted louder this time.

"Ben's been fucking hurt and I think it's serious. Could someone call for an ambulance?" Caz was the first to get out his phone and dialled 999.

"Which service do you require?"

"Ambulance, please." A short pause.

"Hello, ambulance service, can I help you?"

"Yes, my name is Carlton Edwards and I'd like to report an accident on a rugby pitch. One of our players has been injured and I think it's serious. We need an ambulance to Hurlingham Park, Fulham, SW6, right away."

"Could you describe what's wrong?"

"No, I'm at the side of the pitch. I'll just go over to him," and Caz jogged the thirty or so metres, oblivious to the increasing ache in his knees, to where all the players who had only seconds before been locked in mortal combat, were now waiting anxiously. The other spectators didn't know what to do. Some stayed on the sideline, some followed Caz over to the crowd of players. With phone still pressed to his ear, Caz reached the huddle of about seven players kneeling down over the prostrate form of the 26-year-old Ben O'Connor.

Caz had never seen anyone with a broken neck before. Ben's face was blue and getting darker by the second. A trail of thick saliva was dribbling out of his mouth and down the side of his face, his body seeming both lifeless and twitching at the same time. Caz had grown up on stories and films of the World Wars and was familiar with images of dying soldiers, laid out on their backs with lifeless limbs, blood pouring from some gaping shrapnel or bullet wound, eyes staring into space with an expression of both fear and pain. There was no blood, however and Caz couldn't help thinking that the sudden (or was it slow?) ebbing of activity and energy from the slim, elegantly muscled young body of Ben O'Connor reminded him more of the death throes of a shot horse who, realising that a serious and possibly fatal wound had been inflicted somewhere on its body, its wild, rolling eyes just could not *believe* that it was dying.

Barry was hovering over Ben, desperately trying to give the kiss of life. Caz tried to describe the scene to the hospital telephone operator. Ben was gasping for breath and Barry blew air into his mouth for all his life was worth, desperately trying to keep his club mate alive. The telephone operator was saying to Caz, "Stop the mouth to mouth if he's breathing on his own" and Caz kept on saying, "He isn't, this is the only thing keeping him alive!" and in the general confusion and deafening noise of the arrival of the air ambulance, with some of the ladies' team crying, New Quay players, especially the player who had made the innocuous tackle, unable to look,

Hammers from the sidelines trying to cover Ben in coats for warmth, the paramedics arrived and took over.

Once Ben was on a trolley, still clinging on to life and being wheeled over to the air ambulance, Barry, with tears in his eyes through the sheer effort, threw up. A number of the Hammers, both players and spectators, were in shock and Siobhan, who had left the sidelines to see what she could do and was now shaking, reached over to Larry, her recent ex, for comfort.

He recoiled; he didn't want to be touched.

"Do you still think girls should play this game?!" he hissed. "People get *hurt*!!!" and ran off in the direction of his club-mates.

Chapter 48: Indiscretions

Two weeks previously, single malt in hand and back in Milesborough after a visit to his ailing mother, Roger stared at the embossed, hand-written letter, addressed to him at his parents' house, with Anna's ink and perfume all over it ("No-one sends letters anymore, for goodness sake") and again re-read the contents.

"Stell's playing in two weeks time on Sunday at 2 pm. It would be great if you could come along to take some pictures as it would mean so much to her. Unless of course you are too busy..."

"Why did she have to add the last bit?" he protested. "Will I always have to atone for just *one* stupid mistake?"

Even he knew that "just one" was perhaps not 100% true...

From his vantage point at the Olde Swan, Roger could make out the central Milesborough lake, where a magnificent white cob was being surrounded by adoring, far less impressive, greyish pens. He groaned internally as he remembered how his "indiscretions," all those years ago, had arisen.

Mrs Murray, the mother of Darren Murray, whom he had decided he was going to mentor, lived in a nice, two-up, two-down semi-detached rented cottage in a working class but now mostly privately-owned suburb of Milesborough. Everything about the house was neat and well-looked after, even though it was clear that money was not in overabundance. Roger had the feeling, from the well-kept lawn, the meticulously attended flower beds, the immaculately painted dividing line between the two adjacent properties, that Mrs Murray was proud of having made the best she could of the meagre amounts the world had offered her.

A very pretty woman of 30-something, Maureen, as he soon found out, was a secretary who worked as a waitress in the evenings to afford to continue with the Milesborough Prep's school fees. When Roger first appeared at the door, she was convinced that her son had gotten into trouble again and was preparing to scold him before Roger could even get a word in. Now, after the initial worries had subsided (including whether or not Roger was a posh paedophile), she sat in the modest living room ("Dated furniture, tasteful but inexpensive," Roger thought) and just refused to believe him when he announced his plans to give up his time to help her son. Roger had tried to explain that, beneath the inarticulate, unco-ordinated, unsettled, rolly-polly exterior of a boy, lay what generations of army officers had labelled "the right stuff". Under pressure, in the mud and blood and when the bullets are flying, it's that innate strength, that inner bloody-mindedness to not give in to whatever terrible predicament he found himself in, to take charge and *make a difference* that he had recognised in Darren, a quality very hard to find indeed. He couldn't help thinking, "Something I realised I just didn't have when I went to Troubadours..."

"You see, we're just not used to this sort of thing, Sir," Mrs Murray had eventually said, in her faint Glasgow accent, after his words had finally penetrated the wariness and disbelief. She wouldn't stop thanking him.

"Bloody hell, woman, I'm only offering to teach him a bit more than the others, I'm not going to adopt the boy!" Roger heard himself thinking. "And please stop the "Sir," it makes me feel uncomfortable."

When she went to the kitchen to prepare tea, Darren having installed himself at a small desk to paw through war comics, Roger looked around the room. The large colour TV was on, with some holiday programme or another advertising cruises to the Caribbean. There were prints on the wall-paper covered walls of continental vistas, luxury hotels, sunsets, bright suns over picturesque Scandinavian snow-covered landscapes: all things he was sure Mrs Murray had, and would never, experience.

"How could people *live* like this," he thought to himself, "being aware of all the wonders that the world has to offer and knowing that none of them are within your grasp?"

He felt saddened. Here was, to all intents and purposes, a lovely woman who basically, through no fault of her own, was trapped in a limited expectation environment where the things we see advertised everywhere we look: holidays, travel, success, stable family, a husband who lives with you and takes care of you and the children, romance, probably even great sex! are what *other* people do. This would probably carry on for generations.

"It's like being the people under the stairs..." he thought. "People with the "right stuff" given absolutely nothing as a start in life and then people like me who..." Out of self-preservation, his thoughts didn't finish the sentence.

He was staring at a faded print of a slight young man in Scottish Highlanders' army uniform, probably the absent Mr Murray, Darren's father, when she came back into the room, all gushing meekness and apologies: for the tea, the trouble he was taking over her son, the state of her house, for taking up breathing space on this earth. He made up his mind there and then.

"I'm going to show her the good side of life. I'm going to make some of these low expectations disappear. Starting with her son, I'm going to get them to know what success is, what working hard but getting the fruits of your labour is all about. I'll still do the rugby, but my new project is going to be Darren and Maureen Murray!"

It was only a few weeks later that the affair started.

Question: What does one do when one has had 32 years of: being mother to your siblings when still a child yourself; then, barely out of childhood and in order to escape, mother (and father) to your own son; then having to deal with an increasingly violent and mentally disturbed alcoholic, former-soldier husband; leaving your friends and family back home in Scotland to work at two, sometimes three jobs in order to keep a roof over your head; then having some luck and moving away from a horrible, horrible Council estate in London, only to find yourself working just as hard but in a tiny town where you don't know anyone apart from a sick Nanna who needs you?

But the worst part was that, over the last two years, her sweet, loving, angelic little 9-year-old had somehow transformed into a foul-mouthed, moody and hateful 11-year-old who she was convinced simply *despised* her! Darren appeared to hold *her* responsible for not seeing his dad any more, for all the fights he was getting into at school, for all the mickey-taking he had to suffer and the anger and frustration it caused in him which, from the moment she stepped into the house after work, was never more than a few moments away from being fully unleashed on *her*. And after all she had done for him, after all the sacrifices she'd made and how bloody hard she'd had to work! She had only the other day felt her fingers trembling when she inserted the key into her front door, in anticipation of the screaming argument she knew they would have over: not doing his homework, not tidying up the sink, why she was such a "miserable whore with a stupid accent who never did anything" or any one of a number of randomly selected subjects that Darren could employ, at a whim and with no warning. Maureen had never been one for hitting children (partly due to her experiences with constantly changing step-Dads from her childhood who normally never showed any interest in her schoolwork when she'd completed it but who were curiously virtually all exceptionally keen to mete out physical punishment when she hadn't) but, over the course of the years, she had given her son a smack or two for exceptionally bad behaviour (like "accidentally" kicking out a window while practising close-quarters combat, age 7). Now though, she actually did truly believe that if she were to raise her hand to Darren, he would have no hesitation in hitting her back. She'd only recently read in "Who Do You

Do - Magazine of the Stars!" of a 16-year-old who had taken a knife to his Mum...

"Then, all of a sudden, some super-fit Lord decides he wants to "mentor" your son, look after him, teach him, as well as spend time with you and make your life better, just because he's kind and gentle and he looks like a Roman statue!"

Answer: Fill your boots!

Maureen couldn't believe her good fortune. Roger talked about all the places he'd been and the things he'd seen and done. His voice, while he and an extremely attentive Darren discussed schoolwork or rugby and she pretended to be busy in the kitchen, transported her to Paris on a warm spring evening, on safari in Kenya, white water rafting in Canada. Once, for a Food and Nutrition project Darren had been assigned, for which more enthusiasm gushed from her son than for anything in the previous 2 years combined, Roger mentioned a famous restaurant in a London hotel that Maureen had recently read about in "Who Do You Do - Magazine of the Stars!". The words, "I'd love to go there once," seemed to escape from her lips of their own accord.

"I'll take you there, if you like!" was Roger's good-natured response. She never thought it would happen but, true to his word, the next week, there they went. That night had been perfect: the hotel and restaurant seemed to be straight out of a film set, so too were most of the people (women mostly, the men were disappointingly invariably older and much fatter than their escorts for the evening). The waiters bowed and scraped and fawned all over her, the food was amazing (even though not enough of it) and Roger was again the perfect gent when, on the drive back to Milesborough ("An open top Bentley!" she'd gasped), she asked if they could stop for something to eat as she was starving!

The coarse cotton of her every day attire was gradually being replaced by silks and taffetas, on the occasions when he took her to other amazing hotels or restaurants in London and, with the skills he had learned from his wife (the irony wasn't lost on Maureen), he showed her how to wear her hair, her make-up, how to carry herself in high heels, how to be "a lady".

Looking at herself in the mirror of their hotel suite, just before they dined in one of the restaurants again familiar to her from "Who Do You Do" magazine: the silk caressing her skin, the borrowed jewels adorning her ears, neck, wrists, legs elongated by the latest designer high heels, she felt as if she wouldn't be out of place *on* those pages, instead of flipping through them in the minutes she had to herself in between her different jobs. Maureen felt beautiful, desirable, sexy: a woman.

She realised with a strange, resigned lack of bitterness that her whole existence on this planet could have been so different if she'd just had a different start in life, if all the fledgling hopes she'd had as a girl, lying in her bed at night staring at the stars to blot out the latest step-father's drunken snoring, were considered achievable, as goals to which to aspire, as opposed to the empty fantasies of the daydreamers who, according to all the teachers, carers and relatives she'd ever spoken to, "had their heads in the clouds".

She vowed that, unlike her's, Darren's hopes weren't going to be crushed before they were even formed, so she was willing to trade her values: the ignominy of always hiding with "somebody else's man" for the few weeks or months or maybe even years that the affair would last, in order to give that different start to her only son, to change the path down which he already seemed to be heading, as well as enjoying some of life's pleasures for herself. He was getting on better at school and was calmer, more self-assured and so was involved in fewer fights as he was less easy to bait. Roger was showing him direction, giving him a role model to aspire to be, showing him all the qualities necessary to be respected, to succeed. The main thing though was that since Roger was showing Darren he was interested in him, Darren started to believe he was someone worthy of interest. And so did other people.

Friends started visting him at home as being associated with a 1st team front row forward, tipped for the highest honours, was definitely school credit-worthy for some of the less popular boys in his class. These friends, through his school and through the rugby, who would eventually be quite well-placed themselves in British society, Darren was likely to know for the rest of his life and, his mother was absolutely convinced, would grant him access to the top table of opportunity that the country could offer. A large part of this was thanks to Roger.

There was only the tiniest pang of guilt at betraying a fellow female (she'd seen Anna Theakston once and had tried hard to dislike her) but in a straight fight between empathy for the betrayed future ex-partner or support for her son's future, it was a no-contest.

"Aye," Maureen thought to herself, languishing in the deep purple, fine Egyptian cotton hotel sheets, after making love, Roger snoring gently by her side, "My life is definitely changing."

Maureen had probably never heard the words to an old blues song entitled "Don't Advertise Your Man."

The girls at work couldn't help notice a glow about her after her London trysts and a buzz in her eyes (not only due to lack of sleep). They'd even heard Maureen singing to herself whilst skipping - yes skipping! - about the office floor. She was definitely seeing some new fancy man, someone with a bit of money as well judging by the watch, the new clothes, the bracelet, but whom?

Maureen couldn't contain her secret for too long and was relieved to finally spill the beans to her closest work colleagues. Who shared it with their closest colleagues...

Pretty soon, a queue of eager single Mums with snotty Kevins or Mickeys or Billys in tow, with the excuse of being desperate to teach their unruly sons "how to play rugby" - much to the disapproval of the club's alikadoos - but really looking for a male role model (and potential love interest?) was winding its way around the Milesborough Old Boys RFC clubhouse. Their numbers were bloated by various career housewives who, after having transformed their husbands into emasculated workaholics, so they could provide the security of: the kitchen and loft extensions; the two, three, four holidays a year; the private schools and two family cars that were all *completely necessary* to fit into the Milesborough Mum's Scene, now were disgusted by their meek and mild bullocks and wanted to feel the adrenaline rush of being near a tried and tested (as the rumours went) Prize Bull, who could also show their sons how to be Real Men.

Roger had felt like a United Nations voluntary aid worker, handing out food parcels to starving refugees. After the last grain of rice is dispensed, *another* starving village-load come over the horizon. "God, talk about filling the proverbial "gap" in my life," he regretted, no pun intended.

"It was like being at a party where his glass was being constantly topped up with a wine he didn't really like....", he thought and downed the remainder of his whisky.

Chapter 49: Final Game of the Season: Kingston Away

The Hammersmith and Fulham Ladies Rugby team were in a strange mood. They had arrived at Kingston over half an hour later than expected and had subsequently got lost on the normally short walk to the Bushey Park ground. Stell and an extremely red-eyed Gwen were bickering over which direction to take, even though they'd been there many times before. The bright April day was fully living up to all expectations: any type of weather was possible at precisely no notice. The others trudged on through the alternating hail, rain, bright sun and snow. To make matters worse, the weather Gods had decided that a major overnight snowfall would make the afternoon's proceedings even more fun than usual.

There were only forty-five minutes to kick off as the ladies, Danish John and Caz and one or two BAGS walked through the stable door entrance of the Kingston Tusks Rugby Club. Above the general rumblings of the assembling crowd, which for many of the girls was already larger than any game they'd played in before, could be heard the aggressive grunts and groans of the Tusks, in the throes of a full warm-up session on the recently snow-cleared pitch. Stell could make out Fi's short, blonde bob, her stock in trade haircut of the last couple of seasons, slightly to the side of the blue and yellow group.

They hadn't spoken since Fi had jumped ship and the Tusks' impressive run in the league seemed to coincide with her arrival.

It was precisely at that moment that Fi's pre-game stretching routine made her turn to look directly at Stell. Even though the former teammates were at least 50 metres away, she could virtually see a half-smile playing on Fi's lips. Stell turned away.

"She *always* makes me feel like that. "Less"."

Amongst the still arriving spectators, there was a larger than usual contingent of completely inappropriately dressed men (and some women!) sporting bright shorts and shirts, with impossible tans, already well advanced in the lubrication stakes, with a small beer can mountain growing behind them, much to the disapproval of the tutting home support. A short, very well-rounded, orange-faced blond man was holding sway at the centre of the group, talking loudly and excitedly to all who would listen. He broke off to wave to Mrs T.

"Looks like Fi's dad's here already," she thought. She couldn't help herself from scanning the crowd to see if Roger, her ex-husband, had come along to take some pictures as promised. She suspected it would mean so much to her daughter if he had, but as this was highly unlikely, she'd considered it best not to mention anything to Stell as, in the event he didn't show up, her daughter would be impossible that evening, win or lose. Still, she tried to convince herself, it must have been the cold that made the hairs on the back of her neck stand to attention...

In the crowd, Stell recognised several BAGS, plus a small contingent from BetNow! who had come to cheer her on. Geordana caught her eye and waved excitedly. Even Trish, no longer an enemy at work as it would be hugely unpopular to not participate in the Monday morning's Stell hero-worship, managed a smile. Brian and a group of Gwen's colleagues were also there, as well as a handful of Hammers boys who had made the half hour journey from west London. Standing on his own, a few metres away from the boys, she could make out the familiar face of the Hammers Men's 1st team Coach. "Bloody hell," she thought, "They're taking this seriously..."

As the team changed in the small wooden hut in unfamiliar silence, each individual trying to concentrate on the next 70 minutes of what for most of them would be the most important game of their lives, an unspoken sadness seemed to hang in the air alongside the cold. The feelings of those who had witnessed the previous day's incident ranged from steely, silent resolve, vowing to "just get the job done" to red-eyed, jittery nervousness. Nobody put into words what was on everyone's minds: "I could end up like Ben."

The Hammers ladies emerged from the dimly lit changing hut in ones and twos, ready to be taken for the warm-up by Caz. The sun was dazzling, forcing them to squint and shield their eyes from its glare with a protective raised hand. Once the hand was removed and their eyes came into focus, a crowd even bigger than when they had arrived only minutes earlier materialised out of the sun's haze, mostly men come along to support the Tusks in what could be a historic season for their club. Several good-natured boos followed as the Hammers jogged over to the far posts where Caz was waiting.

"We haven't got much time, so we need to get hands warm and the ball moving as quickly as possible," he said. He organised them firstly as a mass huddle, passing the ball amongst themselves while jogging around the 22 as they waited for the stragglers to emerge. They then split into groups of four, passing the ball along the line until it reached the end girl, who popped it on to the girl in front so she could repeat the exercise in the other direction. Caz spoke. "Ladies, we've all been here before. We know what they do," he continued, whilst the exercise progressed. The bellowing and exceptionally loud motivational grunting of the opposition invaded their heads, making it difficult to concentrate, "They stick the ball up their jumpers, trundle forward into our defensive lines and then set up a big rolling mess. They know what we do: we get fast ruck ball out to the backs and run the boots off them out wide." A light shower started; Caz continued:

"They will try every trick in the book, and some not, to stop us from doing what we do. If we do "Our Thang", they stand no chance. Stick to our game plan and we WILL win. Right, now everyone, into a circle."

The Hammers performed one or two more exercises, then split up between forwards and backs. Caz noticed that a couple of players were slow to react, had tell-tale red eyes but more than anything, absolutely stank of alcohol.

"Gwen, Sib, are you OK?"

"I'm fine, honestly," Gwen replied in an unconvincingly cheery voice. Sib said nothing, not wishing to have to remove her mouthguard to avoid gagging.

After Larry had run off the previous day, following the incident at the men's game, Sib was in shock. She had wanted to run after him, probably rugby-tackling him from behind and shout in his face that "SHE needed comforting from HIM!", but her legs just didn't have the strength to even break into a jog let alone a sprint. She'd ended up walking home, very slowly, very deliberately and, ignoring flatmates on her way up to her room, had discovered the litre bottle of Cinnamon Schnapps[104] that had occupied a place on the mantelpiece ever since her Uni'rugby tour to Amsterdam. Larry had found her paralytic on her bedroom floor at 4 o-clock in the morning (after having to climb over the garden fence and break a kitchen backdoor window as no-one was answering the doorbell). As gently as he could, he held her close to him as he tried to get her to the bathroom to clean up, Sib constantly drunkenly mumbling, "You were right! You were right..."

"Forchrissakes, Sib," he whispered, "wontcha giv' iddarist for once. You've got a game to win..."

The team practised their game plan with a couple of minutes "unopposed" drill, running through moves against Caz and the girls who were not in the starting 15.

Stell came back from the "coin toss", which she won ("A good omen," she found herself thinking) and called the girls to her for the pre-match captain's team talk. They linked arms, pulling tightly into a circle, forming an almost impenetrable red, white and blue wall against the increasing rain.

"This has been a fucking mess so far; we've not got much time and Kingston are really fired up for this. But we are the best team in this league, we're the best team in the fucking world and we are gonna prove to everyone, right here and right now, in their own back yard, why we're the best!"

Stell felt the team talk was so lack-lustre, she wasn't surprised when Gwen had to stifle a yawn. It was all going wrong!!!! Even before they'd started it was shite, with the failed "Sensible Night In", the getting lost on the way here, the rubbish warm-up and the accident of the day before that she *knew* was at the back of everyone's minds. Emotional now and fighting back the tears, she pulled herself together, "Right, everyone, on three: a-ONE, TWO, THREE...."

All voices were raised in the traditional war cry: "A-ROO, A-ROO, A-ROO, HAMMERS, HAMMERS, HAMMERS!"

The Tusks' no.10 kicked off high to the Hammers' forwards, the ball holding long enough in the buffeting winds for the catcher, Hannah, to receive man and ball (i.e. the full force of the chasing Kingston pack at the same time), as well as a firm trampling when she went to ground. The ball appeared on the Tusks' side and Fi, in her eagerness to impress her still new teammates, bent to retrieve it. Stell smashed into her.

"Gotcha!!!"

The ball spilled forward.

"Scrum down red ball," shouted the referee, a 70 plus, still fit, former player, with a shock of very well-groomed, white-grey hair. He seemed fairly unbiased.

The Hammers' scrum was crushed as Gwen, in the front row at no.3, completely folded.[105] The ball squirted out to the side, to be pounced on by the Kingston no.9 who just beat Katie to it. The Tusks back row swarmed over both prostrate players, with one or two well-aimed boots at the Hammer, to form a protective wall and the ball was smuggled back, where the Captain Imogen, ably supported by a huge girl whom Caz was sure wasn't around at the first encounter between the teams before Christmas. However, he and his team all knew that the custom of "recruiting ringers[106]" was as old, and as widely practised as the hills.

Kingston had definitely recruited ringers, of which Fi was likely to be one, probably not being eligible for a league game after having represented the Hammers earlier in the season.

"Damn it," he cursed. "None of *our* ringers were available for today!"

A few metres away out on the pitch, the blue surge forward began: the Tusks' maul crushing all in its path. The noise of the home crowd rose.

"Get lower, get lower," Caz screamed. He knew that no one on the pitch could hear him as the cheering crowd were just too loud, but it *did* make him feel better, as if he were doing something.

Instinctively, Stell knew what to do.

She detached herself from the huddle of players inching towards the Hammers' line and smashed in again, at an angle so as to disorientate the maul, with Mands, Mads and Zoe following her lead. The old maul-stop Defence against the Dark Arts seemed to be working!

However, rather than panic and try to counter-push, the Tusks continued wheeling around so they were now closest to the Hammers' tryline with no one in their path.

"Rats, how did they know our defence plan?" Stell thought.

The player to emerge with the ball and to break off from the group, with a clear 40 metre run-in to the tryline, was Fi. She sprinted forward and, just before Ciska, the Hammers' last line of defence, could intercept her, as she always used to do, she suddenly slowed right down and turned to wait for the support, making a pop pass to a pursuing teammate who ran, unopposed, under the posts to score.

5 – 0 (and soon to be 7) Kingston!

Caz tried to run over to his regrouping team under the posts, armed with water bottles, in order to give whatever advice and encouragement he could.

"Coaches must stay in the designated coaching area," he was sternly instructed by one of the Kingston pitch officials. He gave a little smile as he directed the Hammers' Coach back to the 20m x 5m roped off area at the side of the pitch, knowing that Caz had the habit of pretending to be the water boy in order to communicate some mid-game and thus illegal team instructions.

"Bloody hell," Stell said to her team under the posts as the conversion went over. "How do they know all our moves?!" The players collectively looked over at Fi enjoying the congratulatory back-slapping of her teammates as they jogged back to the halfway line for the restart. It was clear to all that this Fi was very different to the selfish one they had both admired and envied in equal measure.

"Forget that girls," Stell continued. "We need to at least compete in the scrums," she looked over admonishingly at Gwen, whose face was enjoying a colour clash of red-rimmed blue eyes offset by green skin. On cue, Gwen rushed behind the deadball line to throw up. The other players couldn't help notice that neither she nor Mel, the no.2 ("Another possible Abandonada?" they thought) who seemed similarly unwell and unfocussed, had on club socks or shorts. Stell made a mental note to deal with them after the game.

The night before the game, Mel and Gwen had gone into the West End looking for trouble.[107] Mel had been able to find a suitable Mr Right Now and had disappeared for the evening, but Gwen's just didn't really measure up to the mark (he was 16 and out in Central London on his own with: hardly any money, no "game" and probably without his parents' permission! She'd ended up swapping texts with a pre-ILY Former Rugger Bugger "Boyfriend" and, abandoning her loved-up teenage heart-throb ("Give him a few years and he'll be fine, eventually...) had taken a night bus to God-knows-where, then a cab, then arrived at FRBB's flat to find him playing X-box with a bunch of mates, all completely pissed but willing to "Share the Taste"[108] of their mate's good fortune. She'd actually contemplated fulfilling their lust-filled fantasies, but something stopped her at the last moment ("Thoughts of ILY? Naaahh....") and ended up drinking them all under the table. When the moment did arrive for her to get into the sack with FRBB, she was actually relieved when he fell asleep before anything could arise. Spending a sleepless night on the couch until public transport services had started the next morning ("Why do Sunday buses have to start so much later than every other day?!!"), with head still spinning from all the shots she'd consumed in a failed effort to build up the courage to go through with her earlier "Gwen Goes Wild in Suburbia!" plan, she'd just had enough time to get home, splash some water on her face (as if that helps...), grab her boots and get to the meet time for the game today. She felt simply awful.

"C'mon girls," Stell added. "We know they'll try to keep it tight, so we need to stop the mauls from rolling." Easier said than done as she simply didn't know how.

"Ladies!" the ref called them to arms again, and their huddle broke up for the restart.

Just as Stell had predicted, the Tusks drove forward in the same old way. The rain had started up again, this time lashing into the faces of the Hammers and the ground below, raked in every direction by the many studs, was impossible to maintain a foothold in. Another try was only delayed by desperate Hammers' defence, but in the churning mud, it was only a matter of time before another maul would continue its relentless drive to the Hammers' line.

Suddenly, Sib had an idea.

Fighting back the nausea and lack of sleep from the previous evening, she grabbed the waist of the nearest Tusk to her and fell over, right at the centre of the heaving, panting, sweating blue and red mass of players.

The marching boots tripped over her, losing their footing in the mud and dragging their linked team mates down with them, burying Sib completely. The referee couldn't work out if the fall were a deliberate attempt to drag down the maul or just a trip.

"Maul not going anywhere, scrum down red put in!"

"Sir, they deliberately brought down the maul!" shouted Rick, the Tusks' Coach. "That should be a penalty to us!"

Although, at his tender age, his eyesight *was* failing and he couldn't be 100% sure the Hammer hadn't committed a penalty offence, the ref was damned sure he "wasn't going to let these whippersnapper Coaches, barely out of short trousers, the like of which he'd seen hundreds of times before," dictate anything to him.

He scanned the ranks of supporters to see if he could pick out the offending Coach. The entire crowd, apart from the guilty party, took a step back. Rick looked to his boots.

"I'm considerably closer to the action than you, young man!" the ref responded. "Let me do the refereeing here, eh Sonny?"

"Yes sir. Sorry sir." He felt like a naughty schoolboy, admonished for speaking out of turn in class.

The next Hammers' scrum collapsed again, resulting in a big mess near their own goal line. The Tusks retrieved the ball and, in tight formation, marched over the tryline for their next score. Only 20 minutes had gone but the Hammers were already 12 – 0 down.

"Coach, what's happening, why aren't they *playing*?" Mrs T, standing next to the Coaches' Technical Area, remonstrated to Caz.

"Two of our front row look as if they're pissed," Caz replied. He was fuming. This was probably the most high-pressure game his team had ever played in and simply, some of the girls just couldn't cope. He had known pressure throughout his playing career and it had never got to him ("Well, almost never.....," he reminded himself). "Of course there were all sorts of things to consider that were probably going on in the girls' minds from yesterday's incident, but to arrive at a game drunk, not even giving yourself the chance to overcome the pressure, was inexcusable," he thought. "A whole season's work gone just like that..."

"Afternoon Miss. Coach." Fi's Dad, James Stanley, had sidled over to the Technical Area to say hello, with only a tiny hint of smugness at the score so far, mixed in with genuine pleasure at seeing Mrs T again, after all these months.

"Did he secretly have a crush on Mrs T, like so many men did?" Caz surmised. "That's what happens when you send a boy to Public School[109]: they become secret Dominatrix fantasists!"

He looked over at Mrs T again, whose nostrils were flaring. "Mind you, if I were a bit older...."

"COME ON GIRLS, WHAT THE HELL DO YOU THINK YOU'RE DOING!!" shattered his subconscious as Mrs T, rising to the "Who's the Most Supportive Parent" Challenge, decided to vocally give as good as she got. Plus a bit more.

The supporters of both teams on the sidelines turned to look at the source of the bone-jarring screech. When they met Mrs T's blue-flinted glare, they quickly looked elsewhere.

Following on from her mother's lead and not cringing at all with the embarassment (she normally would have felt), Stell shouted, "Girls, this is a shambles, we're being pushed over here like we just aren't bothered." Tears of anger and frustration burned in her eyes. She wasn't going to let this slip, but really, she didn't know what to do. However, Siobhan, covered in mud after her recent trampling, was smiling.

"Stell, I know how to stop their maul." The Hammers fell silent. They waited in anticipation.

"We bring it down."

"Illegal, can't do it," was the first response.

"No, no, not *obviously* bring it down, but sort of get it to fall over, like I just did."

Sib explained that, as they had learnt earlier in the season, if they were unsuccessful in preventing the maul from starting, what they should do was to try to get hands on the ball so it could not be smuggled back. Since they couldn't push the bigger Kingston girls into touch, the best thing to do was to subtly fall over and stop the group of players from moving at all.

"But the ref will penalise us," protested Mads.

"He's blind as a bat, he won't see anything if we do it properly," Sib responded. In the absence of any other plan, they decided to give it a try.

The rain suddenly ceased and, as April tends to do, the weather performed a sharp about face. Dazzling sunlight virtually blinded everyone gathered on the rain-soaked, muddy field, splicing through the black clouds which swiftly disappeared to reveal bright, blue skies. A new dawn was breaking for the Hammers!

The Kingston Coach became increasingly frustrated at the Hammers' new tactics, but his protests to the ref did nothing more than increase his insistence that he could see nothing wrong.[110] From every breakdown, a progressively muddy and happy Siobhan would emerge, sporting her most cherrubic "What, *me* Sir?" expression. The penalty count against the home team for dissent was starting to mount and from a quick tap penalty, Katie was able to nip between the complaining and retreating Tusks to secure a try for the Hammers under the posts.

Imogen, the Kingston Captain looked over to her Coach in despair. The game plan of keeping the ball in the bigger home forwards was just not working any more! Rick was in a panic. He knew he had to do something to stem the changing tide of the game but what?

Sophie's kick for the extra two points for the Hammers was blown wide by a sudden gust of wind and the skies darkened again, pelting everyone with a fresh shower of hailstones.[111]

Still, going into half time, the Hammers trailed by only 12 – 5.

Caz walked past the Kingston Coach whilst on his way to the Hammersmith players who were gathering on the touchlines to take on some water, Mars bars and to tend to their various cuts and scrapes. He was in a slightly brighter mood.

"Arguing with the referee eh?" he said, smugly, tutting exaggeratedly. The onlooking crowd held their breath for the expected criminal offence of "gloating". "That's normally *my* job!" he added.

All smiled, more through relief than humouristic content.

Taking advantage of the break, the Tusks' Coach, ably supported by *his* two Touch Judges, headed towards the referee who was puffing hard in the centre of the pitch while the two teams formed their respective huddles, to put into words what many of the home support were feeling.

"Sir, they're dragging the maul down every time! The Touch Judges are flagging but you're not seeing anything! They're chea..."

"If I can't see it, I can't give it!" the referee interjected. He squinted at the Tusks' Coach and reached out a hand seemingly to touch his face. Rick recoiled, bewildered. Someone in the crowd (on the Tusks' side) called out, "You need glasses ref!"

"Oh!" the referee suddenly said. He put his hand in the pocket of his shorts and pulled out the thickest pair of black-rimmed, 1960's-style NHS spectacles ever to have gained a prescription. He put them on – his pupils tripled in size through the lenses - blinked twice, then said to the home trio, "There, that's better, now what were you saying?"

Rick's voice had trailed off to a reflective silence. The emotions of the day had gotten to him. With all that was riding on this seemingly meaningless match between two lower division, amateur teams of a minority sport, he had forgotten the most fundamental rule of rugby, which suddenly slapped him round the face as hard as the hailstones which had re-appeared out of nowhere.

The reasons why rugby players very often triumph in all walks of life could possibly boil down to one simple mantra, initially emblazoned into the consciousness of every tiny child who first picks up the strangely shaped ball and runs with it[112]: "*Play the referee.*"

To non-rugby players, this broadly translates as: "Cheating doesn't exist: if the ref doesn't see it, it isn't a foul."

In every situation: at school, at work, in sport, people have different starting points. Some may be particularly good-looking, intelligent, rich, landed or be fortunate enough to be blessed at birth with a whole host of different, enviable qualities. Others may not. There is thus no "fair" or "unfair" (as we'd all have the same starting point and thus the same chances at what we could call "being successful.") You're given what you are, it's up to YOU to make the most of it. This can lead to the sense of "irrespective": the idea that you will achieve what you set out to as *YOU* are the master of your own destiny. Obstacles are there to be overcome, you adapt yourself to the many different situations you will encounter and use them to your advantage. As Rick's old boss in his first teaching job used to say: "There will be problems, deal with it."

This philosophy has the unfortunate side effect of leaving the individual with a sense that "rules only apply to *other* people" and everything on the way to success is permissible, just don't get caught. Former rugby players can thus either be found at the very highest echelons of office or residing in a correctional facility at her majesty's leisure[113]. Or often both[114].

Rick called his Captain over from the huddle.

"Imogen, when they drag down the maul, let go of the ball."

"Eh," she replied, removing her mouthguard and shaking the built-up spit to the floor.

"I mean it; let them have the ball when the maul goes down. I want you to step away to the side, in between their no. 9 and no.10 and as soon as they try to pass the ball out wide, which is what we *know* they're good at, target the no. 10 and try to smash her."

"Er, either I've got to be really quick to get to her (as she'll be a good 10 metres away), or I'll have to be offside to get there in time."

Then it dawned on her. Imogen's face cracked in a smile. "Coach, are you thinking what I'm thinking?"

"Oh yes...."

The new gameplan was hatched!

In the opposing huddle, the Hammers' half-time talk was taken by Stell.

"We're right back in this, girls!" Smiles now from the collective players as they sensed the tide had turned. Stell continued, "We haven't been able to get the ball, but now we know how to stop them. Once we spin it out to the wings, we can run rings around them and they know it.

"Caz, do you have anything to add?"

"Nope. We're starting to get ball out, but we're really lucky the ref's not seeing how we're doing it. Once we get the ball back though, we need to move it pretty quickly to our fast girls as planned." Leafy, Ciska and Katia, freezing due to inactivity, nodded in recognition. He looked over at Stell and their eyes met. This was the first time in months when no hostility, no animosity, no anger at what *might* have been flew between them. Carlton wanted to hold her hand and squeeze it reassuringly, to communicate to her that he was so proud and that, with her at the helm on the pitch, it would all be ok.

The weather gods had decided that they were going to try to fit the weather to what was going on on the pitch and the sun brightened again, to match the team's mood. The huddle dispersed and the girls fanned out into their respective positions for the start of the second half.

Don't Let Them See You Cry

Hammersmith and Fulham kicked off with renewed hope. If they could steady their scrums (Gwen's face was undergoing the obligatory hangover colour changes of green, to white, then to a type of pink. At this stage, only the "w" of the "white" had been reached, but at least she was recovering), they could get ball out to Sophie at 10, who would feed Lara, Ruth and the fast trio at the back.

At the first breakdown, the Hammers, expecting their adversaries to fall to the floor holding onto the ball, as they had done many times before, were surprised to see Sib on the ground on her own, with the Tusks' pack rolling away and struggling to get to their feet. Katie, pleased at the sudden "clean ball" presented by Sib, picked it up and went to sweep a pass to her no. 10. A blue and yellow wall stood in her way.

"Offside sir!" she cried.

"No it's not, play on!" replied the referee. The glasses had found their way back to his pocket. He felt he looked so much better without them, he thought, stroking his silver mane plus, if they fell off, they'd be covered in mud and might break.

Katie had to take two steps back to avoid the approaching wall, but by doing so, she delayed the pass to Sophie, long enough for the fastest Tusks' forward – which just so happened to be Fi – to reach the pass recipient and scrag her to the floor. The Kingston back row reacted more quickly to the breakdown than the Hammers' pack, who had to turn to retreat the 10 metres while the Tusks' could just rush forward. The boots all over Sophie left her battered and bleeding[115].

In a flash, the ball was scooped up again by the Kingston pack[116].

The blue and yellow herd poured through the gap where the Hammers' Sophie would have been marshalling the defence. The red defenders struggled to plug the breach, by which time it was too late: another try to Kingston. The crowd roared approval as the lightning clapped in unison, the final peal of thunder a fitting accompaniment to the doom and gloom of the Hammers' changing fortunes. The kick for the extra two points was missed, but at 17 – 5 down and with a myopic ref, things were looking as black for the Hammers as the quickly darkening sky.

"Why are we losing? What's going wrong?" Mrs T demanded of Caz.

"The ref can't see that Kingston are hopelessly offside. Katie can't get the ball to Sophie and when she does, Soph's getting flattened. I can't say anything to him as I'm not allowed to leave this area," he said, motioning to his prison ropes. "Whoops," he thought in hindsight, "wrong person to say that to!"

But it was too late. Mrs T marched onto the pitch to confront the ref. The Touch judges considered intervening but, mentally tossing a coin on which course of action would bring the most personal chastisement - Pissed-off Septuagenarian Blind Ref or Formidable Woman-of-a-Certain-Age With Brolly and Small Dog – decided that non-confrontational resolution was the best course of action. They thus examined their flags, hands, sky, anything at all really, but eventually found they could keep themselves fully occupied by concentrating on telling the crowd to keep back.

"Excuse me sir, but what do you think you're doing?" Mrs T addressed the referee. "Don't you know the Kingston forward people are offside all the time and so are stopping our scrum person from throwing the ball to Sophie? I mean, look at the poor girl, she's being trampled black and blue and it's YOUR job to do something about it!!" She paused. "Well, what have you got to say for yourself?"

The bewildered ref didn't quite know what to make of a reprimand from the attractive but fierce-looking woman. "Er, lady," he corrected himself. He tried to stammer a sheepish, "I'll try to watch out for it in the future Ma'am," but thankfully, the heavens opened and the long-expected deluge washed away all thoughts of anything other than shelter. Job done, Mrs T marched back to Caz on the touchline.

"That's told him," she affirmed, more in indignation at having to correct a wrong rather than triumph. Impressed, Caz held his own counsel and thanked his lucky stars he wasn't on the end of one of her tongue lashings.

The worsening weather conditions did not help the level of play, nor the Hammers' plight, one iota.

The ball became a slippery cake of soap which each side took in turns to spill to the floor. Tusks' attacks through mauls became slower and heavier with the cloying mud making forward movement, coupled with the illegal Hammers' counter measures, an impossible slog. Hammers' attacks, if they ever got the ball, never went beyond Sophie at 10 who very rarely had the time to do anything other than avoid the onrushing Fi and other Kingston back row who were living offside. When one or two balls did find their way into the hands of the fast Hammers' backs, the ball was either so slow that the defence was onto them before they could pick up any speed or it was simply knocked on. Errors and infringements began to mount and each team, eventually turned to just hacking the ball upfield for position.

The only source of amusement for the drenched supporters seemed to be in trying to guess to which team the referee would award the many penalties he was giving. The crowd, the rain (and Mrs T) had finally broken down his resistance and, not actually being able to see what was happening in close quarters on the pitch and wanting nothing other than to get into warm, dry clothes in his favourite armchair at home, he began awarding penalties based on whom he was scared of most. At the moment, the tally was in favour of the visitors, who had converted three of them compared to the home side's one, the last one earning two of the Tusks 10- minute suspensions in the "sin bin". Going into the final minutes of the game, the score stood at Kingston Tusks 20, Hammersmith and Fulham 14.

The Tusks had kicked the ball into touch within metres of the halfway line. Hammersmith and Fulham were to take the throw in to the lineout but, with the swirling wind, these had become a lottery.

Stell called her troops in for one last big push. With only minutes left of the most important game of her life, in front of so many doubters and detractors, she felt that her last chance to prove to everyone, to herself, that she could do this sport, was slipping away. She suddenly felt alone.

Before giving her last-ditch "once more unto the breach" captain's speech though, Stell looked around at the 14 other muddy, exhausted faces and paused. She had shared so much with these girls, not just with this team over the course of the last season but with so many different teammates over the last almost 10 years: so much emotion, so many tears, so many times being treated like 2nd class citizens, stuck on a back training pitch or having no showers or changing rooms or having to train on a tiny, unlit hill as there was "no room for the ladies", then all the snide comments from men and women alike questioning her sexuality (as if it were their business!) and sneering at all her commitment, while at the same time they'd slope off with all the best boys anyway, that she was now just *drained*.

"Maybe I should have just not bothered, just stayed at home and gone shopping, or starved myself half my life and worn short skirts, tight tops and high heels and right now, I'd be poncing around some kitchen in my own house pretending to cook, with kids and hubby's money and no worries at all. OK, it wouldn't last for ever, but I'd never have to go through the constant struggle of fighting everyone *every-single-day* just to be the "me" I want to be and now, I'm just tired and want to stop.

"I was wrong, everyone else was right," she concluded. "Who was I to even think that I could be different anyway?"

The 14 other faces were staring at her in anticipation, waiting for her to speak, waiting for a lead.

But that was it.

She wasn't alone.

These 14 other women had gone through, were going through, exactly the same thing. "Every single day someone is telling them, what they can and can't do, but, in this rain and cold and on enemy turf, *here they are*. And they're looking to *me* to lead them! I can't let them down..."

Stell spoke: "Guys, we can really do this. For years, everyone's been telling us that we can't play this game, that we're no good at it, that women aren't good enough or strong enough or can't take a tackle or do a whole bunch of other stuff in every aspect of our bloody lives. Well, this is our chance, our best ever chance, to ram that crap right down their faces."

She looked around again, she could find nothing else to say. Involuntarily though and finding their own way from her heart to her mouth, the words, "I fucking love you guys", emerged as a barely audible squeak.

A few sparks of acknowledgement flickered in the hearts of the team. Some tears sprang to eyes. Sib and Gwen looked at each other, now fully sober and knowing that, instead of, as they had been over the last few weeks, trying to be the people they were when their respective ex-partners still liked them, they were now with *their* team, their girls, whom they'd almost let down by surrendering to other people's expectations of them and basically not taking themselves and their common cause seriously enough. Indeed, not taking their close friends and teammates seriously enough.

Gwen began to cry openly, not through shame but through anger. "What the fuck was I trying to do?" she thought to herself. "*THIS* is who I am! If ILY can't take it then fuck him!"

Sib's confidence had been growing throughout the game as the hangover receded and by now, she was restored to her former, cool, lethal self. She squeezed Gwen by the shoulders: words were not necessary to show that they had both been hurting so badly, but were now back.

Stell's voice had returned. "Girls, we only need one converted try and we're there. Are we going to let them do this to us? To all of our friends and families watching us today. To the boys' teams, to the frigging' men's 1st team Coach for chrissakes! And to Caz."

"And to Mrs T!" Mands added, moving swiftly on. Everyone laughed.

"Are we gonna do this?!" Stell shouted.

"Yes!!!" came the reply.

"ARE WE GONNA DO THIS!" she repeated, much louder.

An even louder, "YES!!!" this time. The excitement crackled through the team as hairs on necks and backs of arms, stood to attention.

"A-ROO, A-ROO, A-ROO, HAMMERS HAMMERS HAMMERS!!!"

On cue, the weather flicked over a page to one marked: "Bright, blue sky, sunlight. Warm even." The wind died down.

With no swirling gale to contend with and the ball now relatively dry after being wiped on the inside of her shirt, Gwen's throw into the lineout was straight and true (for the first time all game). The first three players (two lifters: Mands, Mads and a jumper: Hannah) ran backwards three steps, then forwards to meet the lofted pass. Hannah was lifted so she could make the catch almost a full 4 metres in the air. She immediately threw the ball down to one side in order for Stell to collect it while accelerating in crouched position to charge through the hole in the Kingston forward's defences that their "fake" had created. She was half-tackled though and fell to the ground, twisting her body in mid air so she could present the ball for her supporting forwards.

A perfect defensive wedge was formed over her prone body and this time, Katie could fire off a pass to the war-wounded Sophie, who feigned a pass to Lara outside her to her left and instead, flicked an inside pass to Katia who had come off her right wing. Even though this was the first time she'd touched the ball all game, she held onto the pass and accelerated towards the left-hand shoulder of the Tusks' no. 10. The 10 tackled her, hanging on for dear life as she knew that if Katia were through, with two Tusks in the sin bin, the Hammers would probably score under the posts.

The first person to reach Katia from the Tusks was Fi. She scooped to retrieve the ball but was immediately met by the Hammers' loose forwards swarming all over her and driving her backwards. Her retreat was quelled by the rush of dark blue and yellow, which was countered by a sea of red, the Hammers' tide just being sufficient to enable Katie to dig the ball out from the mass of players and pass off again to her left. The plan to remove the Kingston no. 10 from the defence had been successful, so now all that the Hammers needed to do, bearing in mind that Kingston were two players short in the forwards, was to pass left through the hands of each player in their back line and they would score out wide.

Reading what they were trying to do though and knowing that her troops, by sheer coincidence in Napoleonic blue, were under-manned, Imogen called, "Come right, flat line, push up, PUSH UP!" ordering her Kingston troops to fan out to their right. If they would not be able to stop the next Hammersmith assault, at least they could try to direct it by pushing it towards her right touchline. They would probably outflank her defenders on her right, but with only seconds to go, a score in the corner would still leave them down a point at 20 - 19, with an extremely difficult pressure kick to come. It was risky, but with little choice remaining, it was the plan most likely to succeed.

Stell realised what was happening and yelled out to her forces, again purely by coincidence in Wellington red: "A-ball!" This was a call for the backs to switch the direction of play back towards the forwards, attacking the middle or left flank of the home team's defensive line. "If the Tusks are over-committing left, we can break through right," went through her head. Lara and the hobbling Ruth, who had picked up an earlier knock, performed the "switch" move and the ball was popped to Zoe slightly right of centrefield. She sprinted for the try, through the porous Kingston defensive line on the right-hand side. Thirty metres out, Zoe was brought down by the fullback, who had raced across to cover.

As she hit the deck, Zoe popped the ball up behind her, hoping that the Hammers had followed her run and were in support. The ball went straight to a retreating Fi.

Surprised at her good fortune and the game nearly dead, Fi couldn't help but allow a smile to curl the corner of her lips as she steadied herself to kick for touch. If the ball went out of play now, Kingston would win. However, just before boot connected to ball bringing the glory she craved, Mands, at full force, thudded into her chest. The ball spilled to the floor.

Sib dived to ground and slid through the mud on her front to retrieve it. She was not able to regain her footing though as the rest of the Tusks' back row had caught up with and landed on top of her, pinning her to ground. They would prefer to concede 3 points through a penalty rather than allow the ball to be released and thus a possible 7 points.

But release it Sib did, finding a way, under all those bodies, to twist herself onto her back, freeing her arms and laying the ball backwards to be scooped up by Mel, who was accelerating quickly on still wobbly hangover legs. Fearing she did not have the pace nor the stomach to make it to the line, she shuffled the ball over to her right where Stell had managed to make up the ground from the earlier phase and was now lurking out wide to take the final pass, which would give her a clear run in for the all-important score. The crowd held its breath.

Watching from the sidelines, barely inches away as she caught the ball, stood Roger Theakston.

He hadn't been sure whether or not he should have come. He'd been following the Hammersmith and Fulham Ladies team's performance for months now, with increasing pride and when he had received the letter from Anna, had made up his mind to come to take a few pictures.

Getting back in contact with Estelle, his 8-year-old, messy haired Munchkin, was something he had always intended to do, but the excrutiating, embarrassing silences during the meetings of her teenage years had thoroughly deterred him "until she was older" and "more reasonable." Then she had gone to Uni, then she'd got a job and moved back with Anna, then, well, nothing really. He didn't want to seem like a gushing father who, with nothing better to do with his own life, couldn't keep his fingers out of his children's, so he was waiting for the appropriate moment to show he cared and was there for her.

But Roger knew that the real reason he had stayed away was the disappointment he saw in his children's eyes, similar to his father J's look when Roger had made some silly, schoolboy mistake. All those years ago, he had crushed their tiny hearts, heaping so much embarrassment, no, humiliation, onto his family and exposing as hypocrisy all the values he had tried to instill in them. Now, there was only cold practicality from Jake, burning disappointment transformed into hate from Huggy and from Stell, his Munchkin, well, what really? She had become a woman trying to be a bloke trying to be, well, him?

However, he knew that this rugby thing was extremely important to her, so he could at least share in her obvious delight, celebrating her team's victory with some jolly good photos and, maybe with some common ground on which to try to rebuild the trust he'd shattered, it could be a new start to taking some sort of role in her life. If they won.

But, what would he do if they lost?

Roger had always dreamed of a time when, all three children on his knee, he would tell them how sorry he was for what had happened, how he had wanted to stay in contact but seeing them reminded him of the pain he'd caused, that all he'd wanted to do was help a boy, then a single Mum, then the "helping" had developed into something else entirely. And, as a result, he'd missed the last was it 15, 20 years of his relationship with his children, exposing his feet of clay – his lack of "the right stuff" - to the only people in the world who mattered to him.

However, men are supposed to be strong and definitely not show their feelings – J had drummed that into him since he was a boy – and even if anyone had been interested in hearing his side of the story, he probably wouldn't have told anyway. But no-one was. The children had all since grown up[117] and now, the only options available to Roger to re-establish some form of relationship with them was to try to find common ground.

If the Hammers lost, the conversation with his daughter would be that much more awkward. He would have to try to be the strong one *yet a-bloody-gain*, telling her, a virtual stranger, that everything would be alright. After almost exactly 17 years to the day,[118] Roger just didn't feel he was able to "bond" with Stell.

"Or whatever it is these Touchy-Feely New Men called it," he said.

Without even the small comfort that a reconciliation would allow, Roger's mistakes and his guilt would have to stay inside him for the rest of his life,

"Thank God, she's going to score, she's going to score!" he thought, relieved, drawing himself back from his reverie. He bit his lip in a vain attempt to suppress the excitement welling within him.

Rising from the mud though, a burning need to amend the fumbled-kick giving renewed strength to her aching body, Fi threw herself forward to try to intercept Stell's run and drag her former teammate down before the try-line.

All that training, all those hours in the gym, all that *hunger* that she had had to fight by all that self-brainwashing, then all that jealousy that she could feel off virtually every woman she knew as a result; it had all boiled down to these last few seconds of effort, with everyone: her former teammates, her new teammates, her Dad and all his hangers-on, watching, judging her. "Hoping I'll fail..."

"My body, MY FUCKING RULES!!!!"

Stell saw her from the corner of her eye and, knowing that Fi was a good deal fitter and faster, committed herself, head down, to race for the corner flag. The crowd now cheered support for their respective champions as Fi hurtled across the intervening distance to smash into Stell's legs just before the tryline. Stell's body was flipped over on to her back in the air, but she had just enough momentum to take her torso over the line, grounding the ball with arms outstretched over her head by the corner flag.

Touchdown!

The Hammers lept into the air and the red section of the crowd yelled in delight.

Stell, smile stretching across her muddy face, looked up from the earth to see the Kingston Touch Judge inches away, holding his flag high into the blue skies above her. The referee ran over to him: a few words were exchanged. As if in slow motion, the ref blew his whistle loudly once, while waving his arm in front of his body.

"Foot in touch, no try!" Then two short blasts of the whistle, followed by one long one to indicate the end of the game.

It was now the Kingston fans' turn to erupt, the sound of their jubilation being amplified by the relief from the despair of a few seconds earlier as they surged onto the pitch. The noise was deafening.

Tusks' players were being carried high in the air, and from her prone position, Stell could just make out a blonde-bobbed figure, now detached from her legs, being carried shoulder-high by ecstatic team mates and cheering crowds, in Bobby Moore '66 mode, including a group of drying-out, inappropriately dressed Rhodies, at the centre of which would be, unseen amongst the taller revellers, a short, red-faced Celebrator-in-Chief.

Stell still lay on her back. She couldn't believe what had just happened, it just didn't make sense. She'd scored, she knew that. All they needed to do now was take the kick and if it went over, they'd win. Wouldn't they?

Still uncomprehending, the bright sky was suddenly filled with a lined, much-older-than-she-remembered but still-handsome face.

"What the fuck's *he* doing here?" raced through her mind.

Roger Theakston, seeing his daughter like this, knew it had been a mistake to come. He couldn't drag her from the mud and tell her, "Munch, you were great. I'm so proud of you. It will all be alright, I promise you." Could he?

Stell looked up at the hesitating middle-aged man above her: her father.

"Why doesn't he *do* something?" she trembled, biting back the tears. Too many emotions inside her were swirling around, fighting for attention. She didn't know whether to hug him, burst into tears or lash out a kick to his shins only inches away.

Roger Theakston knew that, in order to extend a hand to his actual child, he had to first embrace his Inner Child. His Inner Child was out to lunch, with a polite notice hung up on the door saying, "I'm terribly sorry, one just doesn't do that sort of thing." He reached for his top pocket instead.

"Munch, don't let them see you cry," he whispered, offering her his silk handkerchief. And then he left.

The tears exploded from every part of Stell's soul.

Pushing her way through the milling crowds, past Caz who was just standing there, not knowing what to do and the other inconsolable Hammers, Mrs T hauled Stell out of the mud and, arm round her shoulders as her daughter sobbed deeply, frogmarched her briskly towards the changing rooms.

In its final act of what had been a fun-filled afternoon, the weather turned the page to "torrential downpour".

Epilogue

Stell, Gwen, Sib, Mads and Caz were all looking over the 1st floor balcony of the Queen's Club, nursing their drinks (Sib's non-alcoholic) while admiring the immaculate lawns, at the end of season Dinner Dance.

"The season hadn't gone anywhere near as badly as it could have and 2nd in the league wasn't a half bad achievement, especially compared to the previous year," Stell contemplated. Plus, Stell had some great photos of the final game, originally emailed from her father but when the sheer bulk of the file had crashed her computer, handed over on memory stick in person by My Roger Theakston himself. They hadn't said much, while he casually threw stale bread to the ducks in Fulham's South Park, near to Fortress Hurlingham, but he seemed even more nervous than she was, "Which was in itself a result," she concluded.

"The old bastard was at least trying to make an effort," she thought and, using the mutual interest topic of the ladies' rugby, they had managed to string together more of a conversation than they had in the previous 20 years. "OK, he was definitely an emotional retard, but he's quite sweet really," went through Stell's mind, especially when Roger seemed genuinely pleased as punch when she suggested he help out at the rugby club by coaching the minis' teams who trained on Sunday mornings just before the ladies' games in the afternoons.

"Oh no!" she realised to her horror, "Dad let loose on Minis' Mums again, aaarrgggghhhh!"

Fears were eased when she remembered the hard-nosed, career Domestic Goddesses of the Fulham Mum circuit. "Poor man won't stand a chance," she came away chuckling. Father and daughter had also promised to attend a new minis' coaching course together during the summer, Stell having decided that she too wanted to "give something back" to the sport before she eventually retired.

Gwen had a new, completely inappropriate policeman boyfriend queuing at the bar for a drinks top up. Not for her another foray into the realms of Mr "Boring but Safe". Her philosophy towards boyfriends, a forever fluid concept in itself, had changed once again to a more stoic approach: "They will eventually leave you anyway, why not have fun with someone you actually fancy in the meantime!" Plus, she preferred the police uniform to the army one any day.

Sib was pregnant with baby Larry (or "Dinko", as Larry liked to refer to him as. Sib had assured everyone that Dinko was only a pre-birth nickname; Larry wasn't so sure, but wasn't looking forward to *that* particular argument...). It had taken them a while (plus a fortune in text messages) to realise that the things they liked about each other far outweighed the things they didn't. If they were both willing to make sacrifices, (Sib getting pregnant and stopping playing rugby), the relationship *could* work. The only proviso though was that Larry would have to agree with everything that Sib said, including whether or not she wanted to play rugby again...

Caz had had a partial reconciliation with his wife Britta. They had agreed to move to Malta, to "try again for the sake of the kids." He was thus, with great regret, leaving the Hammers to start his new life before the new season began. Bets had already been taken on how long it would last, with Mads giving it 5 months tops. She'd got evens.

"I hear Fi's been selected for the regionals," Caz said, avoiding the elephant in the room.

"Was probably a good move to go to Kingston then, to get into the Surrey Coach's good books," added Gwen. She then remembered that the Hammers' Men's 1st team Coach had just been appointed Surrey Ladies' Coach. "Still, no need to let facts get in the way of a good bit of gossip!"

"I hear she hates Kingston though and wants to come back to us," said Sib, gazing longingly at the girls' and Caz' glasses of champagne. "I could murder a drink," she thought, nursing her club soda. Dinko gave her a little kick – "I hope he's not going to be a footballer!" – to remind her of the reason for her abstinence.

"Ah, so that's why she wants to come back!" Gwen said smugly, her gossip justified. "Sod the facts, go with the Fulham jungle drums every time!"

"So, Caz, have you ever even *been* to Malta?" Mads asked, a bit more inquisitively than she would have liked. She didn't want everyone suspecting she had a crush on the Coach. The elephant in the corner of the room got off its chair and coughed politely, for recognition.

"Yeah, why the fuck are you going there anyway?!" Stell finally blurted out. "Whoops! I was supposed to be playing it cool," she admonished herself.

The elephant was doing a jig centre stage.

"Er...." Caz was about to reply.

He had thought about Stell long and hard and, in the end, had decided that tearing up his life and destroying his family for what was clearly a madwoman was not a decision he wanted to make. Well, not for now, at any rate. He looked over at the hair expertly piled on top of her head, the curves that went on for days, the very cute face and the sad, imploring eyes and knew he was making the wrong decision.

Policeboy returned, balancing a tray of five champagne flutes and one soft drink.

"Thanks a bunch, Gwen's ILY no. 376," Sib thought, barely concealing her unspoken contempt for yet another club soda. "And counting..."

"We should go in now, speeches are about to start," ILY chimed enthusiastically.

As Gwen linked arms with ILY, Sib and Mads chatting about kick-boxer Dinko, Stell walking behind them not knowing whether to appreciate a narrow escape ("I've already got one old bastard in my life now, no need for a second!") or to fume and Caz bringing up the rear, they all left the warm, mid-spring evening and trooped off into the Great Hall and the prospect of another season.

(Endnotes)

1 Q: Why do men usually die before their wives? A: Because they WANT to...

2 Reinforced by Jagerbomb chasers, which had seemed such a good idea at the time!

3 So called as, when sometimes too drunk to make it home, the girls from the Hammers Ladies' Rugby Team would often crash at her mother's house. "Mansion" seemed nicer than "Piss Stop Hotel"

4 Sandwiched between the river Thames to the south, the remarkably trendy Chelsea to the east, the even trendier and posh Kensington to the north and Hammersmith (improving, but will take a while) and with good transport links to the City, it had turned out to be an excellent investment decision as it had become the new "in" area of London. The fact that the only reason Mrs T had moved there when she had returned to London was because her old Fashion Designer, work colleague and partner-in-crime Serge's studio had been a few streets down was not something that anyone admiring her foresight needed to know.

Over the last twenty years, Fulham had turned from pink question into the shining light of the inner London gentrification process. Pubs had changed into wine bars or "gastro pubs"; fish and chip shops and working men's cafes into expensive delicatessens and restaurants and everything else into either estate agencies keen to profit from the gentrification or into coffee shops.

5   Or not, it would seem, as the life span of a coffee shop on the Fulham and North End Roads was not long, the said establishments disappearing sometimes in less than a few months. However, they only seemed to be replaced by more coffee shops...

6   A mad person, so called as they tended to want to headbutt random strangers

7   Arch-enemy and nemesis on the rugby team. More on her later

8   You do me, I'll owe you one!

9   Despite having attended almost all the games Stell had ever played in, her mother was still blissfully unaware of what was actually happening on the pitch

10 Many young Antipodeans in the UK, due to the changed lifestyle, food and climate, put on immediate weight on arrival that they only lose once they return back home. This is fondly referred to as "The Heathrow Injection"

11 7 caps in total, one against the All Blacks in which the New Zealanders recorded their highest ever winning margin

12 When children, normally boys, start playing rugby, usually at school, the Games' Master will decide who is going to play in which positions depending on size,

strength, intelligence and propensity for violence. If you are relatively skinny and quick (as well as being of a gentler disposition), you will be placed in the backs (or the "Girls", as referred to by the forwards). The forwards (or the "Donkeys", as referred to by the backs) have a different selection process altogether; the allocation of these positions being probably the only instance when size (as well as personality) does actually matter.

If you are generally gravitationally challenged and enjoy the odd pie or six (i.e. short and fat), plus have spent more time than the average in detention for fighting, you are a natural born front row forward (at the front of the scrum).

The preposterously tall boys are selected for the 2nd row of the scrum.

Those with the physical attributes more akin to Superman (big, strong, fast and probably good-looking as well with perma-gelled hair and the charm and self-confidence that having all the above qualities bring with it) are picked for the back row and the player with the closest resemblance to the Man of Steel is chosen at no.7. The Games Master will then try to imbue The Chosen One with the belief that he alone is hard enough to triumph in the physical confrontations of the forwards, but also fast enough to keep pace with the backs. He is a free spirit, a roaming, omnipresent demi-god who can pop up in any position on the pitch at any time, either slipping through gaps in attack or smashing into the opposition in defence.

None of this pep talk is necessary though as the no.7, since birth, has always been convinced of his (or her) own superiority and is now only mildly pleased that others have finally realised that they are the most important player on the pitch. Or in the club. Or possibly on the whole of God's green earth. Good no.7s aren't made, they are born; it's just not possible for anyone to *make* that much ego.

13 In the WRFU ladies rugby laws, at that level, scrums are only allowed to push a maximum of one metre to avoid potential injury

14 Amanda Pryce-Edwards had always been a bit of a tomboy at school. However, she'd never contemplated the idea of playing rugby as, well, "It just wasn't really the sort of thing young ladies did." In the first year of Uni, after getting rid of the boyfriend from home to whom she'd only sworn undying love a term before, she had discovered the joys of rugby.

Or rather, the joys of rugby boys!

They were fitter, better educated, from richer, posher backgrounds (and thus more chivalrous) and generally significantly more fun than most of the other student boys. If getting drunk, (mostly) getting everything paid for you and having sex with a body-conscious athlete was what student life was about, then what could be better than a rugger bugger? They also would normally eventually get the best jobs through their social circle and so, if you bagged one, you could look forward to a life of shopping and lunches, as well as being married to a sporty hunk.

But it didn't quite work out like that.

After going out with a number of them (or rather, having a series of unfulfilling, drunken, several night stands), it became quite clear that rugby girls were only considered as Short Term Available Bedwarmers and NOT what rugby boys had in mind for anything serious or long term.

It was after a couple of years of this, during her finals, that Amanda Pryce-Edwards discovered rugby girls...

Much more fun, not weird aliens from a different planet who thought in ridiculous, unfathomable ways, but all the good stuff without any of the testosterone filled bullshit. To be around rugby girls, you sort of had to play rugby, but if you're stuck out on the wing, say at no.14 for St Peter's Ladies Rugby Club, the chances of you getting some blood thirsty, super athletic American/ Zimbabwean Mogodon hurtling straight at you with the sole intention of knocking you into sometime next week, are mostly highly unlikely.

Mostly...

15 Actually, in super-slow motion. The dream had decided to really string this bit out.

16 Yes, he had his own knee surgeon

17 A dizzying mixture of high-tempo aerobics and full body work-out delivered with such humour by the permanently smiling, super fit Wayne, that the devoted Fulham Mum following didn't have time to realise they were being worked harder than they ever had during the course of their lives. Well at least since the previous week. The fact that Wayne had a body sculpted by the most meticulous of

perfectionists clearly had nothing to do with his classes' popularity! Fi was a devotee to the class.

18 In Fi's class back home, appearance was everything. Well, actually, not exactly. Not appearance for appearance's sake, but appearance to let all know "I have lots of money"'s sake. With any clothes you wore, or any accessories to clothes, the label in them was more important than what the clothes themselves actually looked like. A designer branded item is so much more "street" than something that looks exactly the same, is possibly made by the same people, in the same developing country for the same tiny wages, but just doesn't have on it the name of some designer, stitched onto a thin piece of material tucked away in a part of the garment so inaccessible that you would have to be on very intimate terms with the wearer to see it.

Alternatively, you could wear clothes that have the designer's name emblazoned on every single visible inch of fabric, as some do, but that's just so "skanky". Or whatever the current word is for "not very well brought up".

For centuries, in many countries, being thin and dark-skinned usually meant you didn't have enough money for food and had to work outside in the sun all day. Rich people were thus invariably lighter-skinned and fat. In recent years though, the availability of cheap, unhealthy food and the reduction in the numbers of people working in the fields had changed this view and, especially in the more industrialised nations, being pale and overweight had become increasingly an image associated with poverty. This had become a major problem for the more affluent as being pale and fat, although it had the advantage of not having to work very hard at it, now ran the risk of people thinking you were actually poor. Thus "tanned and slim" had become the new "pale and fat" for the rich as it indicated "We don't eat chips all day while watching daytime TV and waiting for our Social Security cheques. We are active, have time to look after our bodies and we go on expensive holidays."

A luxury holiday destination just wouldn't be able to stand in the company of other luxury holiday destinations, pint in hand at the bar, if it didn't have an abundance of tanned, athletically muscled beach types surfing the waves, scuba diving the oceans depths, bungee jumping from sheer rock faces or simply lying around being admired. The inhabitants of the Cotes D'Azur, the Maldives, Bondi, Copacobana and Malibu know this and, behind the easy going, laid back, effortless physical beauty that exists at these destinations and many hundreds of others, lie many hours of near obsessive, punishing exercise and dieting regimes.

"Muscle, taut, thin, tanned is the only thing that is attractive."

19 "The Witch" called them "The Africants" as they just couldn't accept that the country they had known simply didn't exist anymore and, for the most part, didn't really do very much but hang around Jimmy Stanley, spend his money and wax lyrical about "the Olde Country".

20 Actually true!

21 Both meant, "a full-of-himself-bighead." Which was pretty accurate

22 Basically what happens is that when a player gets tackled, she has a number of options. If she is on her own and none of her team-mates is within passing distance, one of the options she can take is to go to ground while holding on to the ball. The tackler holds on to the ball carrier and the two make a lovely couple on the floor. Bless. If at least two other players standing on their feet join them, the formation is called a ruck.

Now, the tackled player has, according to the referee at the time as opinions can differ, a certain amount of time to "make the ball available" i.e. to let it go so someone else (not the tackler) can pick it up and continue the game. If the Someone Else, normally a 7, 6 or 8, as they are Supermen who cover every blade of grass etc, is on the same side as the tackled player, then the tackled player has no problem with releasing the ball to him and the attack can continue as planned. If, however, the Someone Else is from the tackling side, the tackled player, after having the stigma of getting tackled burn into her ego, will be damned if she's going to let the ball be meekly handed over as well. Hell no!

She thus may feel the inclination to not let go of the ball. Or at least, kind of give the impression she's letting it go while actually still holding on for dear life (called "killing the ball"). The eagle-eyed referee should see this and give a penalty against the tackled player, but normally before he can put whistle to lips, the tackling side's nos. 7, 6 and 8 are taking justice into their own hands, or rather feet, and trying to persuade the tackled player that it *really* is a good idea to release the ball. This gentle persuasion takes place using their boots.

Conventions do exist with regards to: how hard you can stamp on someone; which parts of the prone, defenceless tackled player's body you're allowed to target; which part of the boot you're allowed to use; the motion of the boot employed against the tackled player's body (dragging the studs along the side of a ball-killer's head is a definite no no. Except for in New Zealand) and all other aspects of this fine tradition of the game, but these are subject to change depending on the country in which the game is played, the part of the country, the club, the level of animosity between the teams playing and many other factors. It is safe to say though, that if you are killing the ball at the bottom of the ruck, you should expect the worst. And you'll certainly get it.

If the 7's, 6's and 8's from both teams get to the tackler and tackled players' ground-level embrace at the same time, one side may attempt to pick the ball up while the other side try to push them over, one side may decide to protect the ball by forming a tortoise-like shell with their bodies over the tackler and tackled, or step over the players on the ground and form a defensive wall just in front of the ball and many other variations. The general rule of thumb though is bloody well get there first - it's so much less complicated!

23 You're able to pass without being off balance or without the oppo clambering all over you

24 Pass on bad ball out of the tackle

25　An activity indulged in by overly-confident young men who, when going out with one girl from a circle of friends whom he knows all fancy him (partly due to the girlfriend's boasts), then subsequently tries to sexually work his way around said circle

26　To whom she certainly gave as good as she got. With no. 5 she actually gave a good deal *more* than she got, but when the magistrate, a Welshman, heard she played rugby, she was let off with only a caution.

27　He had fitted a scrum attachment to the front of his car, so they could practice scrummaging together. She'd "accidentally" left the handbrake off after an argument and the car was scrummaged into the nearest river.

28　He'd joined a rugby team near where he was living in London to meet people other than Aussies from home. However, he'd actually met more people from his class at school on the streets of west London than at his last school reunion.

29　An American military term, meaning New Guys. No-one can come to any cohesive agreement what the "F" stands for

30　The town's second claim to fame was that the principal architect for communist Eastern Europe was originally from Rivenstoke

31　Stokie for, "Good morning?"

32　"Dumb as F#*k London Losers"

33　Halfway in between these two groups were the Returnees (or Stokie-lights). These were the university graduates who *did* come back to Rivenstoke, either through a sense of loss - divorce or a family death - or maybe they had just had enough of the outside world and wanted to come home. The Stokie-Lights were treated, by both sides, with a mixture of envy, suspicion, gleeful ridicule ("London too difficult for ya' was it? I told you you'd come a-cropper but you wouldn't listen") or hopefully just acceptance. A Returnee could thus be regarded as a Stokie or a Dafll, depending on whom he was speaking to and hated by both in equal measure.

34 Public Enemy, "The Invisible Man", Rebirth of a Nation 2006.

35 Which in its simplest form is like a diamond, where one large player at the head of the diamond (say position A) walks forward very slowly right into the heart of the enemy. Other even larger teammates join onto the left and right shoulders of player A (positions B and C), linking arms over the shoulders to form a Roman-legion style phalanx. The ball, in the meantime, is shuffled back, through stubby fingers, to an even larger player at the back of the diamond (position D), normally a no. 8, and the whole troop rumbles forward, bending at the waist to present less of a target. The defending team has to stay behind the lead point of the diamond, in order to remain onside, so it is not possible to nip round to the back and nick the ball.

36 i.e. stopping a maul.

37 i.e. NOTHING

38 Beer. Normally tons of the stuff!

39 But with him probably wasn't - "If you don't like it, get a coat", was his standard rebuttal for any passengers complaining of cold in mid-December. "If it weren't raining or snowing, roof off! Irrespective."

40 The very distinctive Troubadours colours were designed by a group of ex-public schoolboys about 150 years ago with (as legend goes) the sole intention of pissing everybody else off. All the sick-inducing hues one could imagine, grouped together on the playing shirts in quarters for maximum effect and given grandiose names (French Lilac, Magenta, Latin Coffee – you see where this is going?) were a deliberate attempt to stick two fingers up to the rest of the rugby world, saying a collective, "We are posh, privileged boys and superior to YOU! Deal with it." The effect could only be successful though if you could thrash the pants off the enemy, but make it look as if you weren't even trying (hence the need for the extreme training during the summer). The way how the rugby world, in general, dealt with the Troubs effect was by universally hating the club and anyone who donned the infamous colours.

41 At the time Troubs started, rugby was called football and was played for recreation by gentlemen, who very often were fortunate enough to have private incomes. Many of the Troubadours Board of Directors ran firms in the City and could dispense jobs and "means to do very nicely, thank you very much" to promising players, so they could train seriously without the need to indulge in the vulgar practice of having to work for a living. When they retired from playing, they would already be a good few rungs

up the corporate ladder and could thus, if they continued to be associated with the club, continue the employment selection procedure for promising players. The only thing that retiring Troubs felt honour-bound to do and which was tacitly instilled in all who passed through the hallowed halls of the Shelton Memorial Ground, in exchange for the lucrative gravy train that they had fallen into, was to "give something back" to the sport that had given them so much.

With the increasing popularity of rugby football in Victorian England, teams from all over the country began to form and those which did not have access to the cosy "jobs for the boys" network began to claim unfair advantage for those who did. A completely unreasonable and unjustified campaign began, mostly from teams in the North of England, claiming that if a miner or train-driver or builder had to lose wages in order to train and play rugby, drawing in ever-increasing paying crowds; surely he should be able to be paid to play?

The Roman Catholic Church Schism of 1054 has nothing on the Great Rugby Football Schism of 1895. The Northern rugby teams formed into their own league, imaginatively calling their sport Rugby League, where players could be remunerated for their services, while the others formed into the sport now called Rugby Union which, until only very recently, was regarded as amateur (or "shamateur," according to the followers of Rugby League, who were labouring under the belief that getting a job, a car, a flat and "boot money" for away trips was indeed being remunerated for playing). Even though now, the professional era has embraced both codes, the repercussions of this schism between the "Have" clubs and the "Have Nots" can still be felt. To many people, Troubadours was the very embodiment of the "Haves".

42   Apart from in the West Country where they prefer to not be shy when displaying their emotions - it's the only place where he'd played where the supporters actually threw coins at his team – charming!

43   Stell and Fi!

44   Barely restricted violence

45   Which she had: no-one likes a smart arse

46   Surrey region games against other regions

47   Question: if there were no laws, or indeed if a Mad Max situation existed where the only law is unrestricted violence, how violent would the average person be? Every day, Mr or Mrs Average Person faces little frustrations, irritations and sometimes, humiliations. The annoying pedant who insists that due to "procedure" the completely do-able task cannot be done as "the computer says no"; the fellow passenger who, using Sun Tsu "Art of War" tactics, has slipped into the seat on the tube train that our desperately tired feet had been longing for for the last two stops; the boss at work who does everything they can to make your life hell as they know you are better than they ever will be – how many times has the idea of simply punching them in the face and saying the equivalent of "Stitch that, Suckers!" occurred to Mr or Mrs Average Person?

Milton G Stephens

Post-virtually all regimes where the most horrific atrocities are committed, examination of crimes against humanity almost universally shows that most perpetrators were just ordinary individuals who, by some strange quirk of fate, were given the power of life and death over another group. They then dived into their new-found authority with such gusto: settling old scores with people they had known all their lives, paying back for all the frustrations and anguish and disappointments that they had experienced with, when allowed, such unrestricted violence that they even far exceeded their original mandates . After the end of hostilities, those who weren't caught and brought to justice, more often than not, went back to re-becoming the mild-mannered Accountants or Bus Drivers or Teachers and the other completely innocuous people they were before. How does this happen? Do we all have in us everyday frustrations and anxieties that we put away in some dark area of ourselves but which, given the right set of circumstances, can manifest into tremendous violence?

48 "Poo"

49 Rugby players never retire, they just play less often

50 She was on the point of correcting him on the use of the word "we" when a memory of some of her wilder days in London burst into her head, struck an exaggerated pose with one arm raised, lascivious smile curling one corner of its lips, threw its head back and laughed outrageously while exiting through the purple, velvet curtains of her mind

51 Of the "Ever played rugby before? Yes? You're in!" variety

Don't Let Them See You Cry

52 For rugby clubs of a certain size, income from the Minis section: membership fees and new kit every year, constitutes the major part of their revenue

53 He also had no neck, which is a definite benefit for the front row

54 Maybe herself?

55 Out of the mouths of babes and drunks...

56 In fact, some believe that the whole industry of social websites (cruelly dubbed "Retro-shagging") had been created just so women who (luckily/ unluckily?) escaped the clutches of the Shagger when younger could hopefully see him as a latter-day, broken down wreck, in order to justify why their lives were so much better as a result of the choice they had made to avoid him. For those who had slept with him though, and if he were still looking edible, the sexual feelings they had experienced all those years before would come flooding back, leaving them turned on by the distant fantasy and even more frustrated with their present reality

57 Mostly southern hemisphere girls who gravitated towards west London and tended to use it for a base for their Europe-wide travels over the next 2 – 3 years of their visas. They wanted to continue playing rugby at a fairly decent standard, as they had done at home, but on a much more casual basis, so they could easily skip a few training sessions and games here and there for impromptu excursions to Amsterdam, Paris or Berlin

58 Stell had once let slip that, as she was from Fulham, this was her local and preferred football team. They both

concluded that it was OK to like the pagan round-ball sport, but only if they didn't tell anyone

59 Too sissy!

60 A fictional 1970's TV living scarecrow with interchangeable heads, each imbuing him with different qualities. Sadly, none of these included aesthetic beauty

61 Haircut, expensive watch, stylish pen, good highly-polished shoes: all signs that he really was successful (but not *too* successful or the question would be asked: "Whose money is he using to buy all this stuff?")

62 He had sales deadlines to meet!

63 But "But I'm not a mind-reader!" would score precisely NO points, klutz

64 At least 31 times (twice by every player, 3 times by Stell)

65 Not from people like him, but from people like he *used* to be. Years ago. When he was a lad, like

66 "He's not good enough for you!" upon meeting a new boyfriend being countered by, "Why do you want to choose everything for me?!!"

67 The "tortured intellectual" role – that he had never quite got rid of since secondary school - brought up in him the Plato quote: "Those who are able to see beyond the shadows and lies of their culture will never be understood, let alone believed by the masses", but Chelsea were mounting another attack...

68 Anything really, not just the rugby

69 Steady now, don't want to get too self-critical...

70 A bit like the Hot Ugly girl in American 'teen flicks who, just by removing a pair of gawky glasses and letting her hair down, is automatically transformed into a stunning beauty

71 There was a stage 8), 9), 10) and an 11) (involving messy divorce no. 1, boy having to support two families and cracking under pressure, messy divorce no. 2 and acrimony to last for many lifetimes, plus *very* happy lawyers, culminating in them all cursing the name of the establishment in which it all began) but he didn't need to go there just yet.

72 Up until stage 11

73 "La quête", by Jacques Brel: "the inaccessible star" or state of perfect love which, unfortunately, is inaccessible…

74 Which, after purchase, will be used for a maximum of two weeks before being consigned to the cupboard under the stairs for all eternity

75 9.30 am until 11.30 am

76 Yes, they ran two ladies' teams. Unheard of...

77 The Outside Centre (no. 13) was a friend of the 2nd team Winger and so had made sure she was never going to pass to her best mate's rival

78 The spaces close to the ruck, maul or scrum

79 Get involved in the tackling

80 Nickname, honest!

81 A 1970s British television programme. Very, very funny.

82 This is the defensive position on the pitch that should be occupied by the no.7. Attacking different channels means to target areas on the pitch where you think the defence will be weakest.

83 In rugby, as all passes are backwards, if you do not move forward before you pass, you can end up way behind where you started off. The gain line is the line at which you start off and any ground made, is the "gain"

84 Untrue, I just made that up!

85 In strict adherence to the "Toddler's Rules of Possession" i.e. "If I like it: it's mine; If it's in my hand: it's mine; If I can take it from you: it's mine; If I had it a little while ago: it's mine; If it looks like it's mine: it's mine; If I saw it first: it's mine; If you were playing with it but put it down: it's mine; If it's broken: it's YOURS!"

86 A "beasting" is a fitness session designed with no purpose in mind other than to run the participants into the ground. It is so called because the players are worked as if they were beasts and NOT because the trainer would have to be a beast to put anyone through this torture...

87 He knew this because they had said to him, "You're not from round here, you're not welcome in these parts"

88 And violent!

89 During the 19th century, immigration to Argentina from Europe was encouraged and large numbers of Welsh, mostly from the mining community, settled in and around Patagonia, introducing their national sport to the locals who eagerly took to it. Miss Mendez was a direct descendant of these early pioneers.

Don't Let Them See You Cry

90 From the Hollywood film Forrest Gump. He was fast though.

91 Human blood is composed of both red and white corpuscles (erythrocytes and leukocytes), the former is responsible for the distribution of energy, so leads to acceleration and is usually more dominant in sprinters. The latter is used for fighting off illnesses and is often found in the predominance in long distance runners as it leads to stamina. This particular race to the corner flag was a red corpuscle-free zone.

92 "Fat, beer-swilling lesbians with faces like the back end of London buses who only played rugby to sleep with all the rugby boys, from 1 to 15". The obvious contradiction was tactfully ignored...

93 As he had someone even more beautiful waiting for him at... etc etc. I know, I know, it's getting a bit boring now

94 Wives and Girlfriends

95 The scrum is a place where, if freshly shaven, you can quite easily scrape away the sides of your face, a feeling a bit like running over it a few times with a cheese grater. Front row forwards thus did not shave on the mornings of matches and some, so as to not have to bother with the whole shaving thing at all, never shaved. Nor cut their hair (a modicum of protection for the ears). Others opted for the completely shaved head approach, as it made the head easier to use as a weapon. They were also incredibly powerful, having to support a combined mass of sometimes upwards of 900 kgs per team and, if they couldn't support the weight, the whole pile of

bodies could come crashing down on their necks. They were thus either crazy or simply the hardest blokes on the pitch and they revelled in that reputation, adding to it with various off-field antics such as: chewing pint glasses (true); punching opposition forwards much bigger than them (low centre of gravity made it impossible for the taller guy to hit them anywhere other than on the top of their very thick and indestructible heads) and generally being responsible for many completely illegal activities when in the scrum. They were also, unsurprisingly, the most prone to injury, being the only position on the pitch whereby, if you didn't have a properly trained one, the game couldn't continue.

A prop was thus the strongest, toughest, meanest, hairiest, shortest, most testosterone-filled monster in any rugby team.

The front row were also the highest paid, especially the number 3 (tight head prop, where your head is literally squashed in between two hostile enemy heads). Gwen played no. 3.

96 Punching, biting, gouging, kicking, stamping on toes, head-butting, boring heads into exposed necks, twisting the opposition prop like a dreadlock so the equivalent of up to 1800 kgs of human effort could be brought to bear on one spine: why do you think props sometimes pop up out of a scrum?

97 A hard nodule of flesh growing out of leaking spinal fluid at the top of the 2nd vertebrae

98 Of the "'Ere, Lofty, if I don't make it froo tomora', make sure <insert name of beloved here> gets this" variety, whilst handing over sealed, mud-stained envelope.

99 As in, "Ere Lofty, it was me who stole the last cookie from the cookie jar" or, "Lofty, I've never been wiv' a woman before." Poor Lofty probably couldn't wait for the actual battle to start so he could escape from all the whining.

100 If indeed you were impressed by acres of female shoulder, push-up bra assisted breast and thigh, squeezed into tight black, short dresses and trowels of make up, "Which, face it, most men were," Caz thought to himself.

101 See film "Legally Blonde"!

102 Standard procedure. If she'd asked him to buy her the same as he had, she would have seemed a cheap date, which would limit the amount he would have to work to try to woo her. Ordering a much more expensive drink would have set the alarm bells ringing that she was only after his money and he'd be on his guard from then on. She'd pitched her choice of drink just right, for the desired effect.

103 Punching him in the face again being ruled out

104 Too disgusting to drink but too expensive to throw away!

105 If one side of the front row gets pushed back easily, the whole thing wheels around like a spinning top

106 Players who normally play at a much higher level (hence the expression: "He's a dead ringer for <name of famous player>") than the team they are currently playing for, for

which they are not normally eligible, so as to boost the team's firepower. They then take on an assumed name, probably of an existing eligible player who is not as good as they. This widely used practice can be otherwise referred to as "cheating". When at Troubadors and his team didn't have a game, Caz would often turn out for an old club or the club of a friend of a friend, in some meaningless game or another in a league way below his own. It was always a source of amusement to discover, on occasion, that his opposite number on the other team was either a fellow Troub or someone he had played against, of a similar standard, whilst he was at Troubs. He and his adversary would exchange nervous smiles of acknowledgement, knowing full well that the planned easy afternoon's target practice in the lower leagues was about to get a whole lot harder.

107 Well, love really, but "the road to hell, good intentions and all that". You know the drill by now...

108 The "Taste" being her!

109 In England, Public School really means "Private School", as they are open to the public, if you have enough money! I know, confusing.

110 In fact, he could hardly see anything at all...

111 Serves them right for coming to watch a game of rugby at this time of year anyway - after all, they do call them April showers for a reason!

112 Usually straight into the very next child he sees, leaving little Johnny in a sobbing, aggrieved mess on the floor

113 In prison.

114 Bill Clinton was a rugby player (2nd row for Oxford Uni), as was George W Bush (fullback for Yale). We really shouldn't mention that so too was Ugandan dictator Idi Amin (hooker for Sandhurst Military College), known for his murderous brutality, but at least it shows that once a front row forward, always a front row forward.

115 Not an unusual occurrence for Sophie as she was best known in the team for having perfected the art of tackling with her face. Ouch...

116 One of the main differences between rugby and other sports is that only if a limb is seen to be visibly hanging off, or there is an obvious, serious injury, will the referee stop play. Whereas many sportsmen try to feign injury to gain an advantage, rugby players tend to feign not being injured, so as to not appear to be wimps.

117 Putting an end to the "three on a knee" idea!

118 He'd known the correct number of years all the time; he just didn't want to admit it

Milton G Stephens

About the Author

Milton Stephens lives in London with wife and 3 of his 4 children.

Only 6 of them play or have ever played rugby.

www.ingramcontent.com/pod-product-compliance
Lightning Source LLC
Chambersburg PA
CBHW072043110526
44590CB00018B/3011